KU-407-050

9112000435843

ALSO BY DAVE GOULSON

A Sting in the Tale
A Buzz in the Meadow
Bee Quest

DAVE GOULSON

The Garden Jungle

or
Gardening to Save the Planet

VINTAGE

For Gaia, Goddess of the Earth

1 3 5 7 9 10 8 6 4 2

Vintage
20 Vauxhall Bridge Road,
London SW1V 2SA

Vintage is part of the Penguin Random House group of companies
whose addresses can be found at global.penguinrandomhouse.com

Penguin
Random House
UK

Copyright © Dave Goulson 2019

Dave Goulson has asserted his right to be identified as
the author of this Work in accordance with the Copyright,
Designs and Patents Act 1988

First published in Vintage in 2020
First published in hardback by Jonathan Cape in 2019

penguin.co.uk/vintage

A CIP catalogue record for this book is available from the
British Library

ISBN 9781784709914

Printed and bound in Great Britain by Clays Ltd, Elcograf S.p.A.

Penguin Random House is committed to a sustainable future
for our business, our readers and our planet. This book is
made from Forest Stewardship Council® certified paper.

MIX
Paper from
responsible sources
FSC® C018179

Contents

Prologue

This book is about the wildlife that lives right under our noses, in our gardens and parks, between the gaps in the pavement, and in the soil beneath our feet. Wherever you are right now, the chances are that there are worms, woodlice, centipedes, flies, silverfish, wasps, beetles, mice, shrews and much, much more, quietly living within just a few paces of you. Even a tiny garden can contain many hundreds of species of wild insects, small mammals and plants. The lives of these creatures are just as fascinating as those of the more glamorous large mammals or tropical birds that you might see in wildlife documentaries, and are often less familiar. What is more, because these creatures live all around us rather than in some distant, steamy jungle, we can encounter them up close and watch their trials and tribulations, from birth to courtship, copulation and death, all happening right in front of our noses. I recall Chris Packham once saying that he would rather spend ten minutes lying on his tummy watching a woodlouse than an hour watching a glossy television programme about lions in the Serengeti. This book is a celebration of the lives of the little creatures that live in our gardens. I hope that it may also give you some ideas as to the many practical steps that we can all take to increase this diversity, and to encourage even more wonderful creatures into our lives. This can easily be combined with growing lots of healthy, pesticide-free and zero-food-miles fruit and veg, for gardens and allotments can be remarkably productive, places where humans and wildlife can thrive together in harmony rather than conflict. Gardens provide us with a place where we can reconnect with nature and rediscover where food comes from. If we embrace this, we gardeners might just save the planet, and in so doing save ourselves. So join me, in a trip to explore the jungle that lurks just outside your back door...

1

Plants in Profusion

For millennia we humans lived as hunter-gatherers in small bands, knowing nothing of the world beyond our tribal territory, dealing only with what we could see and touch and taste. We harvested berries and nuts, caught fish and game, and later grew crops. For us, the Earth was flat. We did not know or worry about global issues such as overpopulation, pollution or changing climate, and we probably did not try to plan years ahead. Perhaps as a result, our brains do not seem to be well suited to grasping big-picture issues, to understanding and reacting to ponderous global changes that may take decades or centuries to have their effect. Certainly our track record in planning ahead for the long-term well-being of our planet leaves much to be desired.

Even now in the twenty-first century, when our understanding of the universe is vastly increased, the big issues that face us seem beyond our personal scope, unmanageable and intractable. Anything I might do to prevent climate change, stop the felling of rainforests, or prevent the hunting of rhinos for the supposedly medicinal properties of their horns seems trivial and ineffective. As a conservationist, it is all too easy to feel helpless and despondent. Much of my personal inspiration to battle on has always come from the small-scale victories I can achieve in my own garden, for that is a little corner of Earth that I *can* control, that is small enough for my brain to comprehend, and where I can make things right. After a sometimes tedious day in my office at the university, perhaps spent firefighting the never-ending email onslaught as most of us seem to do in place of actually doing anything useful, I gain huge inspiration and enjoyment from going into my garden and getting my hands into the soil. I plant seeds and nurture them as they grow, watering, mulching, weeding, harvesting, composting, and working with the cycle of the seasons. This is the scale on which I work best, when I can see and feel the effects of my actions. For me, saving the planet starts with looking after my own patch.

Since leaving my family home at nineteen I have had six successive gardens over thirty-odd years, starting with a pocket-handkerchief rectangle behind an excruciatingly ugly concrete ex-council house in Didcot, and eventually graduating to my current slightly unkempt but delightful two-acre garden in the Weald of East Sussex. Each one has been very different, in terms of soil, aspect and the plants I inherited, but in all I have tried to gently steer the garden to support the most wildlife possible, learning as I went. In particular, I have tried to encourage bees and other pollinators by providing them with a banquet of flowers and, wherever I can, some quiet places to nest or breed or hole up for the winter.

Wildlife gardening is easy. Plants grow themselves, and bees and butterflies will find them when they flower. Herbivores will appear, slugs, snails, weevils, leaf beetles and caterpillars, and in turn predators will arrive to eat them. Dig a pond and a huge range of plants, insects and amphibians will miraculously and spontaneously turn up, somehow sniffing out the unclaimed water from miles away. Successful wildlife gardening is as much about what you don't do as what you do. This is not to say that a wildlife garden has to be untidy. Many imagine a wildlife garden as an unruly tangle of brambles, nettles and dandelions, and it is true that a laissez-faire garden like this will certainly attract a lot of wildlife, but it is also perfectly possible to have a tidy and beautiful garden that is teeming with life (though tidiness does of course tend to require a little more work). Tidy or unkempt, a tiny courtyard or verdant rolling acres, your garden is probably already home to hundreds, maybe thousands, of wild species.

Just how much wildlife can be found in a garden has been quantified in depth only once in the whole world so far as I know, in suburban Leicester. My PhD supervisor was a chain-smoking, charming old reprobate named Denis Owen, an expert on tropical butterflies who was once married to Jennifer Owen, a lady who was to go on to become one of the great heroines of wildlife gardening. Jennifer spent a good few years of her life, from the 1970s to 2010, cataloguing the diversity of creatures found in her small garden. It was, by all accounts, an ordinary garden, though she did not use any pesticides. There were flower beds, a small lawn, a tree or two and a vegetable patch, in a total area of 0.07 hectares. In this little garden in Leicester she ran a moth trap to attract nocturnal insects, dug in pitfall traps to catch those insects that scurry along the ground, and constructed a Malaise trap[1] to catch flying insects. She also meticulously catalogued the plant life, and any birds or mammals that came through. Over an obsessive thirty-five-year period she identified no less than 2,673 different species, comprising 474 types of plants, 1,997 insect species, 138 other invertebrates (spiders, centipedes, slugs, etc.) and 64 vertebrates (mostly birds).[2] Even more impressive, for most of this period Jennifer was battling multiple sclerosis and now, sadly, much of her garden has had to be paved over to enable access for her wheelchair and for vehicles. Nonetheless, she says that there is still quite a bit of wildlife to be found.

The foundations of a wildlife garden are, of course, the plants; they are the bottom of the food chain, the footings on which everything else is built. The microscopic green chloroplasts in plant leaves capture the energy emitted from a ball of burning hydrogen some 100 million miles away in space. They store it in bonds between atoms, chemical energy, initially as sugars which are then converted to complex carbohydrates, mainly starch and cellulose. The energy stored in the leaves, stems and roots of plants is then transferred to the caterpillars and slugs that eat their leaves, to the aphids that suck their sap, and to the bees and butterflies that drink the sugary nectar in flowers. These creatures in turn might be eaten

---

[1] A tent-like structure invented by the Swedish biologist and intrepid explorer René Malaise, which intercepts any small flying insects and encourages them to throw themselves into a bottle of alcohol. There are worse ways to go.

[2] Jennifer Owen has published a delightful account of the creatures she found over the years in *Wildlife of a Garden: A Thirty-Year Study*.

by thrushes, blue tits, shrews or flycatchers, which themselves provide food for sparrowhawks or owls. Everything, from the gentle croaking of a toad in the garden pond to the frenetic hovering of a kestrel overhead, is ultimately fuelled by light coming from that distant sun. It seems like a preposterously unlikely and precarious system if you think too much about it.

Each creature that feeds upon plants tends to have its own preferences for a certain plant species, and often for particular parts of the plant. The holly leaf miner spends its entire development – which takes just less than one year – burrowing under the cuticle of a holly leaf. It creates a distinctive brown blister before eventually emerging as a minuscule yellowish fly in late spring. It is never found on any other plant species, or in any other part of a holly tree. The caterpillars of the orange-tip butterfly prefer to eat the seed pods of lady's smock, and will eat those of garlic or hedge mustard at a push, but turn their noses up at most other cabbage-family plants and wouldn't dream of eating anything else. There are 284 different types of insects that feed on one part or another of an oak tree: gall wasps, scale insects, aphids, moth and butterfly caterpillars, froghoppers, weevils, long-horn beetles and many more. Each insect tends to specialise in feeding on a particular part of the plant, at a particular time of year, and so the energy resources captured by the tree are divided up by a horde of tiny creatures. Caterpillars of the purple hairstreak butterfly burrow into buds high in the canopy in spring, while those of the green oak tortrix moth live within tubes they roll from the older leaves, gluing them together with silk. Meanwhile, grubs of the acorn weevil quietly tunnel away inside acorns. In this way the insects largely avoid competing with one another, each occupying their own small niche.

A few insects are much less fussy, grazing on the leaves of a range of plants. Known as woolly bears, the caterpillars of the garden tiger moth can eat dandelions, docks, nettles and more or less anything else they bump into. But insects such as these are the exception. Most herbivorous insects eat just one type of plant, or a few closely related ones, and will starve to death rather than try anything else. You might wonder why they are so specific, so adamant about their dietary choice. The answer is thought to be that plants have evolved defences against these herbivores. Some of the defences are physical – tough leaves, spines, bristles and so on – but most are chemical. Over the millennia, plants have evolved a vast diversity of toxins with which they infuse their tissues, intended to repel or poison the creatures that would eat them. Cabbages produce sulphur-rich glucosinolates, the chemicals responsible for the distinctive pungent school-dinner aroma of boiled cabbage, mustard, horseradish and Brussels sprouts. The glucosinolates are not themselves very toxic, but are stored inside the plant cells in little parcels; if the leaf is chewed or crushed by a nibbling caterpillar, or for that matter by the munching of a sheep, the parcels rupture and enzymes within the cell quickly turn the glucosinolates into toxic mustard oils. Most insects cannot cope with these chemicals, and so avoid eating cabbages and their kin. When cabbages first evolved glucosinolates, one imagines they had it pretty easy for a few millennia; but eventually a few insects found ways to overcome their defence. For example, the orange-tip, the large and small white butterflies, and the cabbage stem flea beetle have all evolved chemical means to convert the glucosinolates into harmless compounds rather than mustard oils. Some insects, such as the American harlequin bug and the turnip sawfly, store the glucosinolates in their own tissues to make themselves unpalatable to predators.

Similar sequences of events are thought to have played themselves out over and over again through the 400-million-year evolutionary history of life on land. Any plant that evolves a new chemical defence making them unpalatable has a huge advantage over its tastier competitors, and is likely to multiply and spread.

This then provides a large untapped resource, and it is only a matter of time before by chance a herbivore arises with a mutation allowing it to handle the new toxin. It may be able to break down the chemical, or sequester it in its own tissues. Some toxins act by blocking important biochemical pathways, and insects may overcome this by evolving an alternative pathway to achieve the same thing. Whatever the mechanism, descendants of this herbivore can then thrive and multiply, coming to specialise on this particular plant, since it provides plenty of food and there is no competition. Often the adult insect comes to use the odour of the very plant defences that were intended to deter them as a cue to help it identify where to lay its eggs. The result is an endless arms race, with plants under evolutionary pressure to develop new defences, and insect herbivores following them through the evolutionary landscape, devising solutions to the problems posed by the plants. Since every plant species tends to have different toxins, it pays for their herbivores to specialise; it is difficult to be a jack of all trades, and better to be a master of one. It is these evolutionary games, resulting in tight relationships between herbivorous insects and their preferred food plants, which are thought to have driven the evolution of quite a large chunk of life on Earth. As plants evolve to avoid the nibbling of their herbivores new species eventually evolve, and as the herbivores adapt to track them they too change and become new species. Every plant species ends up with its own collection of specialist herbivores, each of which has its own array of specialist predators and parasites. Some species of rainforest tree have been found to support over 700 species of beetle alone, and there are more than 100,000 species of tree found in our remaining tropical forests, so it is easy to see that plant diversity underpins the fabulous richness of life.

Humans make much use of the diversity of plant defence chemicals; although intended as toxins, in small quantities they have many desirable properties. Some we use as flavourings in cooking; it is largely the plant defence compounds in herbs that give them their flavour. For centuries, the only medicines we had were herbal ones; digitalis is one such example, a heart drug extracted from foxgloves which is lethal at higher doses. Many modern medicinal drugs are based upon plant extracts, and new ones are constantly being discovered. We also use chemicals from plants as natural insecticides, some of which, such as pyrethrum (extracted from chrysanthemums), are allowed in organic farming. Citronella extracted from lemongrass deters mosquitoes. Recreational drugs such as nicotine, cannabis, caffeine and opium (along with quinine, used to treat malaria) are all natural alkaloids produced by plants to deter herbivores. There is no doubt that there are numerous new and useful chemical compounds yet to be discovered in the many tropical plants that have not yet been studied; one of the many reasons why we would be wise to stop destroying tropical forests and the treasure trove of useful chemicals they undoubtedly contain.

You may wonder why I have drifted so far from the garden, but of course there is something to be learned for the gardener here. The plants we choose to grow have a huge impact on the insects which will come to live on them or visit them, and this influences the food that will be available for birds, bats, shrews, and predatory insects such as dragonflies. Everything starts with the plants.

This brings me to one of the biggest debates in wildlife gardening: native versus non-native. The majority of plants grown in most gardens are not native: for example, in a study of sixty urban gardens in Sheffield conducted by Ken Thompson and colleagues from Sheffield University, one-third of plant species recorded were native UK species, the remaining two-thirds being aliens, mainly from Europe and Asia. When compared with derelict land or semi-natural habitats, gardens contained many more plant species overall. Ken's team repeatedly placed one-metre-square quadrats[3] in these different habitats and found that the number of plant species found per quadrat was broadly similar across habitats, but that in the semi-natural areas the cumulative number of species found in successive quadrats tended to plateau after about 120, whereas in gardens it continued to rise. In total, more than twice as many plant species were found in gardens compared to semi-natural areas.

Of course this isn't surprising, for keen gardeners are constantly adding new and interesting plants, impulse buys from the garden centre or seed catalogue, or gifts from friends. It is hard to resist, for these days there is a near-endless and bewildering selection of tempting cultivars of all manner of plants from across the globe. More than 70,000 varieties of 14,000 different plant species can be bought in the UK. If you wish to encourage wildlife, which ones should you go for? Are there some general rules of thumb? In particular, are native wild flowers better than exotic aliens?

Ken Thompson's studies of Sheffield gardens suggest that insect diversity is not noticeably richer in gardens with more native plant species. The best predictor was just the number of different plant species and the volume of vegetation; gardens with lots of plants and more shrubs and trees tended to have more insects. On the other hand, the gardens tended to be rather similar in the proportion of natives. Ken didn't have any gardens that were exclusively planted with natives, or exclusively with exotics, so unless there was a really profound effect of small changes in the proportions of native versus non-native plants on insects he would have been unlikely to detect any pattern. What is really needed is an experiment in which a mix of gardens are created from scratch, some with only

[3] Wire rectangles much used by plant ecologists to study plant abundance and diversity, for example by repeatedly counting the number of plant species within randomly placed quadrats.

natives, some with only exotics, and some with a mix of the two. Perhaps it could be done on a new housing estate where all the gardens are starting from new. It would be great fun to do, but I can't imagine anyone funding such a study any time soon. In the meantime, perhaps the best evidence we have so far is from a study done by Andrew Salisbury and colleagues at the Royal Horticultural Society's gardens at Wisley. They set up small experimental plots with native plants, or close relatives of native plants, or exotics from the southern hemisphere, and they recorded the pollinator visits to the flowers. Overall, natives or their close relatives attracted more bees and other insects than their exotic counterparts. This is not hugely surprising. Some exotic plants have evolved to attract pollinators that do not occur at Wisley, such as hummingbirds, and they hide their nectar at the end of a deep tube where only these long-beaked birds can reach it. These plants aren't likely to get very many visitors (though some of our more enterprising bumblebees might learn to steal the nectar by biting a hole in the side of the flower). On the other hand, most flowers are not so specialised, and bees and butterflies in the UK are not so different compared to those found in Chile or South Africa. A flower that is pollinated by butterflies in Australia is very likely to prove attractive to British butterflies. Plants do not usually protect their nectar with poisonous compounds in the way they do their leaves, since they 'want' pollinators to visit, so there is no need for pollinators to specialise on particular host plants in the way that herbivorous insects do.[4]

---

[4] This is a bit of an oversimplification. Some plants do add traces of bioactive compounds to their nectar. For example, citrus nectar contains caffeine, which bees seem to like, and which makes them whizz backwards and forwards to and from the citrus orchards with the renewed vigour one might expect after a morning cappuccino. Oddly,

I have seen buff-tailed bumblebees in Tasmania, where they were introduced in the 1990s, feeding on clovers from Europe, on lupins from California and on native Tasmanian eucalyptus; sweet nectar tastes just as good no matter where it comes from.

Since most plants have pretty vague and flexible associations with groups of pollinators, something will usually pollinate them no matter where they are planted, and similarly most pollinators are pretty adaptable as to where they gather their food. Hence if your goal is simply to encourage as many pollinators as you can into your garden, then there is probably no need to get too hung up on the origins of the plant. Some non-natives are absolutely wonderful. For example, blue tansy (*Phacelia tanacetifolia*) originates in south-western USA and Mexico, but as a bumblebee plant for a UK garden it has few rivals; bees go mad for it. Giant hyssop (*Agastache foeniculum*), also from North America, will give blue tansy a run for its money (though I find it tends to die in the winter on my wet Sussex clay). Most of us would find it rather limiting if we only grew native plants, but there are of course many lovely natives that also deserve space in the garden. No garden should be without foxgloves, with their majestic spires of purple hooded flowers, and their willingness to grow in sun or shade. Viper's bugloss is also wonderful, and easy to grow if you have a sunny, well-drained spot. Its violet, blue and red flowers drip nectar and are adored by bees of many types. Marjoram and thyme will infuse your garden with the scents of summer meadows, while attracting swarms of buzzing bees, butterflies and hoverflies.

---

rhododendron nectar contains grayanotoxins at sufficient concentration that it can actually kill some bee species, yet honey bees somehow manage to make honey from it and this honey can induce hallucinations or death in humans if consumed in excess.

There is a popular misconception that native flowers are 'weeds', but of course a weed is just a plant growing where the gardener doesn't want it to be. In any case, all flowers are native to somewhere, so there is no fundamental difference between natives and non-natives, weeds and non-weeds. Hence you can remove all the weeds in your garden in a heartbeat, simply by rebranding them as wild flowers. That said, some flowers – including both native and exotics – are prone to self-seeding rather more than you might want. Dandelions provide a great splash of colour in April and May and are very popular with some of our early-spring solitary bees, but their seeds will spread if you have bare patches of soil nearby for them to colonise. My lawn is full of them and I leave them to flower but then pay the small price in having to hoe their many seedlings from the flower beds later in the year. To a sufficiently liberal-minded gardener there is no such thing as a weed, but I'm afraid I have not quite yet ascended to that Zen-like state of acceptance, and so my hoe gets regular use. Rather than attempting to impose my will by brute force, though, I try to gently steer my garden, making a bit of space around the plants I want to encourage, nipping out and pushing back those I want to discourage. Unless you have only a very small garden and/or a lot of time on your hands, aiming for complete control is likely to end only in blistered hands, disappointment and frustration.

From an environmental perspective, the most dangerous weeds are not our native plants but the exotic flowers we grow. Of all the thousands of plant species that we have imported to make our gardens more beautiful, a handful have become major invasive weeds, running amok in our countryside. *Rhododendron ponticum*, Japanese knotweed, Himalayan balsam and giant hogweed are perhaps among the best known and most serious of these pests, forming dense stands that can smother our native vegetation. All were once seemingly harmless garden flowers, imported and carefully tended for their exotic blooms and attractive foliage. From a practical point of view, the best a gardener can do is make sure that these invasive pests don't get a foothold in our own back yard, and use it as a springboard for invasion of your neighbourhood. Of course, the risk that any exotic plant we grow might one day become invasive provides a further argument in favour of growing native plants where possible.

Pollinators may not particularly care where a plant is from, but many herbivorous insects do. As we have seen, plants infuse their leaves with defensive chemicals, and in their native range there are likely to be herbivores that have adapted to overcome these defences. When transported to a UK garden, these native insects are usually left behind. As a result, exotic plants tend to have few herbivores, other than generalists such as slugs and rabbits. You might see this as an advantage, for they are thus more likely to remain unblemished in your garden, but if you want to maximise garden wildlife then you shouldn't mind too much if there are a few aphids, plant hoppers or caterpillars munching away in the herbaceous border. Grow native mulleins (*Verbascum*), and you might be lucky enough to get the beautiful yellow-and-black-spotted caterpillars of the mullein moth. Grow campions, and you will very likely see campion moth caterpillars eating their seeds. Plant meadow cranesbill, and you just might get geranium weevils. These insects are themselves prey for other insects, birds, bats and amphibians, all part of the complex web of life. To me it seems intuitive that planting natives is better than planting non-natives, but I don't see any need to be obsessive about it.

Perhaps more critical than whether a plant is native or not is choosing the best variety. Plant breeders have spent several centuries developing the 70,000 varieties of flowers that are on sale via plant and seed catalogues or garden centres. They have bred them for unusual colours; for example, tulip breeders spent nearly 500 years attempting but never quite succeeding to perfect a black tulip (the variety 'Paul Scherer' is pretty close but look carefully and you will see that it is really very dark purple). They have bred them for bigger flowers, longer blooming periods, extra sets of petals, and for anything else that caught their fancy and which might appeal to purchasers. Sadly, plant breeders never gave much thought to pollinators in this whole process; bees were not their target audience. Yet of course bees and other pollinators were very much the target audience of the wild flowers from which our garden cultivars evolved. Flowers and bees have been co-evolving for 120 million years or so, and the wild flowers that we see today are thus finely honed and often highly intricate mechanisms for achieving efficient pollination. When we start messing about with flowers, altering them for our own ends, we are very likely to impair their function. Rapid artificial selection for any particular trait will often have unintended consequences, so that many of the colourful bedding plants one might buy lack scent, or nectar, or are sterile hybrids that lack pollen, or have flower structures that are inaccessible to pollinators. In my own garden, I inherited a pair of dwarf cherry trees that are a 'double' variety. A normal cherry flower has five petals, arranged as a shallow dish surrounding the anthers that produce pollen, and with nectaries in the centre, providing both food and drink for passing insects. The flowers of my double varieties have, instead, a jumbled ball of twenty petals and no anthers. With all those extra petals they look quite pretty from a distance, but with no anthers they have no pollen, and bees cannot get to the nectaries, so they are of no interest to insects. I have a standard cherry growing nearby which in late April hums with insect life, while the two double cherries are silent. They offend me, for they are a travesty, mutants whose link with the natural process of pollination has been broken. My chainsaw trigger finger has been twitching for several years, but I cannot quite bring myself to cut them down, for a tree is a tree after all, and the world doesn't have enough of them.

Double flowers aren't new. They are naturally occurring mutants that would ordinarily be swiftly selected out from the population, for not attracting pollinators is obviously a huge disadvantage in the wild. Double-flowered roses were described by the Greek philosopher Theophrastus in 286 BC, and they have been cultivated ever since, using cuttings to generate new plants. Most garden roses, including the classic 'hybrid tea' roses that one might give or receive on St Valentine's Day, are double varieties. A queen bee would not be impressed if a drone presented her with one of these. Fortunately, garden centres normally also sell single-flowered roses that are more similar to their wild ancestors and which are great for pollinators.

Many other ornamental plants are commonly sold as double varieties, carnations, camellias, peonies and *Aquilegia* among them. My local Waitrose is currently selling double hollyhocks; the single varieties are great for bees, but these are useless. I want to go into the store and remonstrate with the staff, but I realise that this would be unreasonable and pointless, and that they would probably throw me out and revoke my free-coffee privileges, so I have restrained myself so far. It is a free country after all, and if people want to grow such abominations then good luck to them, but they should at least be aware of what they are doing.

Even among garden flower varieties that do not carry major mutations such as double flowers, there is much variation in their attractiveness to pollinators. The Internet, books and magazines are replete with advice as to the best plants to grow to attract insects. The Royal Horticultural Society published one such list, a very long one including 198 plant genera. The RHS also provides a 'Perfect for Pollinators' logo which can be put on plant labels by garden centres to flag up to customers which plants are on this list. Natural England, the government agency responsible for looking after our natural environment, has also published a list. Not to be outdone, I've put one on my university website. But how good are these lists? Ken Thompson has described the Natural England list as looking 'very much as if it was put together late on Friday afternoon'. Mihail Garbuzov, a PhD student supervised by my colleague Francis Ratnieks at Sussex University, has published a comparison of fifteen such lists, and he highlights a number of common weaknesses. Firstly, the lists are surprisingly inconsistent, with no plants found on every list and a majority of plants found on only one or two lists. This suggests that they may not be entirely reliable, and is certainly likely to cause confusion in any budding wildlife gardener diligent enough to dig out several lists and compare them. Secondly, none of the lists appear to be based on scientific evidence. Ideally, one would plant all of the different varieties in replicate patches alongside one another, and then count how many insect visitors each received through the year. Since different plants thrive in different soils and microclimates, one really ought to repeat this at multiple locations across the country. With 70,000 plant varieties to choose from this would be quite some experiment, and so as with the native versus non-native experiment, it is unlikely that anyone will ever do this. Of course, smaller-scale experiments would still be valuable, and Mihail has been attempting some of his own.

Because the lists are largely based on the personal experiences of the authors, some of whom may not necessarily have great knowledge of the subject (and may sometimes simply be lazily recycling earlier lists), some of the plants included are simply wrong. For example, one list contained petunias, which are scarcely if ever visited by insects, and seem a very odd choice for a shortlist of the best plants for pollinators. Other very attractive plants were missing from most lists; for example, Mihail's field trials have found some types of *Dahlia* such as 'Bishop of Llandaff' and 'Bishop of York' to be great bumblebee plants (something which I have since tried in my own garden and can enthusiastically confirm), but *Dahlia* was not mentioned on most of the lists. Giant hyssop was rarely included, despite being hugely attractive to bees. There is a danger that gardeners might infer that plants not on such lists must be poor for pollinators, but this is not necessarily the case.

One final weakness of these lists is that they usually do not specify a particular variety of plant, often using only a common name such as lavender or a genus such as *Allium*. Lavender includes forty-seven species within the genus *Lavandula*, with some of them represented by a dozen or more different varieties available for gardens, including dwarf plants, ones with white flowers instead of the usual mauve, varieties with variegated foliage and so on. The genus *Allium* contains perhaps 800 different wild species, plus hundreds of garden cultivars, and includes chives and onions, so it is a pretty vague recommendation. Which ones are best? Again, planting them side by side is really the only way to find out. Mihail has done this with thirteen different common lavender varieties representing three different species, and found that there were striking differences between them. Overall, he found that Dutch lavender, *Lavandula x intermedia* (confusingly, a cross between English lavender, *Lavandula angustifolia*, and Portuguese lavender, *Lavandula latifolia*, with no clear link to the Netherlands), is four times better than the more commonly planted English lavender, as measured by the numbers of insects counted per square metre of plant. Even within Dutch lavenders there was more than a twofold difference between the best and worst variety, with 'Gros Bleu' the best of all, and 'Old English' performing worst. While it is broadly true to say that lavender is good for pollinators, it is much more helpful to be specific as to exactly which lavender to grow, and most lists do not include this.

At this point you might be forgiven for feeling a bit bewildered. Who would have thought that choosing plants for your garden could be such a complicated business? Few people are going to have the time and enthusiasm to research which plants and varieties are best in great detail. To make life a little easier, I've included a short list of tried and tested favourites in the back of this book; these haven't all been tested in a proper experiment, but are based on a mixture of Mihail's work, repeated recommendations from others, and my own informal trials; I can say with certainty that they all attract lots of insects in my garden.

An alternative approach to reading lists is to simply go to your local garden centre in spring or summer and let the insects tell you what to buy. Garden centres predominantly stock plants that are in full flower and hence look enticing to potential customers, and also to potential pollinators. Go on a quiet day, ideally avoiding the weekend crowds, and stand still for a moment. Scan across the neat rows of alphabetically arranged herbaceous plants, and you will very likely see movement: bees, butterflies and hoverflies moving among the flowers they prefer, and avoiding the rubbish ones. Given such a wide selection, you can be pretty sure that any plant being visited by more than one insect or getting repeat visits is pretty good. This is much more reliable than going by logos with pictures of bees on them. If you have the money, simply buy the plants the bees are visiting. On the other hand, if you are poor but blessed with patience, take note of the variety and then buy some seeds to grow at home. That way, you can be sure that your plants are free of pesticides and with luck you will end up with so many seedlings that you can share them with your friends and neighbours.

There is really no need to get too hung up on which plants are best for your garden. Any plant is better than decking or paving slabs, and the more plants you have, and the more variety, the better. Include a few of the ones that are really good for pollinators, and perhaps a few native wild flowers and flowering shrubs, and your garden will soon be abuzz with insect life. Persuade your neighbours to grow some too, and soon your neighbourhood could become a sanctuary for these small but vital creatures.

2

The Garden Meadow

To make quince crumble

Ingredients: 400g peeled and chopped quince, 400g peeled and chopped apple, 2 tbsp honey, 100g butter, 100g rolled oats, 100g wholewheat flour, 100g brown sugar, ground cinnamon

1. *Soften quince by boiling in a little water for 5 minutes, then drain.*
2. *Place fruit and honey in a wide, shallow dish, dust on cinnamon to taste.*
3. *Mix butter, oats, flour and sugar by hand, rubbing until it looks like breadcrumbs. Sprinkle over fruit.*
4. *Cook in the oven for 30 minutes at 160°C, until top is light brown and juices are bubbling.*

Quince is a wonderfully aromatic fruit; I don't understand why it isn't grown and used more widely. This dish is fantastic with custard (my favourite) or with vanilla ice cream.

The centrepiece of most gardens is the lawn. Not the flashiest part, for sure, but it usually lies in the middle of the garden, takes up a lot of space, and is used to set off other features such as flower beds to good advantage. We Brits love our lawns. We tend and pamper them, mow them in neat lines and trim their edges with half-moon tools made specifically for the purpose. We play croquet, cricket or tennis on them, and then relax by sitting on them and sipping gin and tonic or Pimm's. What would Wimbledon, the British summer or cream teas be without the lawn?

When it comes to lawns, the phrase 'beauty is in the eye of the beholder' was never more apt. My father loves his lawn, and for him a lawn has to be neat, green and stripy. As a child, I remember watching him scarify it every few months, running a peculiar electric gadget over it that stripped out mountains of moss. I was never sure why he disliked the moss so much, and it seemed futile as it always came back, but nonetheless he persevered. He had a petrol cylinder mower with which he cut neat straight lines up and down every week or two. Today, at eighty-four, he has a small garden, and he still cuts his lawn himself, with a lightweight electrical cylinder mower that I bought him for his birthday. However, now he pays a contractor to visit every month or so in the spring and summer to pour selective weedkillers and fertiliser onto his lawn. Because of this there is no moss, and his lawn is a very bright green monoculture of grass; he is a happy man.

When Dad told me about his lawn care contractor I was intrigued and looked it up. A quick search online revealed an entire industry based on lawn care that had somehow escaped my notice. There are dozens of nationwide companies that will, for a price, take over maintenance of your lawn as they have my father's. They offer to analyse your lawn and diagnose treatment if it appears in any way off colour or indisposed. Their fully trained operatives will not only scarify, but can also offer hollow tine aeration (whatever that might be), pest eradication, top dressing, lichen removal, overseeding, and even a complete lawn renovation programme if you have really let your poor lawn go to the dogs. Rest assured they will swiftly and expertly sort out a nasty case of thatch (accumulated dead grass), chafer grub infestation, red thread (a fungal disease of grass), leatherjackets, moles, or any of a myriad of other threats to the creation and maintenance of that perfect lawn. As one of the websites says, 'It takes time and effort to get the best out of your grass.' Well, quite.

Of course there is an alternative to the pristine Wimbledon lawn, which is much cheaper. You could choose not to call out a SWAT team of highly trained operatives, forgo all of the chemical inputs, the scarification and the overseeding, and indeed do more or less nothing, apart from an occasional mow. You could just see what happens; your own miniature 'rewilding'[5] project. For some of us, the result of doing so is far more beautiful than the classic stripy lawn of which my father is so fond, although this is very much a matter of opinion. It also, I think, very much depends on what you are used to. We humans generally dislike change; we are mostly stick-in-the-muds, who quickly get used to the world as it is and conclude that it should stay that way forever. Having become used to the local park being mown every fortnight, or the roundabouts we pass on our drive to work being kept as a short sward by teams of council workmen with strimmers, we are prone to object if the mowing and strimming ceases. For many people, grass is *supposed* to be short. Anything else is untidy, and the result of laziness or council cutbacks. In many cities in the United States, lawns have to be mown regularly. Local ordinances dictate a maximum lawn height, and you can be fined for allowing your lawn to exceed this, to the immense frustration of US wildlife enthusiasts and conservationists. There is a certain irony that, in the 'land of the free', where one can legally purchase a sub-machine gun, one is not free to let the grass grow.

[5] Rewilding is an interesting new approach to nature conservation that leaves as much as possible to natural processes and minimised human interventions.

Thankfully we do not have such laws here, but nonetheless anyone proposing to reduce their cutting regime can expect complaints, at least to start with. In 2014, Peterborough Council initiated a new regime in which seven areas of city parks were to be left as wildflower meadows, to be cut once per year, and some other areas were designated for cutting just three times per year. They found that this gave them an annual saving of £24,000 in reduced labour and petrol, but they were deluged with letters and emails of complaint. 'The park is horrendous with long grass, how are local children supposed to play in it?' said local resident Stella, while Tariq added: 'How can the city look nice if they are neglecting the parks?' It seems that gardeners also feel under social pressure to comply with the norm and maintain the closely mown status quo. A study conducted by Mark Goddard at Leeds University revealed that most gardeners believed that their neighbours would be concerned or disapproving if they allowed their lawn to grow too long, many fearing that they would receive a complaint. More encouragingly, Mark's work also revealed that these interactions over the garden fence could be a force for good; neighbour mimicry is commonplace, with personal advice from friends, relatives and neighbours emerging as the most important influence over how people gardened. Many felt that their neighbours either admired or imitated their gardening practices, and that this extended to include their efforts to create habitat for wildlife. Perhaps with a little nudging we could get whole neighbourhoods exchanging information on how best to encourage wildlife, and vying with one another to have the most biodiversity, rather than sniping at one another over the length of the grass.

Of course there are good environmental reasons to mow less frequently. Mowing uses energy – petrol or electricity – which costs money and contributes to carbon dioxide emissions. As Peterborough Council found, there are the considerable labour costs to be saved as well. In the case of the homeowner, reduced mowing means less time sweating in the sun behind a dusty mower, and more time sipping Pimm's or lying on the ground watching woodlice. Longer grass is more resistant to drought, so you don't need to water it, again saving a precious resource.[6] There are also dramatic benefits from less frequent cutting for wildlife. A close-mown lawn supports very little life, beyond the odd leatherjacket beneath the soil surface (if you haven't paid for them to be eradicated). The mowing prevents flowering, so there is no colour, and no nectar or pollen for insects. You may think of a lawn as pure grass, and hence wonder what there might be to flower (beyond the grass itself, which of course being wind-pollinated has inconspicuous green flowers). In fact, unless your lawn was very recently laid, it is likely to contain lots of herbaceous plants just biding their time in the hope that they will one day get their moment to flower. Ken Thompson's research on the Sheffield gardens included studies of the lawns; in a survey of 52 lawns they found 159 different flowering plants, with overall numbers of species found per square metre being similar to that found in a semi-natural wildflower meadow. In a regularly mown lawn these plants persist by growing horizontally, clinging to the soil surface, and they reproduce vegetatively through runners and rhizomes. Stop mowing, and they really burst into life.

My own lawn is at least twelve years old, and although I suspect it was originally sown with a simple lawn grass seed mix, it now

---

[6] Even if you do have a severe drought and your lawn starts to look a little sorry for itself, don't waste precious water by turning the sprinklers on. The lawn will recover well enough when it eventually does rain. There are simply too many people using too much water, so that many of our rivers are close to drying up in summer due to excessive water extraction. Much of it simply to keep lawns looking green.

contains daisies, dandelions, buttercups, selfheal, violets, speed-wells, hawkbits, red and white clover, ground ivy, ragwort, bird's-foot trefoil, and lots of moss. I'm sure that a thorough search would reveal many other species. In just a week or so without the mower, the first plants start to flower, but the species are different through the year: dandelions, violets and daisies bloom early in spring, followed by buttercups and clovers, and later in the summer by hawk-bits and selfheal. Right through the spring and summer there is a lovely succession of white, yellow and purple blooms, which of course attract insects: honeybees, bumblebees, mason bees, marmalade hoverflies and many more. It seems a terrible shame to mow it at all, and my wife and I differ on the optimum frequency; I would tend to leave everything to grow and flower for months on end, but Lara prefers a tidier look and gets the mower out when I'm not about. Nonetheless, for most of the spring and summer the lawn has colour, and the movement and sound of buzzing bees.

There is also of course no real need to apply fertilisers or pesticides to a lawn. Grass has managed to survive for millions of years without our help. In a healthy garden there should be a diverse community of insects, millipedes, centipedes, slugs, worms, not to mention countless microbes, living in the soil beneath the turf. If you are really lucky, you might have some ground-nesting bees too, such as the handsome tawny mining bee. A few of these creatures, such as cockchafer grubs, cutworms (soil-dwelling moth caterpillars) and leatherjackets, may feed upon the roots of the grasses, and you might occasionally see a small brownish patch where the grass has withered as a result. You could pop to the garden centre and buy pesticides to pour onto your lawn to kill them, or you could call out the experts, but do you really need to do either? It seems to me that a few small and temporary brown patches are not a great price to pay to have a healthy ecosystem. These soil insects are an important part of the food chain. Leatherjackets are one of the favourite foods of starlings, a species that has undergone alarming declines in recent years, their population having fallen by two-thirds since the mid-1970s. If the dwindling number of starlings don't get them, then the leatherjackets hatch into crane flies (commonly called daddy-long-legs), which are hoovered up by some of our larger bats, along with the adult moths that develop from the cutworms. Adult cockchafers, despite their unfortunate name, are spectacular and beautiful beetles, chestnut brown, white and black with magnificent fan-shaped antennae with which they sniff the air. My youngest son Seth has a pet cockchafer called Colin who at the time of writing is living in a Tupperware box in his bedroom. Why persecute these creatures? It makes no sense to me. Aside from which, any pesticide you apply will kill both the target insects and more or less everything else, doing untold damage to the long-term health of your soil. You will knock out the predatory insects such as ground beetles and rove beetles that help to keep pests such as slugs in check, so you may well end up with worse pest problems in the future. When it comes to lawn maintenance, less is definitely more.[7]

---

[7]   There are many other areas of life in which I would advocate doing less. The best solution to reducing greenhouse gas emissions from energy production is to use less energy in the first place. The best solution to overcrowded roads and traffic jams would be to persuade people to drive less. The most effective way to feed the growing human population would be to encourage people to waste less food, eat less overall, and eat less meat in particular. Sadly it is hard to make money out of doing less, and it is people getting rich that drives political decisions, so instead solutions to these problems tend to focus on building wind farms or nuclear power plants (plenty of money to be made there), building new roads, extra lanes and bypasses (juicy contracts to be won here too), and to do ever more intensive farming (requiring lots more expensive pesticides, fertilisers and heavy machinery).

Most of us value having a lawn area to sit on, play on or drink on, but if you have space you might also try to squeeze in a meadow area too. In a meadow you take the reduced mowing concept one step further, and mow just once (or maybe twice) per year, mimicking the traditional management of a hay meadow. I don't worry too much about Lara's occasionally overzealous mowing of our lawn as the bulk of our garden is meadow and orchard, so when she cuts down the clovers on the lawn the bees only have to move a few metres to find alternative flowers in the meadow. I have created a wildflower meadow before, on a much larger scale in central France, as described in *A Buzz in the Meadow*, but there is no reason why a meadow needs to be large. Meadows used to cover much of lowland Britain; we are thought to have had seven million acres of them in the 1930s, but only about 2 per cent remain today, the rest swept away in the industrialisation of agriculture in the twentieth century. This vast loss of flower-rich habitat is one of the main drivers in the decline of diverse creatures from great yellow bumblebees to corncrakes, but there is now huge interest in restoring and recreating these meadows, and we can all help by creating mini-meadows in our gardens.

A single square metre is a good start if that is all you can spare. There are various ways you can create it, but the easiest is to simply stop cutting (apart from a single cut in late summer, removing the clippings) and see what happens. The vegetation will shoot up, and any herbaceous plants present will soon become obvious as they flower and then set seed through the summer. If you occasional-ly mow around your meadow area it can actually look remarkably neat; the contrast between short and long grass makes the area look managed rather than abandoned. I create the same effect in my meadow by mowing a few meandering paths. It makes walking around the garden feel like going on a small adventure, for by early summer the long grass bounding the paths is waist-high.

If you find that there are few or no flowers in your newly created meadow, then you have several options. You might buy some wild-flower plants from a nursery – field scabious, knapweed and ox-eye daisies are all good choices – and plant them in, clearing the grass around them by hand for a year or so while they get established. Equally, and much more cheaply, you can rear meadow plants from seed in seed trays, pot them up, and then plant them out. Or dig over the area in spring or early autumn and sow a wildflower-meadow seed mix (there are many suppliers, some listed at the end of the book). There is a wonderful little group of volunteers in Stirling in central Scotland who spend their weekends doing just this. They heard me talking on local radio about some bumblebees being 'on the verge of extinction', and I'm honoured to say they decided to call themselves On the Verge. They badger anyone that owns or manages any kind of 'amenity grasslands' (i.e. boring close-mown grass), and persuade them to let the group sow wildflower seeds. At the last count there were fifty-two patches of wild flowers dotted around Stirling, on road verges, roundabouts, public parks, primary-school grounds and rugby-club land. I had a keen student, Lorna Blackmore, survey these plots and she found that the wild flowers attracted fifteen times as many hover-flies and fifty times as many bees compared to neighbouring patches of unmodified mown grass.

There are similar local initiatives elsewhere, from Brighton to Liverpool to Newcastle, but wouldn't it be fabulous if we could do this everywhere? Perhaps the standard training given to every person put in charge of park and road maintenance should include a focus on creating wildflower habitat. We might not be able to replace the seven million acres of wildflower meadows that we have lost, but we could create a network of meadow patches along our roadsides, and creeping through our city parks. I'm sure Tariq and Stella would get used to it eventually, and might one day learn to love it.

Controversially, the mix used by On the Verge contains traditional wildflower meadow perennials and some annual arable
weeds such as poppies and cornflowers. I have also been involved
in meadow creation projects in which we have included some arable
weeds, including one of an eight-acre field at the Royal Society for
the Protection of Birds' Vane Farm reserve in Scotland, in which as
well as poppies and cornflowers we went mad and threw in some
biennial viper's bugloss. You might not think that this sounds terribly controversial, but conservationists can be an argumentative
bunch and sticklers for detail. Poppies are not meadow flowers and
so, for a purist, combining meadow and arable is offensive. If you
are wondering why poppies aren't meadow flowers, it relates to their
reproductive strategy. Life for plants in an established meadow is
fiercely competitive, each fighting its neighbours for light, space and
water. There are few patches of bare ground for seedlings to establish themselves in, and so annual plants such as poppies (which die
each year and rely on the next generation establishing from seed)
tend to be scarce or absent. The poppy is an arable weed, and arable weeds tend to be annual or biennial, growing fast and putting
everything they have into producing flowers and seeds and dying in
the process. This works well in heavily disturbed areas where there is
a lot of bare ground, and so these weedy plants used to thrive in arable
farmland, often mixed with the crop. Sadly, many have declined
as modern seed-cleaning methods and selective herbicides have
enabled farmers to all but eradicate most of them. My point is that
arable weeds and meadow flowers do not normally intermix, so sowing them together is not 'natural' (whatever that is). This gets some
conservationists distinctly hot under the collar, and in the mood to
write sharply worded letters of complaint; the Vane Farm meadow
project was described as 'an abomination' by one local figure.

To my mind this is all a bit daft. The poppies and cornflowers provided a wonderful splash of colour in the first year, when

the meadow perennials (plants that live for more than two years) were busy establishing themselves and scarcely flowered at all. The bees certainly enjoyed the combination, abomination or not. As the sward quickly closed over, the annual weed seeds did not germinate and so by the second year the arable weeds tended to have disappeared, replaced by the biennial viper's bugloss and the perennials which began to flower. By the third year only the authentic perennial meadow plants remained. No harm had been done, and to my mind everything looked jolly pretty throughout.

Interestingly, if a wildflower patch that has been established in this way is ever dug over again, even fifty years later, the poppies will come back. Their seeds are remarkably long-lived and, just like the flowering plants in a closely cropped lawn, they will bide their time for many decades waiting for their chance. Before we started farming the land these arable weeds must have needed this long dormancy as presumably they were dependent on erratic and unpredictable natural disturbance events to provide bare ground for them; maybe rootling by wild boar, or dustbathing by the straight-tusked elephants that once roamed Europe. On Salisbury Plain, the largest area of flower-rich grassland in western Europe, the poppies and viper's bugloss thrive alongside the typical meadow flowers by taking advantage of the disturbed areas created by the army's tanks churning up the soil during the many military exercises carried out there.

Although I don't see any harm in mixing up wild flowers from different natural habitats, I do draw the line at including non-native plants if the aim is to try to replace some of our lost wildflower meadows. Including non-natives is common practice, though, with some suppliers of supposed 'wildflower' seed mixes throwing in North American, Mediterranean and Asian plants: *Gypsophila*, Californian poppies, asters, chrysanthemums, hollyhocks, cosmos, evening primrose and many more. Often known by the odd term 'pictorial meadows', there is no doubt that these mixes are very colourful (some might say gaudy). Pictorial meadows were invented by Sheffield University ecologist Nigel Dunnett, and they have proved very popular. Patches of them have been planted all over the UK, including extensive pictorial meadows around the 2012 Olympic stadium built in east London, where they were admired by millions. Similar mixes are common on rural French roundabouts, and there is even one large patch in the centre of the University of Sussex campus where I work. The one on campus has a rustic wooden sign in front of it, proclaiming it to be a 'wildflower meadow'. This bothers me, because clearly most members of the public that walk past think that these are native flowers. Technically, I guess they *are* wild flowers – but not *British* wild flowers. Even some of the major commercial suppliers of ornamental flower seeds seem to be confused as to what exactly they mean by 'wild flower'. Surely this term implies *native* flowers? But a quick search of the very well-respected seed merchant Thompson & Morgan's online catalogue reveals that many of their 'wild flower' mixes contain a hotchpotch of all sorts of native and exotic species mixed together.

Perhaps I am just being a hypocrite. I can see the inconsistency; why should I be quite happy growing all sorts of exotic plants in my garden but then come over all prudish when it comes to what should be in a meadow? To me, a wildflower meadow means something specific; it is a flower-rich, native grassland, a precious habitat which was largely lost during the twentieth century. It is a habitat that supports a myriad of native species, from Adonis blue butterflies to skylarks to wart-biter crickets, and it cannot be replaced by a mishmash of foreign plants. In a garden setting I don't see any harm in using these mixes, though I don't see any need there either. We are lucky enough to have an absolutely beautiful and diverse native flora, so lovely seed mixes comprising only native species are available for all soil types and conditions. If you are aiming for a wild-meadow area in your garden, or trying to create one in a park or on a roundabout, why would you throw in a bunch of alien plant species?

Let's assume that I have convinced you to try to create your own mini-meadow, using only native species. In the early years you are likely to encounter a problem with luxuriant weed growth, for most garden soils are quite fertile. Docks and nettles often spring up and shade out the prettier plants that you might have been hoping for. Now, there is nothing wrong with docks and nettles; both can support plenty of interesting wildlife, with nettles being the preferred food plant of a number of lovely butterflies including peacocks and small tortoiseshells. However, they aren't especially beautiful, and they are not compatible with creating a flower-rich meadow area. In my garden meadow I have problems with both docks and nettles, along with coarse grasses such as cocksfoot, Yorkshire fog and false oat grass. These grasses are also undesirable species in a meadow as they grow too tall and fast, making large clumps and smothering more delicate plants including many of the flowers. The perceived wisdom is that it is best to cut your meadow back hard two or three times each year for the first year or two, removing the cut vegetation, to reduce the vigour of these more robust plants. I've been trying this with small patches in my garden to see how it goes, and cutting different areas at different times to create a mosaic of patches of different height and age. Judging by the numbers of grasshoppers and crickets I now have hopping about, I am doing something right, though the battle is far from won.

I've also begun experimenting with yellow rattle, a plant which parasitises the coarse grasses and has been found to be a great tool for meadow restoration. It is, unusually for a meadow plant, an annual, but one in which the germinating seedlings create their own space by tapping into the roots of the nearby grasses and sucking the nutrients from them, like floral vampires. The grasses become withered and stunted, leaving room for the rattle and, crucially, for other wild flowers to get established. I've seen a wonderful garden in the Netherlands where a boring mown lawn has been transformed within five years into a magnificent wildflower meadow, jam-packed with flowers, simply by using yellow rattle. The secret, I was told, is to start by cutting the vegetation very short in late summer, sowing the rattle seeds very generously (at least one gram per square metre), and then trampling them in to make sure the seeds are firmly in contact with the soil. Trampling them in with a herd of sheep is said to work even better but isn't practical for most of us.

Even once your meadow is established, it will always need an annual cut. It seems like sacrilege, but that cut really needs to take place when the plants are actively growing and full of nutrients; traditionally farmers cut the hay in their meadows in late June or July so that it was packed with goodness for their animals in the winter. This simple management is what happened to hay meadows for thousands of years, and is what led them to be so rich in flowers. You may not want the hay, but make sure you take away the cuttings as otherwise they will form mouldering clumps that will kill delicate plants beneath and return unwanted fertility to the soil. The cuttings can of course be composted down or used as a mulch in your vegetable patch or flower beds. It may be painful to cut down flowers, but if you don't do it, the thuggish plants will creep back in, as Shakespeare knew:

> *The even mead, that erst brought sweetly forth*
> *The freckled cowslip, burnet and green clover,*
> *Wanting the scythe, all uncorrected, rank,*
> *Conceives by idleness, and nothing teems*
> *But hateful docks, rough thistles, keksies, burs,*
> *Losing both beauty and utility.*
>
> *Henry V*, Act 5, scene 2

Most of us would have to agree that the stripy green, regularly mown lawn still has its place. Watching Andy Murray and Roger Federer skip through knee-high meadow flowers to play their next stroke might be amusing for a while, but would almost certainly not find the approval of the Lawn Tennis Association. However, for the sake of the planet and our blood pressure, let's try to relax our grip on grasslands wherever we can. Mow lawns as infrequently as possible, avoid ever blitzing them with chemicals, leave some areas to turn to meadow, and embrace the cockchafers. Colin, long may you live, and may your offspring thrive and multiply.

3

Earwigs in my Orchard

To make cider

Ingredients: apples, yeast (optional)

1. *Crush apples (any type will do, including windfalls; each variety produces a cider with a different character and flavour).*
2. *Squeeze out juice (tricky without your own press, though I know of a local farm shop that will crush and press your apples for £1 per gallon of juice).*
3. *Add cider yeast to juice, stir.*
4. *Cover tightly, but allowing the carbon dioxide produced by the yeast to escape.*
5. *After about 3 months, siphon into bottles.*
6. *Enjoy at your leisure.*

I love making my own cider. It is the simplest process, requiring only apples and yeast as ingredients, and there are few pleasures to match sitting in the garden in the afternoon sunshine in spring, listening to the birdsong, and drinking chilled home-made ciders from the previous autumn.

Earwigs don't have a great press. There is no Earwig Preservation Trust, nor ever likely to be unless they are given a thorough image makeover, and that is what I am going to attempt here. First, let's examine the popular view of the humble earwig. They are slender, brown, scurrying insects, armed with a conspicuous and fierce-looking set of pincers at their rear end which they can raise up and jab at you menacingly if you are foolish enough to try to pick one up. They commonly secrete themselves in nooks and crannies in damp old houses and garden sheds, popping out and scampering about when least expected in a way sure to cause alarm in anyone who isn't fond of insects (which, sadly, is almost everybody). If you grow your own fruit and veg you will often find them squeezed between the leaves of a lettuce or leek, or hidden among the bunches of blackcurrants and grapes, and I have found that few things are more certain to disconcert one's guests at a dinner party than an earwig scuttling out of the salad bowl (though of course they should be delighted at this living confirmation that you haven't been spraying their food with pesticides). Earwigs can be crop pests, damaging blossom in spring and nibbling on soft-skinned fruits such as strawberries. For many decades it was common practice to spray orchards with insecticides specifically to kill the earwigs.

As if all this isn't enough to ensure universal revulsion for these little creatures, there is an old superstition that earwigs favour sneaking into our ears while we sleep, presumably the origin of their name. I imagine that they might well have occasionally sought shelter in old-fashioned wigs too, though it is thought that the 'wig' part comes from an old word for 'wiggle'. Lurid stories whispered in the school playground tell of unfortunate souls who were driven mad by an earwig lodged deep inside their ear, incessantly wriggling and tickling. In more elaborate versions the earwig lays eggs and rears her offspring inside, or even burrows into the brain for a snack. For all of these reasons, earwigs are almost universally loathed and even feared. Little wonder, then, that the Earwig Preservation Trust has yet to be founded.[8]

The reality, of course, is somewhat different. Firstly, let's be clear, earwigs don't climb into our ears to breed, and nor do they consume our brains. There is no recorded incident of any such behaviour, though once in a blue moon I'm sure an earwig must have accidentally found its way into an ear.[9] What is more, those fierce pincers are actually quite feeble (hardly surprising, given the diminutive size of the insect), and are completely incapable of doing harm to a human, though you will feel a mild pinch if you let one nip you. They are used by the earwig in defence against predators such as ground beetles, and are deployed extensively in courtship, during which the male uses his pincers to gently tap and caress the abdomen of the female.[10]

---

[8] Sadly, should the EPT ever be created, it will be too late for the giant earwig of St Helena, the world's largest earwig species which came in at a smidge over 8cm long, with a truly whopping set of pincers which made up about one-third of its body length. It lived in deep burrows among nesting seabird colonies on this remote Atlantic island, and the females were said to be devoted mothers. Unfortunately most of the seabirds have been wiped out by invasive rodents, which may also have eaten the earwigs. The last living specimen of this gigantic beast was seen in 1967, fifty years ago as I write. Rest in peace, giant earwig.

[9] If you have a fear of insects crawling into your ears, you would be better to be concerned about cockroaches, which seem more partial to ear occupancy. According to May Berenbaum's excellent book *The Earwig's Tail*, one particularly unfortunate soul was once admitted to an American hospital with a cockroach in each ear.

[10] Male earwigs have elegantly curved pincers, while females have straight pincers. Gruesome experiments have shown that removing the pincers from males makes them entirely unable to persuade females to mate with them. Poor earwigs.

The female often turns and nibbles his pincers seductively, and if all is to her liking she may eventually choose to mate, something that takes several hours. Interestingly, the males of many species of earwig have two penises, but they only use one at a time during mating. Perhaps the male's pondering as to which penis to use adds to the lengthy duration of courtship and copulation.

So, earwigs pose no direct threat to us humans (and shouldn't we be just a tiny bit embarrassed to have ever thought that they might, given that we are about 750,000 times bigger than them, pound for pound?). But they are still pests, right? A quick search on the Internet will confirm this, for there are dozens of articles on how to 'control' (i.e. kill) earwigs. The bottles of insecticide in your local garden centre often show a picture of an earwig among the images of other pest insects that you might be hoping to dispose of, including terrifying and life-threatening creatures such as ants, spiders and flies. You can also kill earwigs with sticky traps or poison baits sold for the purpose. You may therefore be surprised to learn that the latest evidence suggests that earwigs are overwhelmingly beneficial, useful insects, acting as major biocontrol agents: they are significant predators of genuine pest insects, particularly aphids. Earwigs are omnivores, but given the chance they prefer animal prey, and aphids are perfect bite-sized snacks for them. Experimental exclusion of earwigs from apple trees in orchards – which can be achieved by putting a band of sticky 'tanglefoot' glue around the trunk to prevent the earwigs from climbing up – has been found to result in an increase in woolly aphid populations to more than three times that found on control trees with earwigs. Earwigs have been estimated to eat as many aphids each year in apple orchards as could be killed by three rounds of spraying with insecticides. They are also voracious predators of almost all other insect pests found in apple orchards, including codling moth, leaf rollers, scale insects and psyllids. Given that each spray might cost £60 per hectare, and that there are 14.5 thousand hectares of commercial apple orchards in the UK, that makes the humble earwig potentially worth about £2.6 million to the economy each year. And that is just for apples – presumably earwigs are helpfully scoffing aphids in many other crops too, in fruits such as pears, cherries, and plums, and in vegetable crops, though this is much less studied. We should certainly see earwigs as our friends in the garden, just as we do ladybirds and lacewings. If occasionally our earwigs cheekily nibble an apple blossom or bite a hole in a strawberry, we should see it as a small price to pay for all the good they do.

Unfortunately, many commercial orchards do not have any earwigs. Earwigs are ubiquitous insects, and would naturally occur in good numbers in any orchard, but they are easily eradicated with insecticides. It is generally the case that beneficial predators of crop pests breed more slowly than the pests they feed on. Aphids, in particular, breed spectacularly fast, giving birth to live young which themselves have developing offspring inside them when they are born. Earwigs, on the other hand, have just one generation a year, with each female producing maybe fifty or so offspring. Having mated in the autumn, she lays her creamy, oval eggs in a burrow in the ground towards the end of winter. She tenderly cares for them, standing over them and guarding them against predators. She regularly inspects the eggs, gently picking them up and adroitly spinning them round with her forelegs while nibbling them to remove any dirt or traces of fungus, ensuring that they are entirely clean. When they hatch she cares for her young brood, known as nymphs – small, grey-coloured versions of herself – shepherding them together like a mother duck with her ducklings. Only when they moult again does she evict them from home, deciding that they are now old enough to be independent (and occasionally eating one that refuses to get the hint – if only humans could threaten that). From then on they have to look after themselves, foraging at night and hiding during the day in any crevice they can find. They must survive right through the spring and summer to then themselves mate in the autumn. If they are living in a commercial orchard then the odds are against them, for orchards are conventionally sprayed with many pesticides throughout the growing season. It is a vicious circle; the sprays kill the earwigs and most of the pests, but the pest populations quickly recover, and before long the pest problem is worse than it would have been if the farmer had not sprayed (technically this is known as 'pest resurgence'). What's more, other 'secondary' insect pests spring up, ones that were not previously common enough to be a problem but have become more numerous because they too are now free from their natural enemies. The fruit tree red spider mite, for example, is rarely a pest in unsprayed, organic orchards, but its population explodes if its natural enemies are decimated with sprays. With the original pests resurging and outbreaks of secondary pests, the farmer then has to spray again, and again, and again, wiping out any remaining earwigs, lacewings, hoverflies and beetles that might otherwise have been disposing of his pests for him, and locking him into a cycle from which it can be difficult to escape. If the farmer stops spraying, it might take years for populations of predators to recover because of the slow rate at which earwigs breed. Also, despite having a perfectly serviceable pair of wings tucked away on their backs,[11] earwigs almost

[11] The scientific name for earwigs is *Dermaptera*, meaning 'skin wing'. Like beetles, the forewings of earwigs have evolved into a hardened case which protects the soft, membranous hindwings that are folded beneath. Flight is thought to be one of the key evolutionary innovations that helped insects to come to dominate life on land, but earwigs appear to be unaware of this and stubbornly refuse to put their wings to use. Despite having a garden full of earwigs I have never seen one fly. Those that have witnessed it say that they aren't very good at it, presumably the result of a lack of practice.

never fly, so recolonisation of an area in which the earwigs have been eradicated will be very slow unless they are given some assistance.

It is hard to find data on exactly how many pesticide sprays are typically used on commercial apples – I suspect because growers might be embarrassed for such data to become widely known. With a lot of digging around I have found data collected by the Department for the Environment, Food and Rural Affairs (DEFRA) in 2004 on pesticide use on Cox apple orchards in the UK. The average orchard received thirteen fungicide sprays, five plant growth regulator sprays,[12] five sprays of insecticides, two herbicide sprays, and one spray with urea. Many of these sprays involved applying mixtures of different pesticides, for forty-two different chemicals were used in all. The main insecticide used was chlorpyrifos, a compound which belongs to a chemical family known as the organophosphates, nerve agents developed by the Nazis to kill people. Organophosphates are known to damage nerves irreversibly and impair brain development in foetuses and young children even at very tiny doses, and globally are currently estimated to cause acute poisoning symptoms in about three million people per year.[13] Among the other insecticides most commonly used was a neonicotinoid, one of a group of chemicals which are known to be very harmful to bees. In contrast, according to the DEFRA survey, just one-tenth of 1 per cent of

---

[12] Chemicals that mimic plant hormones and are used to thin the fruits and speed up ripening.

[13] In a 2015 study by Greenpeace, 83 per cent of 109 conventionally grown apples on sale in European supermarkets were found to contain one or more pesticide (you may be surprised that it is not more). Fourteen per cent of apples contained the organophosphate nerve agent chlorpyrifos. Seventeen organic apples were also tested and none contained pesticides.

non-organic UK apple orchards were taking measures to encourage biological control agents such as earwigs or ladybirds as an alternative to chemicals. Those rosy, shiny apples on the supermarket shelf got there as a result of environmental carnage. We are all familiar with the adage 'an apple a day keeps the doctor away', but if you really want to look after your health, and that of the environment, you might think about buying the slightly less glossy and more expensive apples from the organic section, or better still, grow your own.

It was because of my love for cider rather than any fondness for earwigs that I discovered the joy of growing apples, and now apples have become something of an obsession for me. You might wonder what there is to get so excited about. The apple is perhaps the most commonplace and familiar of garden trees; many people have one and don't even bother to pick the fruit, just allowing them to rot on the lawn (which is not such a bad thing – blackbirds and a host of insects will enjoy munching them right through autumn into early winter). To my eternal mystification, those same people may buy apples in plastic bags from their local supermarket, even while ripe fruit hangs on the tree in their garden.

Mundane though apples might seem, our association with them goes back to ancient times and they crop up regularly in myths and legends from across the Old World, many of which involve apples bestowing health or even eternal life. The Norse god Thor was said to gain his immortality from regular consumption of golden apples from the garden of Asgard, though sadly this hasn't been mentioned in any of the recent Hollywood films. One of Hercules' tasks was to steal the magical golden apples from the Garden of the Hesperides, which were guarded by a hundred-headed dragon. A jealous row over who should receive a golden apple given by the Greek goddess Eris 'to the most beautiful' is supposed to have started the Trojan War. Apples are also sometimes associated with sinfulness, perhaps simply because the Latin word *malus* means both evil and apple, potentially leading to an awful lot of confusion. The Old Testament does not actually specifically mention apples as the forbidden fruit eaten by Adam and Eve, but almost every painting of them uses an apple (a few use a pomegranate).

Legends aside, it seems that apples originated on the flanks of the Tian Shan mountains on the border between Kazakhstan and China, where wild forests of them still grow to this day, unaided by pesticides, their seeds spread by bears. The familiar fruit of the apple tree is of course a seed dispersal mechanism, intended to tempt a hungry bear or other large mammal to eat it entirely, with the hope that some pips are passed out undamaged and at a distance from the parent tree, along with a healthy dollop of fertiliser to help them grow. Alternatively, some animals might discard the uneaten core, as we humans generally do, perhaps deliberately avoiding the pips, which contain small quantities of the toxin amygdalin.[14] Bears are well known to have a sweet tooth (as both Winnie-the-Pooh and Paddington would attest), and so it may well have been selection by bears for the sweetest fruit that resulted in the progenitors of the apples we love today.

That apples originated in Kazakhstan was not discovered until relatively recently, by the Russian scientist Nikolai Vavilov (1887–1943). The apple forests of Kazakhstan were at the time unknown to the outside world, and it was Vavilov who first described them. He noted that the fruits of these wild apples, classified with the scientific name *Malus sieversii*, were highly variable in size,

[14] Amygdalin releases hydrogen cyanide once ingested, but the amount in a few apple pips will do you no harm at all. There has been one reported death, when someone inexplicably took it upon themselves to consume a cupful of apple pips.

shape, colour and sweetness but that some of them were remarkably similar in appearance to domesticated apples (technically known as *Malus domestica*). Before Vavilov, it had been assumed that domesticated apples were descended from wild crab apples (*Malus sylvestris*), the fruits of which are much smaller and more sour than those of domesticated trees. Vavilov very sensibly hypothesised that *Malus sieversii* was a more likely ancestor. Almaty, the largest city in Kazakhstan, used to be known as Alma-Ata, meaning 'father of apples' in Kazakh, which surely gave Vavilov an enormous clue. Vavilov was a geneticist and plant breeder – he travelled the world in search of the wild ancestors of crops, collecting seeds which he hoped could be used to breed better crop varieties. Sadly, he fell foul of Josef Stalin, who used Vavilov and other scientists as scapegoats on whom to blame widespread famines which had actually resulted from his forced collectivisation of Russian farming. Vavilov was imprisoned and starved to death in jail. Fifty years later, modern genetic techniques revealed that he had been as accurate as William Tell with the apples; our domestic varieties are primarily descended from *Malus sieversii*.

So far as we can tell, the Kazakh apples were first domesticated 4,500 years or more ago, back in the mists of prehistory. As trade routes developed through Kazakhstan, apples, seeds or grafts must have been transported both east and west, and there is evidence that apples were being cultivated in the Caucasus and Middle East by 4,000 years ago. Alexander the Great is reported to have found dwarf varieties of apples (popular today for their ease of picking) being grown in Kazakhstan in 328 BC. Apples quickly became a staple food in many of the cooler parts of Asia and Europe, particularly because under cool conditions the fruits can be stored for many months. Some varieties will keep right through to spring, providing an invaluable source of carbohydrates and vitamins at a time of year when, historically, other food supplies were likely to be running low.

Genetic studies suggest that there was some interbreeding between the Kazakh apples and European crab apples during Greek and Roman times, and perhaps this has helped to create the vast array of nearly 7,500 apple varieties that are known today. Yet how many varieties have you ever tasted? Most supermarkets stock perhaps five or six, and these same varieties are found everywhere: Golden Delicious, Granny Smith, Fuji, Gala, Pink Lady and so on. These modern apples tend to be juicy, sweet and crisp, all of which is fine but they are also all rather similar to my mind.

Modern varieties, the ones that dominate the supermarket shelves, were developed during the age of pesticides and typically have little resistance to fungal and insect pests. Varieties such as Pink Lady are hard to grow without a barrage of chemicals, and once a farmer has invested in planting them he is locked in for years, for grubbing up and replacing the trees is expensive and requires several years before the new trees are fully established and producing fruit. In contrast, older varieties tend to be much better at looking after themselves; they had to be, for they were grown without any chemical help. They are also wonderfully variable, each with its own history, distinct flavour, aroma, colour, texture, and keeping and cooking properties. It seems to me rather sad that so few of us have ever had the chance to taste more than a dozen or so of these old heritage varieties, many of which are far tastier than anything the supermarket can provide. Luckily, a great many of these old varieties still exist, and there are specialist nurseries that can supply them, bare-rooted by post in the winter months as maiden or two-year-old trees, or as young potted trees at any time of year, though at a higher price. If you have space in your garden you have a choice of many hundreds of apple variety to choose from; the only problem is deciding which ones to grow.

In 2013 I moved to East Sussex with my family, and we were lucky enough to buy an old cottage with a big garden. It had two gnarled Bramley apple trees, full-sized, maybe five metres tall, crusted in lichens and bending under the weight of fruit in autumn, plus an unhealthy Discovery tree producing red apples pockmarked by scab. The rest of the garden was mostly lawn with a few shrubs. I decided to plant an orchard, using old varieties. I wanted full-sized trees, not the stunted, dwarf varieties grafted on to slow-growing roots that are now grown commercially. Traditional orchards used full-sized trees, but their apples have to be harvested by hand and using ladders, which is too labour-intensive for the modern world so instead contemporary commercial orchards usually consist of neat rows of those stumpy dwarf trees that Alexander the Great spotted more than 2,000 years ago, because they can more easily be harvested.

I figured I had room for about forty different apple trees, each of a different variety, and I spent weeks poring over websites and nursery catalogues to decide which ones to go for. I soon came to the conclusion that my two acres were nowhere near enough, although for the moment it will have to do. I could spend the rest of this book talking about the ones I did buy, and the ones I wish I could have squeezed in, but I guess I should realise that not everybody is quite as interested in apples as I am. However, I cannot resist telling you about a few of my absolute favourites. Let's start with the oldest. Court Pendu Plat is known to have been grown in France in 1613, but it is widely believed to have been brought to France by the Romans. Apple varieties have to be cultivated by grafting – cutting a twig from a tree and attaching it to a young rootstock – as they do not breed true from pips. Hence the tree in my garden is the *exact same individual* as the ones grown in France

400 years ago, and perhaps the same as the one which produced apples eaten by Julius Caesar and his legions on his expeditions across Europe. I find that astonishing.[15] Court Pendu Plat apples are flattened, with red-and-orange-striped skin and an intense flavour. The texture is altogether quite odd, with something of the graininess of a mature Cheddar cheese. Some authorities maintain that it tastes better if cut with a knife rather than bitten, but I can't for the life of me notice any difference.

D'Arcy Spice are crisp and aromatic apples, with a unique, nutmeg flavour claimed by some to be reminiscent of mince pies. The first records of them are from Tolleshunt d'Arcy near Colchester in about 1785. This variety was traditionally picked on Guy Fawkes Day and hung in bags from the trees for eating through the winter. The apples are small and ugly, green and brownish, and heavily russeted (slightly furry to the touch). I can't imagine a mainstream supermarket ever dreaming of putting them on the shelf, which is a great shame, for they are delicious. What's more, they keep right through to May, so with careful choice of the right trees you can have home-grown apples to eat for all but about ten weeks of the year.

[15] Bramley apples also have a fascinating history. A girl called Marry Ann Brailsford planted some apple pips in her garden in Southwell, near Nottingham, in 1809. A tree grew, and the house was later bought by a butcher, Matthew Bramley, in 1846. Ten years later, a local plant breeder named Henry Merryweather recognised the tree as an unknown variety and asked for some cuttings, naming them after the butcher. Of course the variety became very popular, but the original tree is still there. When ninety-one years old, in 1900, it was blown over in a storm but it sent up new shoots and is still bearing fruit more than 200 years later. Every single Bramley apple in the world is a part of this same plant.

Which brings me neatly to Devonshire Quarrenden, a glorious scarlet apple that is one of the earliest apples to ripen, in late July or August. This is another very old variety, dating back to at least 1690, and enormously popular in Victorian times. They have a distinctly strawberry flavour when eaten straight off the tree, and produce a fantastic red-tinged juice.

And then there is Pitmaston Pineapple, producing small yellow apples that somehow taste nutty, honeyed and of pineapple, all at once. There is Sops of Wine, a tree so abundant in purple pigment that the leaves, petals and even the timber are purple throughout, along with the skin and flesh of the aromatic apples, which when thinly sliced make a very attractive addition to salads.

I could go on, as I am sure you can tell, but I will mention just one more, one that I haven't yet planted, but which I would love to acquire and squeeze in somewhere among my growing forest of trees (if only I had a bear to live amongst them). Knobby Russet is an old Sussex variety, and is perhaps the least appetising apple I have ever seen. I cannot better a description of the fruit that I chanced upon online: 'most grotesque … so deformed as to be unrecognisable as part of any living organism'. No doubt the manager of my local supermarket would run screaming at the sight of it, but I'd love to taste one.

It is four years since I planted my trees, and I am quite literally now gathering the fruits of my labours. Not every tree has begun flowering or fruiting, for full-sized trees fruit later than dwarf varieties, but most have, and each year I get to try new ones. Among others, my Ashmead's Kernel, Crimson King, Beauty of Bath and Cornish Gilliflower have stubbornly refused to flower as yet, but perhaps this spring will be the one. What treats are in store for me.

For the moment, the bulk of my apple crop is from the mature Bramleys. These two trees each produce about 400 kilos of apples every year, enough to feed apple pie or crumble to a small army, should one be passing. Most of them go to producing a zingy, tart cider which has the unusual side effect of making my scalp sweat. Gathering, crushing and pressing the apples every autumn is a family affair; we first gather the apples in barrows, wash them off with a hose, and chop them in quarters. They then have to be minced in a manual crusher, which has a heavy spinning flywheel on the side, driving rotating teeth that bite through the apples, spraying juice and pips into the air and attracting the last of the autumn wasps. My three boys fight over using this until their arms begin to ache and the novelty wears off – which doesn't take long – and then it is up to me. Once the apples are crushed to a pulp they go into the press, a cylinder of chestnut staves mounted in a heavy steel frame, with a long steel handle and a ratchet mechanism on top to drive down a heavy wooden plate, causing cloudy brown juice to boil out from between the staves and into a bucket beneath. It is glorious, sticky, blistering work, rewarded by regular gulps of the wonderful liquid, a drink which bears little resemblance to the cartons of bland, pasteurised apple juice from the supermarket. I add a sprinkle of cider yeast, but this isn't strictly necessary; apples naturally have wild yeasts on their skin which will ferment the juice, but the end result is a bit more reliable if you add commercial yeast. The juice then goes into big vats in the shed to bubble away until Christmas, by which time the sugars will have turned to alcohol and the yeasts and solids settled out to leave a clear, golden cider, as pure and natural a product as one can imagine. The squeezed, dryish pulp is much enjoyed by my assortment of hens and Bourbon Red turkeys, though they can't eat all of it so I sprinkle the rest as a mulch on my vegetable beds. Nothing goes to waste.

Soon I will be able to make cider from other apples, including the cider varieties I have planted. Some of these are 'bittersweets', such as Dabinett, absolutely vile to eat but said to add a wonderful richness and depth to the flavour of cider. I've also planted a selection of perry pears, pear varieties that produce rock-hard and completely inedible sour fruit. Perry-making is said to be much harder than making cider, with the perry far more susceptible to spoilage by bacteria, but I can't wait to have a go.

Given the barrage of pesticides sprayed on commercial orchards, one might think that apples and pears are delicate, difficult plants to grow, but they are not. I spray nothing at all on my trees; the only management they get is a mulch of lawn clippings around their base, and a plastic guard around the trunk to stop my multitude of wild rabbits from chewing off the bark in winter. The plastic guard doubles up as a home for hundreds of earwigs. All of my trees are healthy. Perhaps one in one hundred of my Bramley apples has scab, and maybe two in one hundred have codling moth burrowing inside them. Ninety-seven per cent of the crop is perfect, without my doing anything at all.

Of course my garden is not a commercial orchard. If you plant hundreds of acres with apples you are likely to have far worse problems with pests than I do in my two acres, as you are providing the pests with a huge patch of their favourite food. The same is true of any large-scale monoculture, be it fields of wheat, barley or oilseed rape, or orchards of cherries, almonds or mangos. If you attempt to grow a huge patch of just one plant species, maintained free of weeds, then it will be inhospitable to most forms of life. But if you happen to be one of the few insects that have specialised in feeding on that particular crop, such as the cabbage stem flea beetle, which loves nothing more than chomping on oilseed rape, then it must think that all its Christmases have come at once when it happens across a fifty-acre field of oilseed rape. The parasitoid wasps and carabid beetles that might otherwise predate the flea beetles are usually scarce or absent in these large fields as, for most of the year, there is nothing for them to eat, and in any case they have usually been taken out by insecticide sprays. There may be some in the hedges surrounding the field, if it hasn't been permeated with spray drift or flailed down to a stumpy remnant, and there will be lots in any unfarmed areas nearby, but like the earwigs these insects breed slowly and spread into the field from the edges far too slowly to have much effect on the flea beetles. Hence the flea beetles make hay while the sun shines, given virtually unlimited food and freedom from natural enemies. Any crop grown like this is prone to huge outbreaks of pests, and in these circumstances reaching for the pesticide spray might seem like the only option. But there are better ways, as we shall see.

Let us return to the apple orchard. Apples certainly can suffer from plenty of pests, including codling moth, green apple aphid, rosy apple aphid, red spider mite, apple leaf curl midge, apple leaf miners, apple blossom weevils, apple sawfly, and many more. In fact, left unsprayed, an old apple orchard of full-sized trees is a teeming mass of life. More than 2,000 arthropod[16] species have been found in British apple orchards, and 2,500 species found in apple orchards in Hungary. More than 20 per cent of the entire British fauna of 'true bugs' (technically known as Hemipterans) have been found living on the leaves of just three apple orchards in south-east England. About a quarter of the arthropods are potential pests, which means that there are more than 500 possible pests for an orchard owner to worry about. On the other hand, another quarter are natural enemies of these pests, and will keep most or all of them in check, given half a chance. The remaining half are benign to the trees, doing no measurable harm nor predating pests. Together, this

---

[16] Arthropod means 'jointed foot' and includes insects and their relatives such as spiders, mites, scorpions, millipedes, centipedes and crustaceans (crabs, lobsters, barnacles, woodlice, etc.). About three-quarters of all the species on Earth that have so far been described are arthropods.

throng of insects form a complex food web which also supports larger creatures such as many birds, bats, shrews, mice, hedgehogs and so on. There is a natural balance, so that no one creature comes to predominate. All of this can be very rapidly destroyed with a few sprays of insecticide, and once that has happened the few surviving pest insects shift into overdrive.

When I was at university in the mid-1980s, I was taught about 'integrated pest management' or IPM for short. Enthusiastic but naive overuse of synthetic pesticides such as DDT and organophosphates in the 1940s and 50s had led to devastating environmental and human health problems which were brought to the world's attention by Rachel Carson in her book *Silent Spring* in 1962. IPM was developed as a response to these problems, a system of pest management intended to dramatically reduce pesticide use. Before pesticides, farmers used many other techniques to control pests, and the goal of IPM was to use a sound scientific understanding of the biology of the pests to develop a suite of control measures that sought to minimise environmental harm and treat synthetic pesticides as the last resort when all else had failed. In the 1980s this was considered the gold standard for pest management to which all farmers should aspire, and this is still true to this day, although in the intervening thirty years depressingly little progress has been made towards this being the norm.

One of the central planks of any IPM strategy is 'scouting' – not tying knots in ropes or fiddling with one's woggle, but regularly examining the crop to spot any developing pest problem. Sadly this vital part of IPM is often forgotten in modern industrial farming. Since a central tenet of IPM is that pesticides should be used as a last resort, they should never be sprayed prophylactically, or by the calendar. It is common sense to check that there is actually a problem before spending money on treating it, yet scouting is surprisingly scarce in modern farming, not least because much farming is now done by contractors who do not live on or near the land. As a result, many sprays are applied that are not necessary. Some pests cannot easily be monitored simply by looking at the crop, for they may be nocturnal and hidden out of view during the daytime. Adult codling moths are very hard to spot in an apple orchard, but they can be monitored by using pheromone traps, which contain a synthetic version of the female moth's own sex pheromone. Simple cardboard triangles bated with pheromone and lined with sticky glue can be hung in the trees and provide a good indication of the size of the moth population. Larger amounts of the pheromone can be used to disrupt mating; the male moths cannot find the females if the whole orchard smells of sex pheromone, presumably leaving the males confused and frustrated. This is all a bit of a faff for the farmer, but far preferable to blitzing everything with an insecticide that will wipe out both good and bad insects.

Some pesticides are applied to seeds before the farmer buys them, and these are necessarily being used prophylactically to defend against a pest that may not actually be there when the crop is growing in the field. What's more, just because a pest is present does not mean that it is time to spray. Often pests may exist at low density in a crop without measurably reducing the yield. Even when their numbers rise to a point where the crop yield is being reduced, it will not be cost-effective to spray if the cost of buying and applying the spray exceeds the value of the increase in yield that may result. It does require detailed research to establish what the economic threshold for spraying is, but this has been calculated for most crops; for example in the USA, an average of five codling moths per pheromone trap is deemed to be the point at which action is needed. As yet such calculations do not attempt to factor in the hidden environmental costs that are often associated with the pesticide application, such as damage to bee populations or pollution of streams.

Of course, before pesticides were available most crop pests were controlled by their natural enemies; in orchards this would have been the 500 or so species of predatory and parasitic insects, plus various insect-eating birds. It is relatively simple to encourage some of these valuable insects. Our dear earwigs can be given a helping hand by providing them with places to hide during the day. Some forward-thinking orchard managers have tried creating earwig refuges, which can be made by stuffing bundles of straw into wire-mesh cages, or pushing rolled-up sheets of corrugated cardboard into bottles, jars or tin cans and hanging them from the trees. Such refuges, placed in local woodland for a few days, can then be moved into an orchard that has lost its earwig population, but of course there is little point in doing this if you plan to spray again with insecticides.

I have found that some of the very best homes for earwigs, aside from my plastic tree protectors, are solitary bee 'hotels'. These provide holes of about 8mm in diameter in a block of wood or in a bundle of bamboo canes, intended for mason and leafcutter bees to nest in. If placed on the trunk of a tree they become overrun with young earwigs in the spring, which appear to find holes of this size very much to their liking and hang out in messy gangs like teenagers on spring break. The holes tend to fill with earwig frass (excrement), and not surprisingly this seems to repel the bees, which presumably prefer less odorous and crowded accommodation. If you would rather your bee hotel was actually occupied by bees then it is best to place it on a wall or fence, for earwigs seem less frequent in such places, probably because there are no aphids and few other insects for them to eat. Of course the ideal is to have both, to encourage the mason bees to pollinate your apples, and to encourage the earwigs which will sally forth from their grubby digs at night to eat the pests.

Other natural enemies of pests can also be deliberately introduced, such as predatory mites, some of which are available from commercial suppliers, though it is generally best to encourage wild, native insects of local provenance. In an unsprayed orchard there may be as many as five predatory phytoseiid mites per leaf, and these tiny but ferocious predators are the main enemy of the red spider mite. The red spider mite has become one of the worst pests of apples since pesticidal sprays were introduced; it was unheard of as a pest before that, because the predatory mites naturally kept it in check.

Managing pests effectively with minimal or no pesticides requires a good understanding of the biology and behaviour of the pest. For example, the adult codling moth emerges in spring and lays its eggs on the leaves of the tree. For the first few days of their lives the tiny caterpillars graze on leaves, before selecting an apple and burrowing inside. After chomping away inside the apple for several weeks, the larvae reach full size and crawl out and down the trunk to find a dark crevice in which to spin a cocoon and eventually pupate. If you are going to try to kill them with pesticides, there is just a narrow window of opportunity, those few days while they are feeding on the leaves. Once inside the apple they are beyond the reach of sprays (unless you wish to use systemic insecticides and then have apples that are impregnated with insecticides at harvest). Scouting via pheromone traps can be used to identify exactly when this window is; for example, in Switzerland a national pest forecasting system uses scouting and a mathematical model which takes into account daily temperature to predict exactly when the optimum time to spray is. If you are going to use pesticides, it is best to use them wisely. Some Swiss growers prefer to apply a granulosis virus instead of a chemical; this biopesticide multiplies in the caterpillar and eventually dissolves it from the inside. It may sound gruesome, but this virus only affects codling moth and its close relatives, and so is harmless to most insect life and to us.

Codling moths can also be managed by tying layers of corrugated-cardboard strips around the trunk of the trees. When climbing down the trunk in late summer, the fully grown caterpillars find that the layers of cardboard provide just the sort of crevices in which they like to spin their cocoons. The cardboard can be stripped off in winter, any earwigs shaken out, and then either burned or, better still, soaked in a bucket of water to kill the codling moth caterpillars and then composted. Simple tricks such as this are easy to use by anyone and cost almost nothing, but they do take time and effort. Modern farming employs very few people, and tasks that need to be done by a real person walking through the crop have largely been done away with as being inefficient. IPM is more labour-intensive. But then, there are now seven and a half billion of us humans on the planet, soon to be 10 billion. We are not short of labour. Rural communities throughout the developed world have collapsed through mechanisation of farming, but perhaps we need to think about going back to farming systems that involve more people in growing food. This is a theme I shall return to later.

Aside from avoiding harm to those vital natural enemies such as earwigs, there is another compelling reason to avoid pesticides in the orchard. Apples require cross-pollination; most apples will produce little or no fruit unless their flowers are visited by an insect carrying pollen from a different apple variety (since other trees of the same variety are actually just branches of the same individual plant, in terms of their origin and genetics). Effective pollination is not just necessary for a fruit to develop; the quality of pollination can also prevent deformed fruits, and increase the sweetness and mineral content, and improve the keeping properties of some fruits such as apples and strawberries. For example, a strawberry flower has many stigmas, the female parts of the flower, and if just a few are pollinated the resulting strawberry is small and deformed. Saleable strawberries require visits by insects that will spend time diligently probing the flower to pollinate every part. In parts of south-western China, farmers now hand-pollinate their apples and pears as overuse of pesticides has all but exterminated bees of all types. China may be a long way away, but signs of something similar have been detected much closer to home. A recent study on Gala and Cox apple production in the UK suggested that farmers are currently losing about £6 million in potential income because the quality of their fruit is being impaired by inadequate pollination; the 'beepocalypse', as it is sometimes called, may not be so far over the horizon.

Take pesticides out of the equation and a plethora of bee and fly species will turn up and happily pollinate your apples, usually bringing in pollen from a neighbour's garden if you haven't got a suitable pollinator tree of your own. Typically, about two-thirds of the pollinators that visit apple blossoms are solitary bees, mainly mason bees and mining bees, some of which are on the wing only in the spring, timing their life cycle to hit the spring blossom period for apples, hawthorn and blackthorn. Because they are spring specialists and have a short period in which to stock a nest with food and lay their eggs, these spring bees have to be hardy and capable of foraging in inclement weather, so they are far more reliable pollinators for apples than honeybees. Honeybees prefer warmer climates to ours, and are liable to sit in their hives having a sulk when the weather turns chill and breezy – which is most of the time in a typical British spring. Solitary bees differ from honeybees in many other ways, not least in their tendency to forage close to home. Most go no further than one hundred metres or so from their nest to find flowers, whereas honeybees can go several kilometres in search of food. This difference may be in part because a solitary bee can't risk being away from her nest for long, since it is unguarded. In her absence it might be taken over by a competitor, or a cuckoo bee might sneak in and lay her own eggs, so it is unwise to be gone for long, whereas of course a honeybee hive with its thousands of workers always has someone on guard duty. The large size of honeybee colonies also means that they must travel further to find enough food for all of them.

Because solitary bees don't like to travel, it is important to provide them with nest places in your garden; that way, they will be on hand to pollinate your fruit trees and vegetables. Some, such as red mason bees and leafcutter bees, can be catered for with those bee hotels, so long as there aren't too many earwigs. These are bee species that naturally nest in holes in dead trees or in the hollow stems of shrubby plants, but they very readily adopt artificial holes, and these are well worth providing as red mason bees in particular are great pollinators of apples.

I have often wondered what the natural pollinators of *Malus sieversii* are, in those bear-frequented Kazakh forests. Probably they are similar species to those in Britain, but who knows? Perhaps one day I'll get the chance to follow in Vavilov's footsteps and find out. I'd better go soon, for Vavilov would be disheartened to learn that the apple forests he discovered were largely destroyed in the second half of the twentieth century. In the 1950s, Nikita Khrushchev pushed the clearance of vast areas of 'virgin lands' to increase cereal production, and the apples and bears were hard hit; it is estimated that 80 per cent of the forests were cleared, and now only fragments persist. Vavilov was ahead of his time in recognising the irreplaceable value of conserving plant genetic resources to provide material for breeding crop varieties with improved characteristics such as better resistance to diseases and pests. These wild apple forests must contain many genes that could prove valuable in apple breeding, and it would be madness to lose them. There is hope that at least some of the remaining forests will be protected, for the Kazakh government now formally recognises their value and a new protected reserve has been set up, but media reports suggest that encroachment of urban areas continues to result in deforestation.

We cannot easily do much about the forests and bears of Kazakhstan, but we can still do our bit. Given the threats to the apple's wild progenitors, it is all the more important that we look after the full diversity of domestic varieties. Plant an apple tree. If you have a small garden then go for one of those dwarfing rootstocks on which the trees grow to no more than four feet tall; they can be trained along a wall, so taking up almost no space. A specialist nursery can sell you any of the varieties I have mentioned, or any of hundreds more. If you have room for just one, what about going for a Howgate Wonder, a splendid dual-purpose cooker and dessert apple that keeps until March? Whichever one you choose, you will be helping to look after a plant that has been providing us with food for millennia, and you will be creating a new ecosystem which in time may come to support hundreds of different insect species. Best of all, you will be able to enjoy the timeless pleasure of picking and eating your very own apples, straight from the tree.

4

The Toxic Cocktail

To make yacon & Stilton Waldorf salad

Ingredients: 1 large yacon, peeled and cubed; 3 apples, cored and cubed; 1 lime; 100g mayonnaise; 50g crème fraiche; 50g dried cranberries; 50g ripe Stilton; 50g toasted walnuts

1. *Put the yacon and apples in a bowl, squeeze on the lime juice, crumble in the cheese, add everything else and gently mix. It could not be easier.*

Yacons are a new discovery for me, a very easy to grow plant from the daisy family that produces big crops of huge crisp tubers, tasting somewhere between a pear and a radish. Nice raw, stir-fried, roasted or casseroled.

The UK is far from perfect, and we might often bemoan the deteriorating state of our environment and the seeming lack of any willingness among politicians to plan long term, but at least give thanks that we don't live in the USA. As if having a misogynist science-hating climate-change-denying president (at the time of writing) and enforced lawn-mowing were not bad enough, it is also common practice to drench urban and suburban areas with insecticides, either dropped from aeroplanes or sprayed as a toxic fog from large tankers that patrol the streets. There is no opting out – the police may be called if you try to prevent your garden from being sprayed. In the many areas where this occurs there is little point in trying to garden for wildlife, or plant bee-friendly flowers – all you would be doing is providing a death trap, luring butterflies or bees to their slaughter.

I have been contacted by distraught wildlife enthusiasts in Sacramento who have had their gardens repeatedly drenched with insecticides by contractors hired in by the local authority. The spraying is supposed to target the Japanese beetle, a rather attractive copper and emerald-green scarab beetle which, as you might surmise from the name, originated in Japan. It was accidentally introduced to the east coast of the USA over a hundred years ago, and has been spreading westwards ever since, with a handful turning up in Sacramento in 2011. Japanese beetles spend most of the year as grubs underground, eating grass roots; they are related to Colin the cockchafer, and similarly can produce brown patches on lawns. The adults live for just a few weeks but nibble the leaves and petals of many ornamental plants, and also have a particular taste for vine leaves. California has a thriving agricultural industry, including a very profitable wine industry, and fear that these beetles might become significant pests led the California Department of Food and Agriculture to launch an eradication programme. Unfortunately, the invading beetles had been found in suburban gardens, so it was these that were targeted with a barrage of insecticides; garden citrus trees were sprayed six times per year with a pyrethroid insecticide, other garden trees were sprayed three times per year with carbaryl (an insecticide which is a likely human carcinogen), while lawns were drenched with imidacloprid (a neonicotinoid neurotoxic insecticide which will poison the soil for years to come). Spraying was done in the daytime, when butterflies and bees would be active; it is hard to imagine how any insect could survive this onslaught.

In response to protests from local residents, these three chemicals have now been replaced with a newer pesticide known as Acelepryn (technically a chemical with the tongue-twisting name chlorantraniliprole). Acelepryn is billed as providing 'season-long control from a single application' of pest insects such as caterpillars, beetle grubs, adult Japanese beetles, weevils and more. Remarkably, it is also claimed that the chemical has 'no known adverse effects on beneficial and non-target organisms including earthworms and honeybees' according to the manufacturers, Syngenta. If this were true it would be a remarkable trick. No one has yet invented a pesticide that can tell the difference between pest insects we might wish to kill, such as pea aphids or Japanese beetles, and the large majority that we ought to avoid harming, such as bees or hoverflies. Whatever the manufacturers may claim, it is inconceivable that hosing a garden with a potent insecticide will kill only the pests and leave bees and other beneficial insects unharmed.

There would seem to be other problems with Acelepryn. Its half-life in soil (the time it takes for half of the chemical to degrade) can be up to 924 days, depending on soil type. This means that it will accumulate in soils if used every year, for most of last year's dose will still be left when the next batch is applied. This is why it gives 'season-long control': a single application makes the soil toxic for years to come. On top of that, the technical data also states that Acelepryn is 'highly toxic' to aquatic organisms. There is no value in having a garden pond if you live in an area that is being treated with this chemical, unless a lifeless toxic hole in the ground is your cup of tea. In short, this chemical has a bunch of undesirable properties. I'd be willing to bet that, twenty years from now, Acelepryn will have been banned from use in gardens, once enough evidence accumulates that it is harming wildlife. It will then be replaced by yet another chemical, and so the cycle will continue, while nature continues to vanish.

Funnily enough, despite all of these efforts, the Japanese beetle has survived in Sacramento; they are still turning up, presumably because there are quiet corners of land which are overlooked by the sprayers where the beetles can multiply. Entomologists at nearby University of California Davis have suggested that eradication is probably impossible, and that a more gentle approach using phero-mone traps and biocontrol agents to manage the pest rather than trying to kill every last one might be more sensible, but their view does not yet seem to have been heard.

If the butterfly-loving residents of Sacramento feel hard done by, they can at least console themselves that their gardens are not yet subject to pesticide bombardments from aeroplanes. In south-east-ern USA, dropping clouds of insecticide from planes is intended to eliminate the mosquitoes that spread the Zika virus, certainly a more serious threat to human well-being than the Japanese beetle. Infection of pregnant mothers can lead to birth defects, notably microcephaly (a small brain and head), although most people who contract the Zika virus experience nothing more than a mild and brief illness. The birth defects are obviously terrible, but nonethe-less the reaction to the arrival of this disease in the USA seems to have been disproportionate and poorly thought through. Even before Zika, it was common practice in Florida and Louisiana to blanket-spray insecticides to kill mosquitoes, with some 14 mil-lion acres being sprayed every year, particularly targeting big urban centres such as Miami and New Orleans. When the Zika threat emerged in 2016 these efforts were redoubled, and nearby states began spraying too.

The insecticide of choice for use in this situation is an organo-phosphate known as Naled. The Cornell University 'Extension Toxicology Network', an online pesticide database, lists a disturbing catalogue of toxic effects of Naled on humans. It describes Naled as 'moderately to highly toxic [to humans] by ingestion, inhalation and dermal absorption'. Edited highlights of the effects on humans include: 'When inhaled, the first effects are ... bloody or runny nose, coughing, chest discomfort, difficult or short breath, and wheezing ... Eye contact will cause pain, bleeding, tears, pupil constriction, and blurred vision. Following exposure by any route, other systemic effects may include ... nausea, vomiting, diarrhea, abdominal cramps, headache, dizziness, eye pain, blurred vision, sweating, and confusion.' As if that was not terrifying enough, it goes on to say: 'Severe poisoning will affect the central nervous system, producing incoordination, slurred speech, loss of reflexes, weakness, fatigue, involuntary muscle contractions, twitching, tremors of the tongue or eyelids, and eventually paralysis of the body extremities and the respiratory muscles. There may also be involuntary defecation or urination, psychosis, irregular heartbeats, unconsciousness, convulsions and coma. Death may be caused by respiratory failure or cardiac arrest.' There have also been suggestions that exposure to pregnant women might lead to autism or other mental disabilities in children, but as far as I can tell this remains speculative. What is beyond doubt is that Naled is quite an unpleasant chemical, and ideally not one that most of us would wish ourselves or our children to be doused in from a passing aeroplane.

Of course I am being deliberately alarmist in reciting this long list of symptoms. The counter-argument is that the doses that the residents of southern US cities receive are small, and on paper should not be enough to produce any but the mildest of the symptoms described above. This is the position of the US Environmental Protection Agency, but in Europe the regulatory agencies take a different view and have banned Naled, while the governor of Puerto Rico (which has the Zika virus) has also prohibited its use. Understandably, some suburban residents in south-eastern US are deeply concerned, and there have been street protests in Florida against the spraying. When different agencies view the same toxicological data and draw opposing conclusions, what are ordinary people supposed to think? It is very hard to predict what the long-term consequences of regularly exposing tens of millions of people to low doses of this chemical might be. If even a tiny fraction of them are adversely affected, might this not amount to more people than are harmed by the Zika virus?

Whatever the costs and benefits to people, it is clear that this spraying carries a huge environmental cost. At 8 a.m. on 28 August 2016, aerial spraying of Naled began over the county of Dorchester in South Carolina. It was in response to four cases of Zika virus infections in people in South Carolina, although all of those were people who became infected on visits outside of the state. There was no evidence that a single mosquito in South Carolina was carrying the virus at the time, but the spraying was intended to prevent the disease getting into the mosquitoes and hence infecting more people. When commercial beekeeper Juanita Stanley went to check on her forty-six beehives that morning, almost every bee was dead – perhaps two and a half million bees. Dead bees carpeted the ground and crunched underfoot, while a few survivors were trying to drag the corpses clear of their hive entrances.

According to the manufacturer of Naled, the chemical is 'highly toxic to bees exposed to direct treatment on blooming crops or weeds'. To minimise the risk to bees, it is recommended that Naled should be applied at night, and is not to be applied more than two hours after sunrise or two hours before sunset, limiting applications to times when bees are least active. The sprayers in Dorchester County followed this advice (8 a.m. was within two hours of sunrise), but on a warm day in August the bees are fully active and outside the hive visiting flowers by this time, and so they got a full dose. The advice would appear to have been wrong.

Juanita received no warning of the spraying. It was apparently announced a few days earlier on Facebook, but she had not seen the post. Much of the acrimonious debate following this incident focused on the inadequate notice given, and in future the authorities have agreed that they will not rely on social media when announcing spray dates. If Juanita had been warned she could have closed up the hives the night before. This would obviously have been much better for Juanita and her bees, but it is missing the bigger picture. The south-eastern United States is home to an extraordinary diversity of insect species, undoubtedly comprising tens of thousands of them: bumblebees, dragonflies, butterflies, ladybirds, hoverflies, lacewings, fireflies and many more. These insects are not on Facebook, and there is no one to tuck them away at night before a spray. The two and a half million honeybees that Juanita lost are a drop in the ocean of countless trillions of insects that must be killed every time an aeroplane passes over dropping a cloud of insecticide. These are pollinators, pest control agents, recyclers, and food for umpteen species of birds, bats, lizards and frogs. Such insects comprise about two-thirds of all known species, so these spray applications are wiping out the majority of life. All to kill the one species of mosquito, *Aedes aegypti*, that transmits Zika.

Ironically, this spraying isn't even particularly effective. Infectious-disease expert Duane Gubler of Duke Medical School found that adult *Aedes aegypti* spend a lot of time in or under buildings, or perched under the canopy of trees and shrubs, where they are sheltered from the falling spray. Unlike many mosquitoes they are not active at night, instead feeding mainly in the early morning or late afternoon, so that night-time spraying is largely pointless. In any case killing a portion of the adults has little long-term effect as they reproduce very quickly. Removing their breeding places is a much more effective control measure, for mosquitoes breed in small puddles and often use water that has collected in discarded plastic rubbish, old car tyres, blocked gutters, bird baths and so on. Adding small insect-eating fish to ponds also works very well. Likewise, encouraging bats by putting up bat boxes; the little brown bat can eat up to 1,000 mosquitoes in an hour (but is likely to starve if an area is carpet-bombed with insecticide). Aerial spraying seems to be more of a symbolic gesture, visible proof that the authorities are taking action to protect citizens, rather than a practical means of control.

Sadly, it seems that my Sacramento friend and the protesters in Florida are in a minority, for many US citizens are in favour of having their yards doused in chemicals. Indeed, they are actually willing to pay for it. A couple of years ago I attended a US conference on protecting pollinators in gardens and was shocked to discover that, just as some UK residents employ a contractor to tend to their lawn, some US residents actually hire contractors to regularly visit and hose down their garden with insecticides. One of the speakers, entomologist Mike Raupp from the University of Maryland, showed pictures of operatives blasting the shrubs in a suburban garden with insecticides using what appeared to be something akin to a fire hose linked to a large tanker. These sprays are targeted primarily at pests of garden plants rather than mosquitoes. Mike said that he had tried to suggest that this prophylactic spraying was unnecessary, and that perhaps more carefully targeted applications only when there was a severe pest problem would be better. One homeowner replied that he did not feel that he was getting value for money unless he could see that his garden had had a thorough soaking and that the pesticide was, quite literally, dripping from the garden trees. Perhaps he also loves the smell of napalm in the morning.

Some regard pesticides as entirely unnecessary, as poisons that are destroying wildlife, and believe that all should be banned. Others regard them as a valuable tool that is needed if we are to feed the world. But drenching suburban areas with them is completely nuts. It certainly does huge damage to garden wildlife, and probably poses risks to human health. It also threatens the long-term viability of the pesticide, for the more any pesticide is used the more likely it is that insect pests will become resistant to it. It is just like antibiotics; overuse, either by doctors dishing them out indiscriminately, or farmers using them prophylactically on crowded and stressed farm animals, has accelerated the appearance of 'superbugs', bacteria that are now resistant to more or less all known antibiotics. In exactly the same way, unnecessary use of pesticides simply hastens the appearance of insect pests that are immune to them. Hence even ardent supporters of pesticides should argue against their use for purely cosmetic purposes in gardens – unless, of course, they actually manufacture the pesticides, in which case eliminating urban use would impact on sales.[17]

In any case, plants are pretty good at looking after themselves. They have their own defence mechanisms – spines, bristles, tough leaves, and natural chemical defences. Garden plants generally only suffer badly from insect pests if they are stressed because they are not suited to the local climate or soil. Take a walk in the woods and the flowers, trees and shrubs you see are generally healthy; they

---

[17] You might think that the manufacturers of pesticides would have a strong interest in preventing the evolution of resistance to their products in insect pests. However, the company that brings a new pesticide to market gets a fixed period during which it has the exclusive right to manufacture it, typically between ten and fifteen years, depending on the country. This is the window during which the parent company has to make back the considerable amount of money it invested in developing the chemical. Once that period is over, other companies can start making it, and so the price and profit to be made drops. Hence it may actually be in the interests of the manufacturer for their own product to become obsolete after about fifteen years, so long as they have a new pesticide ready to roll out as its replacement. Bad for the environment, but good for profits.

are well adapted to their environment. On the other hand, if you try to grow an acid-loving blueberry or rhododendron in a chalky, alkaline garden soil, it will not thrive. The plant will be sickly and, too weak to invest in defences, it will be vulnerable to insect pests. You might try to grow nectarines or peaches, but in the UK it is really too cold for them and they will rarely do well. In short, if you have a garden plant that is repeatedly and heavily infested with pests, you are trying to grow the wrong plant. Wherever you live, on chalk, clay or peat, in Cornwall, Clapham or the Cairngorms, there are certain to be plenty of better choices that will be able to look after themselves.

Even if your garden plants do occasionally suffer a bit from slugs or caterpillars or aphids, does it really matter? I still have some hybrid tea roses in my garden, hangovers from a past owner that I have yet to dig out, and they often get a few aphids on them, but so what? I could go for the nuclear option and blast them with an insecticide, or I could leave them. The very worst outcome is that I might end up with a few more aphids and perhaps a few less flowers on my roses as a result. Is that such a catastrophe? Similarly, my broad bean crop usually gets black bean aphids on it by mid-spring. These insects breed fast, and soon form dense clumps near the growing tip of the plant, often guarded by ants that milk them for honeydew. It looks bad, and I might be tempted to rush out and buy an insecticide spray, but instead I do nothing. Within a week or two there are always clusters of orange ladybird eggs, and if I am lucky there are also lines of delicate pearly lacewing eggs, each laid at the top of a slender stalk to keep it out of reach of the ants. The ladybird eggs hatch into burly, black, spiky larvae that shrug off the attacks of the ants and munch away voraciously at the aphids, consuming up to 5,000 in their short development. The assassin-like larval lacewings are armed with scimitar-shaped jaws with which they impale their aphid prey.[18] Tiny black parasitoid wasps arrive, smaller than the aphids but equipped with a long, sharp egg-laying tube with which they stab their prey, inserting a single egg into each aphid that will soon hatch and devour its host from the inside. Hoverfly larvae also grab their share. These blind and transparent maggots resemble nothing more than an animated bogey. They find their prey by smell and then use their hooked mouthparts to ensnare them, sucking out their juices and discarding the empty husks. Soldier beetles, which until this time have been feeding on the yellow umbels of my lovage plants, are attracted over to the beans by the surfeit of food on offer – these rusty-red, elongate and leggy insects are omnivorous with a hearty appetite for aphids. At night, the earwigs emerge from their crevices to lend a hand. Each bean plant becomes a battleground, but the end result is always the same; the aphids are slaughtered, the ants eventually retreat, and all that remains is a sticky mess of honeydew and 'mummies', the petrified corpses of aphids from which parasitoid wasps have emerged. I'm sure this sometimes reduces my bean harvest, but I still seem to get plenty of beans, enough to freeze bagfuls and keep us going all winter. My succeeding summer crops never seem to suffer from aphids, perhaps because the predators that bred up among the beans fan out among my other vegetables. Had I gone for the apocalyptic option of the pesticide spray, there would be no predators, and I would probably suffer from recurring aphid problems through the year.

Of course, since you are reading this book, I'd hazard a guess that you use few pesticides in your garden (if you are lucky enough to have one). Perhaps you use none at all and have gone entirely organic. You may well be trying to make your garden wildlife-friendly,

---

[18] Some lacewing larvae decorate their backs with the remains of their prey, and this seems to fool guarding ants into thinking that they are giant aphids and hence should not be attacked.

stocking it with bee- and butterfly-friendly flowers, putting up bee hotels and so on. Sadly, you might still find that there are pesticides in your garden, ones that you have inadvertently brought in. Take a walk around your local garden centre and you will see a mouth-watering display of gorgeous plants on display. Some are specifically labelled as bee- or pollinator-friendly, with a picture of a cartoon bumblebee on the label, sometimes using the Royal Horticultural Society's 'Perfect for Pollinators' logo. If you like hearing the buzz of bees in your garden, and want to do your bit to help our wildlife, you might well be tempted. Indeed, I have often spent a small fortune myself on potted plants when I only went to the garden centre to buy a pack of parsnip seeds. The big DIY and supermarket chains are similar – somewhere by the main entrance you will usually see a range of colourful plants in plastic pots and trays, some of them labelled as bee-friendly.

If, like me, you've ever succumbed to the temptation to buy these plants, you may be somewhat concerned by the results of research performed in my lab by visiting PhD student Andrea Lentola from Italy. I had a suspicion that these ornamental plants were just too perfect, and had heard plausible rumours that the greenhouses in which they are mass-reared rely heavily on pesticides. I wondered whether these plants being sold as 'bee-friendly' might not be so friendly after all, and so in 2016 I launched a bid for crowd-funding[19] to support some research to find out. The public were very kind and collectively coughed up nearly £8,000, enough to pay Andrea's tuition fees and the costs of the research. Andrea and I

[19] Getting funding for scientific research is increasingly difficult, and any project which has the potential to offend powerful industries is particularly unlikely to receive funding, even from government research councils. Crowd-funding has emerged as an alternative means to fund small projects on subjects which the general public deem worthy of their support.

drove to the nearby Wyevale garden centre and filled a trolley with lovely plants: campanula, catmint, lavender and scabious, among others. We bought only those on the RHS list, and most had their 'Perfect for Pollinators' logo. Under the guidance of our in-house chemist, Professor Liz Hill, Andrea set about the tedious business of extracting nectar and pollen from the flowers, and screening the nectar, pollen and leaves for a broad range of pesticides. In the meantime I toured around some other big-chain retailers, Aldi, B&Q and Homebase, buying more bee-friendly flowers for Andrea to process. It took Andrea several months to get through collecting the samples and running them through some very expensive analytical equipment that lurks in a windowless basement room at Sussex University (gas and liquid chromatographs linked to tandem mass spectrometers, if you should be interested).

The results were depressing. Most of the plants contained a cocktail of pesticides, usually a mixture of fungicides and insecticides. I wish I could say that I was surprised by the results, but sadly I wasn't. Only two out of twenty-nine plants that we tested contained no pesticides. Twenty-two of them, 76 per cent, contained at least one insecticide, and 38 per cent contained two or more insecticides. One flowering heather plant contained five different insecticides and five different fungicides – a veritable toxic bouquet. Seventy per cent of the plants contained neonicotinoids (insecticides that are notorious for their harmful effects on bees and long persistence in the environment).[20] Although neonicotinoids were the most common

[20] Neonicotinoids are not all equally dangerous to bees. Three have been identified as particularly harmful, and have been banned by the European Union from use on flowering crops to protect bees: imidacloprid, thiamethoxam and clothianidin. For the technically minded, 38 per cent of the plants contained imidacloprid, 14 per cent contained thiamethoxam and one plant contained clothianidin.

insecticides we found, there were others, both pyrethroids and the organophosphate chlorpyrifos. Some of these pesticides are quite persistent and are likely to be detectable in the plants for a few years. Enough detail; you get the picture. Plants sold as 'bee-friendly' are usually stuffed full of pesticides.

This seemed to me to be pretty scandalous. Clearly these plants were not 'bee-friendly' at all. Well-intentioned gardeners, hoping to encourage pollinators in their plot, were buying plants laced with pesticides and poisoning the very insects they hoped to help. I'm no legal expert, but didn't this contravene the Trade Descriptions Act? The use of the 'Perfect for Pollinators' logo was a marketing ploy, taking advantage of the increasing interest amongst gardeners for looking after wildlife[21]. I couldn't help but wonder whether the retailers had known full well what was in the plants they were selling and had turned a blind eye, or whether it was simply ignorance.

Our results were published in spring 2017 and caused quite a stir. Several national newspapers ran the story, and on the back of it Friends of the Earth launched a campaign focused on persuading plant retailers to ensure that their 'bee-friendly' plants are free of neonicotinoids. B&Q acted quickly and positively, promising that from February 2018 they would prohibit their suppliers from using neonicotinoids. Aldi declared that they had stopped using neonicotinoids in October 2016, just after we bought the plants from them. Other organisations were less positive. The Horticultural Trades Association, which represents the gardening industry, instead went on the offensive, trying to play down and undermine

---

[21] Since writing this, the RHS have changed the logo to 'Plants for Pollinators', implicitly acknowledging that the plants may not be 'perfect', but this seems to me to be sidestepping the issue. Actually taking action to reduce or eliminate the pesticides in these flowers is surely what is needed, and it would be nice to see the RHS taking a lead in this.

the significance of our findings. In an online article it claimed that the three neonicotinoids banned by the EU on flowering crops are not used in horticulture (which would seem from our results to be simply untrue). It then argued that the concentrations of pesticides we found were at 'low levels', and that we only sampled from 'a very restricted area of the country'.

Let's have a closer look at their criticisms. Firstly, the concentration of the pesticide is of course important. Modern analytical techniques are very sensitive and tiny concentrations can be detected. Perhaps the concentrations we detected were all too low to do any actual harm? For neonicotinoids, the concentrations typically found in the nectar and pollen of treated crops such as oilseed rape are in the range one to ten parts per billion. This is indeed a minute amount, but exposure to such concentrations has been found to impair bee navigation, reduce egg laying and learning, and suppress the immune system. In a study with bumblebee nests we found that giving them pollen with six parts per billion of neonicotinoid was enough to reduce nest growth and resulted in an 85 per cent drop in the number of new queens produced by each nest. In the ornamental flowers we found the neonicotinoid imidacloprid at up to a maximum concentration of twenty-nine parts per billion, clothianidin at thirteen parts per billion and thiamethoxam at 119 parts per billion. In other words, concentrations far higher than those known to harm bees. The claim that we only sampled from a 'very restricted area' is pretty absurd. It is true that we sampled from stores near Sussex University, but these are huge chains with an international supply network. Is the Horticultural Trades Association really suggesting that this problem is peculiar to East Sussex?

Luckily the Friends of the Earth campaign gained real traction and very soon most of the big-name chains, including Notcutts, Hilliers, Wyevale, Dobbies and so on, had all agreed to withdraw neonics. By the end of the summer the only major ornamental flower retailer that was not on board was Homebase. Friends of the Earth set up an 'online action', whereby members of the public were asked to contact Homebase and ask them to change their policy on using neonicotinoids. After 18,000 people did so, in November 2017 Homebase finally announced that it too would be ceasing to sell plants treated with neonicotinoids by the end of 2018.

It makes a refreshing change for scientific research to directly lead to decisive changes in practice. It is perhaps the only piece of research I have ever been involved in which has led to such a clear response, and I should be delighted, but at the risk of sounding churlish I am not. I would argue that, by focusing on neonicotinoids, Friends of the Earth and all of the garden centre chains are missing the bigger picture. Neonicotinoids are undoubtedly bad for bees, but what about all the other chemicals? If I buy a plant to feed to bees I don't want it to have been drenched with a pyrethroid or organophosphate insecticide either. Both are highly poisonous to bees, and organophosphates are exceedingly toxic to people too – this is the group of nerve agent chemicals that currently kill about 200,000 people per year. Even fungicides have been found to harm bees; some seem to block the detoxification system of the bees, rendering insecticides up to 1,000 times more toxic, while others are thought to damage the bee's gut flora, which are vital to health.

Promising to withdraw neonicotinoids is all very well, but what will the growers use instead? They might use more pyrethroids or organophosphates, which would not be a great improvement, or they might use new chemicals that are quietly appearing on the market. While the pesticide industry has been fighting a rearguard action over neonicotinoids for the last twenty years, it has been preparing the alternatives. They all have tongue-twisting and eminently forgettable names: cyantraniliprole, sulfoxaflor and flupyradifurone are now on the market (I suspect that these names are deliberately complicated and hard to remember or pronounce as a strategy to discourage discussion about them). All three of these chemicals are neurotoxins, the latter two targeting exactly the same neuroreceptors in the brain of insects as do neonicotinoids. They are also all systemic (i.e. they spread through the tissues of a plant), just like neonicotinoids, and so if they are used on any plant that flowers they will end up in the nectar and pollen. All three are highly toxic to bees. Indeed, in almost every respect sulfoxaflor and flupyradifurone look like neonicotinoids, but their manufacturers are very keen to claim that they belong to quite different, newly invented classes of chemical. Neonicotinoids have a bad reputation, one that is best left behind. After all, it would be a bit obvious if, while we were busy banning neonicotinoids, we were registering new neonicotinoids for use. How dumb would that be?

For the moment, my days of buying garden centre plants are over. I don't want the lingering worry that I might be accidentally poisoning my bees, hoverflies and butterflies. It would be nice the see the Royal Horticultural Society showing some leadership here, for it is their logo that is used on plants full of pesticides. Throughout the media coverage of this issue and the Friends of the Earth campaign, the RHS kept a very low profile. It seems to me that they should stipulate that any plant sold with their bee logo should be free of insecticides, better still free of pesticides of any type. Anything less is a fudge. Until the gardening industry gets its act together, I'd suggest buying plants from organic nurseries. They aren't common, but some are online. Alternatively, and with lower carbon footprint, grow plants from seeds or, if you haven't the patience, plant-swap with your friends and neighbours.

OK, so I hope I've persuaded you not to buy and spray pesticides in your garden, and to beware of those showy garden centre ornamentals for the moment at least. There is just one more thing that you might want to think about before you can declare your garden pesticide-free. There are currently eight and a half million dogs in the UK, nearly as many cats, plus a million or so pet rabbits. If you don't have a dog, cat or rabbit, you're off the hook; feel free to skip on a paragraph or two. If you do have one of these animals, you may occasionally treat it when it catches fleas, or indeed you may treat it for fleas even if it doesn't have any. The latter may seem a bit odd, but is common practice. If you take your dog to the vet for any reason, many will attempt to sell you a prophylactic flea treatment. It is a bit like the polish or water-repellent spray that shoe shops often try to sell you whenever you buy a new pair of shoes; you don't really need it, but it seems rude to refuse. The most common flea treatment is a 'spot on', meaning you drip it on the back of the animal's neck. One can also buy collars impregnated with insecticide. In both cases the active ingredient is often imidacloprid, a name that should sound familiar by now – it is a neonicotinoid, one of the ones banned by the European Union from use on flowering crops, the very same stuff that we found in 38 per cent of our ornamental plants and that is highly toxic to bees.

The dose your vet will advise you to drip onto your medium-sized dog every month is 250mg, enough to deliver a lethal dose to about 60 million honeybees or about sixty partridges (the dose in the impregnated collar is nearly twenty times higher at 4.5g). Of course this isn't necessarily a problem unless 60 million honeybees or sixty partridges suddenly decide to eat your dog, both of which would seem to be unlikely events, but one cannot help but wonder: where does this toxin go? Neonicotinoids are persistent in soil and plants, present for months or years, but where they go when they are applied to a pet has not been studied at all, so far as I can find. The instructions say to part the fur and drip the chemical onto the skin. To protect the whole animal against fleas the pesticide can't stay on the neck, so presumably it is absorbed to some extent into the body, or perhaps it spreads over the surface of the skin. This treatment is advertised as suitable for use on lactating dogs with pups, and the instructions explain that it will confer protection to the pups. I can't find any explanation as to how the protection of pups is supposed to work, but this suggests that the chemical is systemic in dogs just as it is in plants, and so is passing through the mother and into the pups in her milk. To get into the milk, they must be penetrating the skin, so what happens when you stroke the dog, affectionately ruffling the fur on the back of its neck? What happens when your child gives the dog a hug, burying her face in the animal's pelt? And when you grab the dog's collar, if it is wearing one impregnated with insecticide? In each case, presumably some of the neurotoxin is passed to your skin, and penetrates it.

If neonicotinoids are in the milk, I would guess that they are also likely to be in the pet's urine, which is then sprinkled onto your garden, or into the local park or hedgerow when you take the dog for a walk. If so, then we know that the chemicals will be absorbed by the roots or leaves of any plant they touch, and will go into the pollen and nectar if that plant bears flowers. If you have a small garden where your dog or cat regularly urinates, perhaps it is not such a good idea to allow the clover and dandelions to flower. In recent studies at Sussex University we have put bumblebee nests out into urban Brighton and repeatedly found imidacloprid in the food they collect. This might be coming from the 'bee-friendly' plants that people have bought from their local garden centre, or it might be coming from these flea treatments applied to our pets – we do not yet know.

It isn't just bees that are threatened. One would guess that, since these flea treatments are water-soluble, they readily wash off the pet. Although there appear to have been no scientific studies of the environmental fate of imidacloprid dripped onto pets, there is one study of fipronil, a related insecticide with similar properties. Volunteers who were treating their dogs with fipronil were asked to bathe them, and then the bathwater was tested for the insecticide. Hardly surprisingly, a large proportion of the chemical was found in the water – up to 86 per cent in one case of a dog washed soon after treatment. The authors of the study suggest that this might be harmful to aquatic environments downstream of the waste-treatment works to which bathwater goes. A bigger worry for me is what happens when the dog goes out in the rain or jumps in the garden pond to cool off – something my dog does every day in summer. If most of 250mg of imidacloprid were to wash into a pond or stream that could devastate the aquatic insect life. Let me bore you with some quick back-of-an-envelope calculations. A concentration of six parts of imidacloprid per 10 billion of water is enough to kill the aquatic nymphs of the slate brown dun mayfly, so 250mg is enough to render 417,000 litres of water toxic to mayflies. It would take about six dogs treated with a spot on to render an Olympic-sized swimming pool toxic to mayflies (or, if all the chemical washed out of the collar, one single dog wearing an impregnated collar to make three such swimming pools toxic).

I imagine that you are already wondering what the human health risks are here. If you treat your pet with imidacloprid, you will undoubtedly contaminate yourself and your family with tiny quantities of neurotoxin. This doesn't sound like a great idea, but you should bear in mind that these chemicals are a lot less toxic to people than they are to insects. Weight for weight, imidacloprid is very roughly 1,000 times more toxic to an insect than it is to a vertebrate (rats are the standard test organism, the assumption being that humans are just big rats so far as the effects of toxins are concerned). For obvious reasons no one has ever done an experiment to measure the lethal dose in humans, or for that matter in dogs. So, some more quick maths suggests that if four-billionths of a gram of imidacloprid is enough to kill a honeybee weighing one-tenth of a gram,[22] then a human-sized honeybee would be killed by about 3mg of imidacloprid, while killing a real human might require about 3g. That is twelve times the amount you might drip onto Rover each month, and of course you are only likely to be exposed to a tiny fraction of the chemical you apply to the dog. Unless you drip a year's supply straight down your throat, or decide to eat the dog's treated collar, you won't get a lethal dose. So, phew, nothing to worry about.

I have a suspicion that you aren't convinced, just as the pro-testers in Florida aren't happy at being doused with Naled, and rightly so. It isn't quite so simple. There are a number of factors which make this issue far from clear-cut. Firstly, you won't just be exposed to imidacloprid and other neonicotinoids via the family pet. A recent study revealed that there was imidacloprid in about half of Spanish red wines – and there is no reason to suppose that Spain is atypical. A global study of honey on sale in shops found neonicotinoids in three-quarters of the samples (often at concentrations known to be harmful to bees). Neonicotinoids have been detected in tap water in the USA, and my research group at Sussex University has found them – at very low concentrations – in well water on an organic smallholding in the UK. Given that they

---

[22] I should explain that toxicity is usually measured by giving test organisms different doses of a chemical and, after twenty-four or forty-eight hours, seeing how many are dead at each dose. At the highest doses most or all die, at low doses none die, but somewhere in between is the 'LD50' – the dose at which half of the animals die (the 'lethal dose which kills 50 per cent'). The LD50 of imidacloprid in honeybees is about 4 nanograms (four-billionths of a gram).

are very widely used on diverse crops, including staples such as wheat and many horticultural fruit and vegetable crops, they are likely to be in many foods. It is more or less impossible to escape them, and it is also impossible to work out exactly how much we are exposed to in total. This exposure will be happening continuously, throughout our lives, over months and years. Anyone born during or after the mid-1990s (when neonicotinoids started to be used) is likely to have been regularly exposed to tiny, varying doses from conception onwards. Maybe this is fine, maybe it isn't – we simply don't know.

On top of all this, we aren't just exposed to one pesticide at a time. The study of neonicotinoids in global honey found two different neonicotinoids in nearly half of the samples. Other studies which have screened honey for other pesticides often find ten or more, mixtures of different types of insecticide, fungicide and herbicide. I love honey, and still eat it regularly on toast for breakfast, but I know that I am consuming a complicated cocktail of pesticides. When I can find it I buy organic honey, which must be better, but I often wonder how any beekeeper can be sure his bees haven't come into contact with pesticides, given their ubiquity and the fact that honeybees fly several miles to find food. There is no reason to suppose that honey is especially bad; the bees are simply gathering nectar from farms and gardens, picking up the many pesticides that are being used. More than 500 different pesticides are registered for use in the European Union, so there are plenty for them to bump into. A 2017 survey by the European Food Standards Agency found pesticides in just under half of all food samples. You won't be surprised to hear that fruits are particularly heavily contaminated, with grapes being among the worst culprits. More than three-quarters of grapes tested were positive, with most containing multiple residues. One sample of grapes from Turkey contained nineteen different pesticides. Tasty.

We are more commonly exposed to some pesticides than others. Neonicotinoids are among the most frequent chemicals in samples of food, but probably the pesticide we consume most of is glyphosate (often sold as Roundup), a weedkiller and the most-used pesticide in the world. Controversy has raged over this chemical, which in 2015 was declared by the World Health Organisation to be a carcinogen. Counter-arguments suggest that the doses required to cause cancer are far higher than those we are likely to be exposed to. What is undoubtedly true is that we are all consuming glyphosate all of the time. A 2016 study of more than 2,000 Germans found glyphosate in the urine of more than 99 per cent of them, with particularly high levels in children. Three-quarters of them had glyphosate concentrations in their urine that were five or more times the acceptable safe limit in drinking water. This near-universal exposure is hardly surprising, since glyphosate is routinely sprayed onto many staple crops such as wheat just before harvest, and hence it turns up in everyday foodstuffs such as bread, Cheerios, chocolate cookies, Ritz crackers and Kellogg's Special K cereal, among many others. Like it or not, unless you buy exclusively organic food, you are very probably urinating weedkiller.

There is one more thing to throw into the toxic mix. Pesticides aren't the only man-made chemicals that we are exposed to on a regular basis. In fact a government inventory of chemicals sold in the USA since 1979 lists a staggering 85,000 different compounds. The average American woman uses twelve personal-care products a day (soaps, lotions, toothpaste, shampoos and so on) containing 168 different chemicals. Men use about half that amount. These chemicals include acrylamides, formaldehyde, phthalates, hydroquinones and many others, including known and suspected carcinogens, and endocrine disruptors (chemicals that interfere with the normal functioning of the numerous hormones that regulate our bodies). Many of these chemicals are readily absorbed through the skin. We encounter other potentially harmful chemicals in flame retardants, food packaging, plastics, cleaning products, paints, even in shower curtains. Farmed salmon often contain polychlorinated biphenyls (though their manufacture has been banned for forty years), and wild tuna often have accumulated mercury in their tissues. One would go mad if one worried too much about it all.

The primary defence offered by those who make the many chemicals to which we are exposed is usually to argue that they are harmless at the dose we receive. As with the neonicotinoids, typically the amounts in our food, or detected in our blood or urine, are a small fraction of that which will kill us (at least in the short term), and hence we are assured that we have nothing to fear. The problem with this reasoning is that our understanding of toxicity of pesticides is mostly based on short-term toxicity tests, often conducted over just twenty-four or forty-eight hours.[23] If the bee, rat or partridge is alive and kicking at the end of the test then all is well. If there is particular concern over a chemical's safety for people, then longer-term chronic exposure tests might be carried out on rats, typically lasting ninety days. All of these tests use just one chemical at a time. We assume that effects on humans can be extrapolated from effects on rats, that the result of long-term exposure over decades can be predicted from short-term studies over days or weeks, and that studies of the effects of exposure to cocktails of mixed pesticides can be predicted from studies of the effects of one chemical at a time.

A second line of argument which is often trotted out to defend pesticides is the 'nature fallacy'. Many people have an intuitive belief that natural is synonymous with good, and that by implication

---

[23] Surprisingly, many chemicals used in cosmetics and other everyday household products have never been subject to any kind of safety testing.

unnatural (e.g. synthetic chemicals) is bad. Following this principle, organic farmers are allowed to use pesticides that are naturally occurring, such as pyrethrum, the chemical that is extracted from chrysanthemums. They are not allowed to use synthetic variants of pyrethrum, many of which are widely used by conventional farmers. I can't see much logic in this. There are many naturally occurring chemicals that are exceedingly harmful, such as botulinum toxin, arsenic and nicotine. Indeed, botulinum toxin and tetanospasmin – the toxin naturally produced by tetanus bacteria – are the two most poisonous compounds known to man. As we have seen, plants have evolved all sorts of chemicals to deter herbivores, such as the mustard oils in cabbages, and so many foods we routinely eat contain natural toxins. Conversely, some man-made chemicals are enormously valuable, such as the many synthetic antibiotics developed since naturally occurring penicillin was discovered by Alexander Fleming. It is simply not true that natural is necessarily good for you, or that natural pesticides are innately better than man-made ones. This is often used to bash the organic movement over the head, which is unfortunate as it rather misses the point of organic farming. Organic farmers strive very hard to use no pesticides at all. In the UK, if an organic farmer wants to use pyrethrum he has to apply for written permission from the Soil Association[24] to do so, providing it with a detailed plan as to how he intends to minimise any risk to pollinating insects. In contrast to a conventional arable or horticultural crop, sprayed with dozens of pesticides each year, most organic crops are not sprayed at all. That is the key difference.

To return to the 'nature fallacy': the argument goes that natural toxins are just as bad as synthetic ones, and hence we should not worry about being exposed to the synthetic ones. I'm sure you

[24] The regulatory body for organic growers in the UK.

don't need me to point out that this is not a convincing argument. Just because some naturally occurring chemicals may be harmful to one's health does not mean that adding lots of extra synthetic chemicals on top isn't going to make things worse. Consider also this: synthetic pesticides have killed hundreds of thousands of farm workers over the decades. So far as I can ascertain, no organic farmers have ever died from contact with the very limited suite of chemicals they sparingly use.

If all this leaves you unconvinced that peeing weedkiller is fine, the final line of argument in defence of pesticides is to point out that, in the developed world, life expectancies are higher than they ever have been. Consuming these chemicals can't be so bad if most of us are making it well past eighty. The logic of this argument is also weak to non-existent. Of course we are living longer than we used to, but that is clearly due to massively improved health care, more stringent health and safety laws, a stable supply of food, and a host of other factors. Very few of us in the UK now die during childbirth, of starvation, by catching cholera, or getting accidentally mangled in a steam-powered threshing machine. Nobody knows whether we would be living even longer if we weren't exposed to pesticides, phthalates and so on. Some suspect that the rise in neurodegenerative diseases such as Parkinson's and Alzheimer's is due to long-term exposure to neurotoxic pesticides. Perhaps the rise in behavioural disorders such as attention deficit hyperactivity disorder (ADHD) in children might also be due to these toxins. In mice, the neonicotinoid imidacloprid has been found to promote weight gain, so perhaps this is contributing to the global obesity epidemic. Once again, we simply don't know. For obvious reasons we can't take, say, 2,000 people and randomly select half of them to be exposed to pesticide mixtures for several decades while somehow preventing the other half from being exposed, yet this is the sort of experiment one would need to do to obtain a definitive answer (and even then pesticide companies would no doubt find fault if they did not like the results).

Instead, epidemiologists try to tease apart the causes of ill health by following the fates of large cohorts of people, measuring whatever factors are of interest. Theoretically, one could measure exposure to pesticides of a group of volunteers through their lives, looking for correlations between exposure to particular chemicals and subsequent disease, but it is fiendishly difficult to separate out correlation from causation in these studies. For example, suppose one found that those eating some or all organic food, and hence having low pesticide exposure, tended to live a little longer. Aha, proof at last, you might say. But of course it would not be. Those eating organic food might also (at a guess) tend to eat less meat and more tofu, come from safe, middle-class neighbourhoods, be more health-conscious and do more exercise, go to yoga classes and have more cucumber facials. It could be any of these factors that explains their long life, or indeed one of an infinite number of other correlated factors that the epidemiologist didn't think to measure.

Since it seems unlikely that we will have a definitive answer as to whether routine exposure to chemical mixtures is bad for us any time soon, it seems to me pretty obvious that the wise option is to try to minimise exposure. Buy organic food if you can, grow your own if you have any space, and avoid Turkish grapes. You just might live a longer and healthier life. Follow this advice and even if, one day, it somehow emerges that all of our fears about pesticides and human health were unfounded, then the worst problem you will have is that you may feel a little foolish. You can console yourself with the fact that, by buying organic, you supported more environmentally friendly farming, and that by growing some of your own food you saved a bit of money while getting some fresh air and exercise. As a worst-case scenario that doesn't sound too awful to me. On the other hand, if one day a clear link between exposure to particular pesticides and, say, Alzheimer's disease is uncovered, you'll be very thankful you took my advice.

There is one final route of exposure to pesticides that is very hard to avoid. You may use no pesticides yourself, refuse to drip neurotoxins onto your dog, and buy mainly organic food, but you cannot control what your local authority does in your streets and local parks. You may be walking along the pavement or in a local park, perhaps with your children, and encounter someone with a tank of liquid on his back and holding a spray nozzle with which he is blasting the pavement. Alternatively you might encounter a council workman on a sit-on sprayer driving along leaving a trail of wetted tarmac or gravel behind. There are usually no warning notices to tell you what is happening or to keep you away. If you are lucky enough to miss the actual spraying, the signs that it is happening are all too evident in all our towns and villages: strips of yellow, dying vegetation along the path or road verges and along the edges of school playing fields and parks through spring and summer. Our towns and cities may not be bombed with insecticides, but huge amounts of herbicides (mainly glyphosate) are sprayed to keep pavements tidy, to stop weeds encroaching on footpaths and so on. The exact amount used in parks and gardens in the UK appears to be unrecorded, but a recent study estimated that, globally, about 80,000 tonnes of glyphosate are applied each year for 'non-agricultural use'. This is an awful lot of chemical to use for purely cosmetic purposes and it is entirely unnecessary.

More than twenty-five years ago the small town of Hudson in Quebec introduced a local law banning the use of all pesticides within the town limits. Hudson led the way, and today there are more than 170 towns and cities in Canada, including Vancouver and Toronto, that are pesticide-free. Eight out of the ten Canadian provinces have also banned cosmetic use of pesticides. Inspired by this, and with growing concern over the safety of pesticides, other towns around the world have followed suit. France has 900 *villes sans pesticides*, including Paris, and the French government recently announced the introduction of national legislation banning the non-agricultural use of all pesticides from 2020.

These towns and cities are still standing. They have not been overrun with cockroaches, flies and nettles. In recent years I have visited Toronto, Copenhagen and Paris, all of them pesticide-free, and there were no signs that this was causing an epidemic of pests or weeds. To be honest, I was slightly disappointed that there were not dandelions sprouting everywhere from the cracks in the pavement, that the Eiffel Tower was not becoming encrusted in clambering brambles and vines, and that the parks in fact looked tidier than those in pesticide-doused London. The explanation is that there are many effective pesticide-free means of controlling weeds, if they must be controlled. Some towns have set up community groups that hand-weed in parks, engendering pride and a sense of community among the local people. Vinegar also works reasonably well as a weedkiller and was trialled in parts of Bristol, but claims in a local paper that it made the area smell 'just like a fish and chip shop' led to this option being abandoned. Glastonbury Town Council recently banned herbicides following successful trials of a hot foam system, which uses a biodegradable plant extract as a foaming agent and cooks weeds by engulfing them in steaming soapy suds.

In the UK, there are campaigns to make cities such as Brighton and Bristol pesticide-free, but none have quite got there yet. The cause is being championed by Pesticide Action Network, a small but very well-informed organisation who can provide advice on alternatives to chemical pesticides. If major cities throughout the developed world have been managing perfectly well for decades without pesticides, why can't we in the UK? There is nothing stopping it, other than conservatism and inertia. Wouldn't it be wonderful if every city, town and village were pesticide-free?

5

The Buzzing of the Bees

To make sauerkraut

Ingredients: cabbage (any crunchy type), salt

1. *Finely slice or shred 1kg of cabbage, discarding wilted outer leaves, and place in a bowl.*
2. *Sprinkle on 15g of salt, then mix the two thoroughly with your hands, squeezing and massaging the cabbage for about five minutes. Some juice will begin to come out.*
3. *Place cabbage and juice in a large jar, squashing the cabbage down with your fist. Weight the cabbage down with a clean stone (e.g. a large beach pebble). Cover the jar mouth with cloth, tied with string or held with a rubber band.*
4. *Leave for four to ten days in a cool dark place. Natural lactobacillus will ferment sugars, making the mix bubble – this is good!*
5. *Eat, or put a lid on the jar and refrigerate – the kraut will last for months, and is jam-packed with healthy bacteria. Delicious with just about any savoury dish.*

We may not have to worry about the bees for much longer; help is at hand. They could soon be redundant, for they are to be replaced – by robots. No, seriously. Teams of scientists in far-flung places from Japan to Indonesia to the United States are working on it as I write.

There really have been a number of scientific papers published in recent years discussing the possibility of building miniature flying robots to replace bees and pollinate our crops for us. Clumsy prototypes have been tested and some seem to crudely work, although most still rely on a human to control them from a remote handset, and some seem more likely to chop flowers to pieces with their tiny rotor blades than to pollinate them. Regardless of these shortcomings, media coverage has heralded the imminent retirement of the bee and a brave new world in which tiny metal and plastic drones buzz from flower to flower. If crops could be pollinated this way, farmers wouldn't have to worry about harming bees with their insecticides. With wild bee populations in decline, perhaps these tiny robots are the answer?

While I can understand the intellectual interest and challenge of trying to create robotic bees, I would argue that it is exceedingly unlikely that we could ever produce something as cheap (i.e. free) or as effective as bees themselves. Bees have been around and pollinating flowers for more than 120 million years; through the random tinkering of evolution they have become exceedingly good at it. It is remarkable hubris to think that we can replicate or improve on them. Consider just the numbers: there are roughly 80 million honeybee hives in the world, each containing perhaps 40,000 individual worker bees through the spring and summer. That adds up to 3.2 trillion bees, give or take. They feed themselves for free, breed for free, and even give us honey as a bonus. What would be the cost of replacing them with robots? Even if the robots could be built, complete with charged power pack and control devices, for one penny each (which seems absurdly optimistic), it would cost £32 billion to build them. And how long would they last? Some would malfunction, some would get caught out in the rain or get lost, some would be damaged by wind or spiders' webs or curious bee-eaters. If we very optimistically calculate the lifespan of a robo-bee at one year, that means spending £32 billion every year (and continually litter-ing the environment with trillions of tiny robots, unless they could be made biodegradable). What about the environmental costs of manufacture? What resources would they require, what carbon footprint would they have, what energy source would power them? What would happen when terrorists or the Russians hacked into the drone control system and turned them against us? Real bees avoid all of these issues; they are self-replicating, self-powering, essentially carbon neutral, and unlikely to be subject to mind control by Vladimir Putin any time soon.

Thus far I have glossed over a vital further point. Not all pollin-ation is done by honeybees. Numerous other insects pollinate crops and wild flowers, including butterflies, beetles, moths, flies, wasps, sawflies and many more. In more exotic climes, hummingbirds, parrots and bats help out, and even occasionally lizards and mar-supial mice. These pollinators come in all sorts of different shapes and sizes suited to different flowers. It has been calculated that honeybees contribute at best one-third of crop pollination in the UK, averaged across crops, and that we have in the region of 4,000 other species of pollinator. So we wouldn't just need to replace the 3.2 trillion honeybees. We'd also need to replace countless trillions of other pollinators. All to substitute creatures that currently de-liver all of our pollination needs and those of innumerable wild plants for free.

Declines of bees are symptomatic of larger issues. It is not just bees that are declining; almost all wildlife is declining in the face of massive habitat loss and pollution across the globe. Even suppos-ing we could create robot bees cheaply enough for it to be viable, should we? If farmers no longer needed to worry about harming bees they could perhaps spray more pesticides, but there are many other beneficial creatures that live in farmland that would then be harmed: ladybirds, hoverflies and wasps that attack crop pests, worms, dung beetles and millipedes that help recycle nutrients and keep the soil healthy, and many more. Are we going to make robotic worms and ladybirds too? What kind of world would we end up with? Do we always have to look for a technical solution to the problems that we create, when a simple, natural solution is staring us in the face? We have wonderfully efficient pollinators already; let's look after them, not plan for their demise.

Luckily, the gardener can play a vital role in doing exactly that. Suburban areas can be great for bees, compared to most of the countryside. Of course there are areas of tarmac, concrete and buildings, decking, paving and gravel that are more or less devoid of flowers, but there are also gardens packed with ornamental flowers, next to abandoned gardens full of dandelions and brambles, vacant industrial lots overgrown with buddleia and willowherb, and railway embankments carpeted in marjoram and teasel. In my own research, we have found that bumblebee nests grow much faster in gardens compared to the countryside, and that there is a higher density of bumblebee nests in gardens compared to farmland. What's more, we discovered a few years ago that plants get better pollinated in gardens compared to those in farmland, and that farmers with fields near gardens benefit from bumblebees spilling out from the gardens to pollinate their crops.

A bee's-eye view of the importance of gardens for insects is revealed by some fascinating research done by Maggie Couvillon and Francis Ratnieks at Sussex University. The honeybee is unique among bees in performing its famous waggle dance,[25] in which a bee communicates the whereabouts of a good patch of flowers to

---

[25] The waggle dance was first explained by Austrian scientist Karl von Frisch in 1927, but had been observed long before. The dance was described a hundred years earlier by Nicholas Unhoch, who attributed it to the bees indulging in 'pleasures and jollity'.

her nest-mates. She walks in a straight line, waggling her body excitedly, before looping back to the beginning of her run. Each time she loops back she alternates between turning left or right, so that her overall path traces out a figure of eight, which might be repeated up to one hundred times (presumably depending on how enthusiastic she feels about the patch of flowers she has found, something she also expresses through the vigour of her waggling). The length of the straight part of her dance indicates the distance to the flower patch, and the angle of her run from vertical indicates the angle of the flower patch relative to the current position of the sun. All of this is done in the pitch black of the interior of the hive. As if that were not remarkable enough, if she performs a large number of runs over an extended period of time she gradually changes the angle of her run to account for the shifting position of the unseen sun.

If the bees are set up in an observation hive (where the comb is sandwiched between sheets of glass so that the bees can be observed going about their business), then humans can decode these dances, and plot the locations to which bees are attempting to recruit nest-mates. This is pretty tedious work as you might imagine, for the observer has to sit for hours on end, armed with a ruler and protractor, measuring the length and angle of every waggle dance. Maggie and an army of undergraduate helpers did exactly this for weeks on end in the spring and summer of three consecutive years, recording over 5,000 waggle dances made by honeybee colonies housed on the Sussex campus just outside Brighton. The coded location of each dance was plotted onto a map of the local area to see which places the bees were recruiting their nest-mates to visit. The results were fascinating. In spring the bees didn't go far at all, most staying within 600 metres of their hive and foraging mainly on the university campus and in Falmer village next door. In autumn the foraging distance was also quite short, perhaps because many of the honeybees were feeding on ivy[26], which is pretty common on campus and in the surrounding woodlands. In contrast, it seems that in summer the bees had to go much further afield to find food. Some headed south-east to Castle Hill, a lovely chalk grassland nature reserve located about two and a half kilometres distant from campus, while many headed in to Brighton and its suburbs, some of them travelling three or four kilometres to visit the gardens and parks. My point is that gardens are already pretty attractive habitats for bees, worth them flying four kilometres to reach. However, we gardeners should not be complacent, for there is always room for improvement, and bees need all the help they can get, given the problems they face in the farmed countryside.

Perhaps driven in part by a growing realisation that towns have lots of flowers, the last few years have seen a huge growth in interest in urban beekeeping. I think this has also been stimulated by media coverage of bee declines, and a desire among members of the public to help. Taking up beekeeping seems like an obvious way to boost the local bee population, and in recent years beekeeping associations have been swamped by newcomers wanting to do beekeeping training courses. This has proved to be especially popular in cities, encouraged by reports that honey yields from hives kept in central

[26] Ivy is an underappreciated and sometimes maligned plant. It is often accused of damaging brickwork (to some extent true) and strangling trees (not true), but on the plus side its inconspicuous little green flowers are very attractive to many insects, the berries are a winter food source for birds, and the dense foliage provides ideal roosting and nesting sites for many birds and hibernation sites for insects such as the lovely brimstone butterfly. It is also one of the only food plants of the appropriately named ivy bee (*Colletes hederae*), a pretty little striped bee that invaded Britain from the Continent in 2001, and has since become very common in the south.

London, in European cities such as Amsterdam and also in US cities such as Birmingham, Alabama, were much higher than those gained in the countryside. Some beekeepers were getting yields as high as 36kg per hive per year, more than twice the average from rural hives (which normally produce about 11kg, although it varies a lot with the weather and location). As a result of this urban bee mania, there are now hives perched on top of swanky hotels, art galleries and restaurants, even on top of a custard factory. In the USA, Second Lady Karen Pence recently announced that she was going to do her bit by keeping honeybees in the vice president's garden in Washington DC. I imagine that the Pences' garden may be quite large, but urban hives can be fine placed in small gardens at ground level – as long as there are tall fences or hedges around the hive which force the bees to fly upwards before they head off in search of food, so preventing streams of low-flying bee traffic from bothering the neighbours. So, there is nothing to stop you; wherever you live, as long as you have some kind of garden, courtyard, balcony or rooftop space, you can keep honeybees. If you can't be bothered or don't have the time to actually learn about and look after the bees yourself but like the idea of having them in your garden or on the top of your hotel, then there are companies in London that will rent you a hive or two, install and maintain them for you, and give you a cut of the honey, for a price. There have even been claims made that eating your own honey, or honey produced very locally, is an effective treatment for hay fever. I've not seen good evidence to support this, and it doesn't make complete sense since the plants that bees visit are mostly not the wind-pollinated ones that generally cause hay fever, but perhaps there is something in it.

Whatever the underlying causes, the number of registered hives in London more than doubled between 2008 and 2013, from 1,677 to more than 3,500, making approximately one hive per square kilometre, which is about ten times the UK national average. The

UK capital leads the way in everything from banking to bees. Great news for the honeybee.

Or perhaps not. As Francis Ratnieks recently pointed out in an article published in the *Biologist*, there may now be too many honeybees in London. A survey of honey yields in 2013 revealed that yields from London hives had fallen to an average of 8kg per hive, compared to the national average in that year of 11kg. The explanation is of course pretty obvious. There are only so many flowers producing nectar and pollen, and the increase in numbers of hives has not been accompanied by an increase in the extent of flowers. Francis's colleague Karin Alton calculated that each hive would need the equivalent of one hectare of borage plants (a great food source for honeybees) through the spring and summer – which few homeowners or, for that matter, custard manufacturers are likely to be able to provide. Thus by keeping a hive without providing sufficient flowers, each extra beekeeper places an extra drain on the nectar and pollen supply. Keeping honeybees is not in itself going to help the bees; it may even be actively harmful to them.

This surplus of honeybee hives isn't only a problem for the honeybees and their owners, but is also likely to be causing problems for wild pollinators living in our cities. It isn't just the honeybees that depend upon those floral resources. There is plentiful evidence that wild bumblebees fare poorly in places where there are too many honeybees. The worker bumblebees tend to be smaller, and their nests grow more slowly. This is probably mainly because of competition for food, but honeybees can also spread disease to wild bees, particularly if their colonies are poorly maintained by amateur beekeepers who are beginning to lose interest in their latest fad. Disease such as deformed wing virus and the invasive Asian gut parasite *Nosema ceranae* tend to flow out of honeybees and into wild bee populations, transmitted via shared flowers just as human diseases can be spread if we glug from a shared bottle of wine.

A lavender bush covered in a buzzing mixture of bee species can be a hotbed for the spread of disease.

In short, the problems that pollinators face in the modern world cannot be addressed by encouraging more people to keep honey-bees. To give a slightly silly analogy, suppose you owned a game park in Africa and you notice that your pride of lions were starv-ing, and that there were few antelope left for them to eat. Would you conclude that introducing more lions was the solution? Karen Pence may mean well, but her efforts are misguided. She is not alone; there have been many recent 'save the bee' campaigns that have promoted beekeeping. The Co-op's 'Plan Bee' seemed to be based on the premise that honeybees are the only type of bee, and that encouraging more beekeeping on all of their farms would solve bee problems. If one of the major problems that bees face is lack of flowers, then keeping more of them is not the answer; indeed, it will make things worse. Planting more flowers is a far better way to help the bees than trying to keep more bees. Aside from anything else, planting flowers helps lots of species, not just honeybees; in the UK, potentially as many as the approximately 4,000 species of native pollinator.

I have already talked a little about the many plants that can eas-ily be grown to encourage bees and other pollinators. If you can, try to grow a selection of flowers that will cater for different types of insects. Foxgloves and aquilegia have deep flowers suited to long-tongued bumblebees such as the garden bumblebee; lavender and catmint are perfect for the shorter-tongued bumblebees, while bor-age and thyme are superb for honeybees. The plate-like umbels of hogweed, angelica and wild carrot are great for some of the smaller solitary bees, beetles and hoverflies. Honeysuckle and buddleia will cater for moths and butterflies. Some plants, such as marjoram, seem to be attractive to more or less everything. The more diversity of flowers you can squeeze in, the more creatures you will please.

Try also to have plants that flower successively through the year, from lungwort and pussy willow in early spring to Michaelmas daisy, ivy and sedums in the autumn. Of course, unless you have a vast garden you won't be able to provide food for everything all of the time, but don't stress too much about this. If there are periods when there isn't too much in flower in your patch, the insects will whizz off to your neighbours' gardens and hopefully will find something to keep them going. And if you can gently persuade your neighbours that they might like to grow a few more bee-friendly flowers, you might be well on the way to turning your whole neighbourhood into bee paradise.

Aside from food, the other thing that wild bees need is somewhere to nest. Just as different bees prefer different flowers, they also have quite different preferences for nest sites. Most bumblebees nest in cavities beneath the ground, often using old rodent burrows. They are opportunistic and will take advantage of all sorts of man-made spaces, commonly nesting in cavity walls, using the airbricks to enter, or going under decking, patio slabs or the floors of garden sheds. They need insulation – moss, fine grasses, hair or feathers – and usually recycle an old nest made by a previous occupant of the hole. Some bumblebee species will happily nest above ground, using old bird nests, or entering the eaves of houses and nesting under the loft insulation. I have heard of an early bumblebee nest in the fluff collected in the back of a disused tumble dryer. Tree bumblebees, a new arrival in the UK in 2001,[27] have been bucking

---

[27] As luck would have it, I caught the very first UK tree bumblebee, in the village of Landford on the edge of the New Forest in 2001. This species is widespread in Europe but had never previously been recorded in the UK. I was pretty confused when I first saw it, for it is a distinctive species with a chestnut thorax and black-and-white abdomen that cannot easily be mistaken for any of our native bumblebee. I sent it to the

the downward trend shown by other species and thriving, in part perhaps because they love to nest in tit boxes and we UK gardeners are very accommodating in providing plenty of these.

There are plenty of commercial bumblebee nest boxes on the market, but they generally do not seem to be the kind of des res accommodation that bumblebees are looking for. Most are wooden boxes that approximately resemble tit boxes but are intended to sit on the ground rather than be nailed to a tree. When investigating a promising hole in the ground in which they might nest, most bumblebee queens tend to land next to it and then explore the hole on foot. A hole in the vertical side of a wooden box is difficult to enter this way, and for the majority of bumblebee species that prefer to nest underground it probably does not look enticing. Some of the better designed bumblebee nest boxes attempt

---

Natural History Museum for confirmation. The species has since become very common and spread as far north as Scotland, even crossing over to the Isle of Man. We have no idea how it crossed the English Channel in the first place; presumably it was a natural invasion, but it could have been accidentally assisted by man. I was also the first person to sight this bee north of London, near Harpenden in 2003, leading to half-joking suggestions from colleagues that I had a supply in my pocket and was spreading them around the country, but I can promise that I wasn't (even had I been so inclined, bees don't fare well in pockets). In fact one of my PhD students, Jane Stout, described seeing a bee in my garden in Southampton in 1998 that fitted the description of a tree bumblebee, but in the absence of a photograph or specimen I assumed that she had imagined it. With hindsight the tree bumblebee might well have been quietly living in southern England for a while before I caught the first 'official' one. So far as we know, this species is not doing any particular harm so I guess we should welcome these European immigrant workers.

to overcome this issue. The Rolls-Royce of bumblebee nest boxes is made by George Pilkington, an eternally cheerful and proudly Scouse ex-policeman who now makes a living by building and selling wildlife products, including wormeries, solitary bee hotels and bumblebee boxes. His boxes have the entrance drilled into a sloping wooden surface, making it easier for the bees to enter on foot. He also provides detailed advice on how to disguise the entrance with moss so that it looks more like a mouse hole in a mossy bank, which is much more what a bumblebee might naturally be looking for. However, tempting the queens to come inside is only half the battle. Unless they like what they find when they get there then they won't hang around, and it is here that providing cosy bedding is vital. Again George has his tricks. He travelled to Norway to meet Atle Mjelde, a bumblebee expert who has been designing bumblebee boxes since 1968 and has successfully persuaded most of the Norwegian species into them over the years. Atle taught George how to sculpt a ball of soft nesting material with a small cavity at the centre, using kapok or upholsterer's cotton (never cotton wool, which the bees get tangled in), and then to encase that in an outer layer of fine hay. Inside his nest box George places this cosy bundle on a layer of vermiculite, intended to absorb excess moisture. He will happily supply his boxes with detailed instructions and all the materials – kapok, hay – and he can even provide vermiculite soaked in mouse urine, thought to help lure in the bumblebees by providing the authentic smell of an old mouse nest.[28] George really does go the extra mile. In his own garden in Liverpool the majority of his boxes are occupied; seven out of ten at the last count. In Norway, Atle says he gets between 50 and 100 per cent of his boxes occupied every year.

---

[28] George's products can be found online under the company name Nurturing Nature.

Being a generous chap, George sent me one of his boxes to try out. I carefully installed it at the bottom of my garden two years ago, collecting balls of moss from our old roof to create an idyllic-looking mossy bank to disguise the entrance. I followed the instructions carefully, rolling the upholsterer's cotton into a hollow ball, layering it in hay and nestling it on a rodent-scented bed of vermiculite. Surely no broody bumblebee queen could resist? I've been waiting ever since – not a damned thing, nada, nothing, zilch. I'm so sorry, George, I really wanted it to work. Maybe I've just been unlucky so far, or maybe my nest-bedding preparation skills are inadequate. I'm still hoping.

I've also tried my own home-made bumblebee nests of various types. I made a stack of old wooden pallets, stuffed the spaces with loft insulation, and used roofing felt to keep the rain out, thinking that this might provide cosy dry cavities that bumblebee queens might appreciate. When I built a new garden shed, I left a series of gaps between the bottom course of bricks, each leading into a wooden box that I constructed on the inside, each box equipped with a hinged lid so I can peek in to see what is happening. Dotted around the garden I've built simple nesting chambers out of old bricks and paving slabs. At the last count, I think I now have thirty-five different bumblebee nests of various types, all with soft bedding, some with mouse-scented vermiculite and some without to see if it makes any difference. The pallet stack has proved enormously popular as a nesting place for wood mice, but does not seem to appeal to bumblebees. The boxes in the garden shed were soon occupied by spiders, woodlice, earwigs and more mice. The brick-and-slab chambers seemed very popular with toads, violet ground beetles, the obligatory mice, and a couple are regularly occupied by shrews which shriek excitedly at me if I lift the lid. Of course these creatures are all welcome, even if they are not what I was hoping for. Excitingly, there have also been some bumblebees. The nests in the shed have twice been occupied by buff-tails; one nest died while quite small, but the other thrived and produced new queens before being ravaged by a mob of hungry wax moth grubs. One of my brick-and-slab nests was occupied by common carder bumblebees which seemed to be eventually ousted by a wood mouse, though it may be that the bees died of other causes and the mouse took advantage of the empty nest and the ready supply of honey. Three bumblebee nests in four years, two of which died early, isn't a great success rate but I'll keep trying. Perhaps George's nest box will finally be occupied next year.

It is fun trying to tempt bumblebees to nest in these artificial chambers, and it would be great for research if we could do so reliably. I have a pipe dream of sitting in a camp chair in my shed observing the comings and goings of half a dozen or so nests (which on reflection probably seems a little bit of a bizarre dream). Perhaps when, like Atle, I've been doing this for fifty years I might get half of my boxes occupied, but it seems unlikely to become reality any time soon.

So far as the bees are concerned, it probably doesn't matter. Every year I discover several natural bumblebee nests in my garden. This year there was an early bumblebee nest in one of my compost heaps, a buff-tailed nest going down what appeared to be a mole-hole in the lawn, a carder nest in the tussocky grass in my meadow and another in a pile of hedge clippings I'd forgotten about, and two tree bumblebee nests in the loft. There are very likely to have been others that I didn't discover. My strong impression is that my garden, and probably gardens in general, provides lots of nesting places for bumblebees. If they were desperate for somewhere to nest, presumably they would be more interested in the accommodation I painstakingly build for them. If I am correct in this, then trying to make artificial nest boxes that work is probably not a very effective way of helping bumblebees. I'd suggest sticking to providing them with lots of the right kinds of flowers.

In marked contrast to bumblebees, providing homes for solitary bees can be very effective and rewarding. The term solitary bee isn't especially helpful, for in the UK it is generally used to refer to any bee that isn't a honeybee or a bumblebee (these being social bees that live in a colony with a queen and her daughter workers). It is a catch-all term for an eclectic group of about 250 different species with diverse life cycles and confusingly containing a few types, such as the sharp-collared furrow bee, which actually live in small colonies and hence are not strictly solitary. When it comes to nesting, the different 'solitary' bees have very different ideas as to what makes the perfect home. Some, such as the mining bees (of which there are no less than sixty-seven different species in the UK), tend to burrow into the ground, as you might guess from their name. When I was a teenager, our neatly mown lawn in Shropshire was home to hundreds of tawny mining bees. Each female would excavate her own vertical burrow, creating a spoil heap of soil grains resembling a miniature volcano in the grass. I used to love peering down into the burrows, for when not out foraging for food the females would sit just inside the nest entrance looking upwards, presumably guarding their nest against cuckoo bees or other tawny mining bees that might steal their home. Other mining bee species seem to prefer to nest in bare ground, often using the edges of wheel tracks on farmland. Even the truly solitary species seem to nest close together in aggregations, though whether this is simply because suitable areas for digging nests are few and far between so they have to squeeze into them, or because they get some benefit from nesting together is unclear (I'd guess the latter). These nest aggregations can be very busy with bee traffic, sometimes so much so that members of the public become alarmed. Ivy bees in particular often seem to nest at high density, and the groups of nests attract large numbers of males looking for mates. They grab the poor females as they come and go from their nests, sometimes forming balls of males around them in a frenzy of lust. Sometimes beekeepers are called out to deal with the 'swarm', but there is little that they can do, and indeed nothing that needs doing. Ivy bees are entirely benign; one can stand in the middle of a busy nest aggregation and the bees will pay you no heed. Francis Ratnieks has caught females and forced them to sting him, but says that the stinger has trouble penetrating human skin and is barely noticeable.

Other solitary bees prefer to nest in horizontal holes above ground; for example, holes left by beetles burrowing into dead trees, or the hollow stems of plants such as rose, bramble, elder or raspberry. Some mason bees will burrow into soft mortar in an old wall, and in nature use steep clay banks and sandy cliffs. A few solitary bees have more specialised accommodation requirements. Three species of mason bee, including the very handsome red-tailed mason bee, will only nest in abandoned snail shells, preferring medium-sized shells of species such as *Cepaea* (variably-coloured, often stripy snails that are common in gardens). Having stocked the shell with pollen and laid her eggs, the female red-tailed mason bee will spend hours carefully hiding the shell under a small pile of pieces of grass and leaves that she collects, presumably to prevent her nest from being stolen by another mason bee or attacked by some enemy such as a parasitic wasp. I have watched these bees laboriously dragging and rolling their chosen shell, much larger than themselves, along the ground, taking hours to move it just a few centimetres. They say that location is everything when it comes to property. It wasn't clear to me what was better about the final location compared to where the shell was to start with, but presumably the bee was looking for something beyond my perception.

Boosting nesting opportunities for mining bees isn't easy. I have tried scraping off the vegetation from small areas of my meadow, leaving bare patches of my red clayey soil in the hope that mining bees might be tempted, but with no success. An abandoned sandpit

I made for my youngest son seems to have worked better – I have had a few plasterer bees and furrow bees burrowing in there. I've also scattered empty *Cepaea* snail shells onto the sand, for I would love to find red-tailed mason bees in my garden, but I'm pushing my luck since they tend to occur mainly on chalky soils such as the South Downs, which are about ten kilometres to the south. On the other hand, providing nest sites for mason bees appears to work remarkably well. The red mason bee in particular seems to be very easy to tempt in to occupying man-made holes; all they need is a roughly horizontal hole of about eight millimetres in diameter. Including some that are a bit smaller will encourage some other bee and wasp species too, such as yellow-faced bees, slender yellow-and-black mason wasps (which stock their nests with caterpillars) or even smaller red-and-black sphecid wasps (which tend to stock their nests with tiny flies or spiders).[29] These creatures generally don't care if the hole is square or round, or whether it is made of wood or glass or plastic, though some say that they do better in breathable natural materials. Mason bees will happily nest in a block of oasis – the green foam used by florists – if you poke holes in it with a pencil. Or you can simply drill holes in any existing wooden structures, such as fence posts, the wooden corner posts of a garden shed, or the trunk of a dead tree. I recently drilled holes in the wooden pallets I use for my compost heaps, and that seemed to work. The deeper the holes the better, within reason; the bees will certainly use the full depth of holes up to twenty centimetres deep, which is as far as my longest drill bit will go. The deeper the hole, the more offspring they can squeeze in. An alternative to drilling holes is to cut bamboo into lengths and tie them in bundles.

[29] Many solitary wasps such as these stock their nests with prey that they have paralysed with a sting, ensuring that their offspring has a pile of fresh, living food to consume at their leisure.

Whatever they are made from, it seems best to site the holes in full sun, ideally on a wall or fence. Height doesn't seem to be critical; anywhere between fifty centimetres and three metres above the ground seems to work fine for my mason bees.

If you haven't the enthusiasm to make your own mason bee 'hotel', there are dozens of designs sold in garden centres and online. Some work very well, others not so much. The sad truth is that wildlife products are often very poorly researched, and designed more to appeal to the human eye than to their intended occupants. A common mistake is for the holes to be too wide; I was given as a present a bee hotel with holes that are all twelve millimetres in diameter. No bee has gone near it for they prefer snug lodgings; open-plan accommodation is not for them. Some hotels use bamboo but the manufacturers have not taken care to avoid or drill out the nodes – where the hole is blocked – so bees cannot get in very far. George Pilkington is also critical of designs in which the bamboo has not been cleanly cut or the holes smoothly drilled, leaving a ragged edge which he says can damage the wings of the mason bees. Of course he makes and sells his own design of solitary bee hotel, and this I am relieved to be able to report works very well. (In case you are wondering, I do not get a cut of his sales, and have no ambition to get a job as George's marketing manager.) I have one of his hotels attached to my garden shed, and it is full of mason bees every spring. It has one huge advantage over most other designs I have come across in that it has a viewing window on each side. With a normal hotel, one can watch the female bees coming and going, and the male bees sniffing about for a mate, but one has no idea what is happening inside. With a viewing window one can keep an eye on progress, and my kids love to peek in.

The female mason bees start by lining the tunnel with wet clay from damp corners of the garden which they mould into little balls and carry in their mandibles. In dry weather they struggle to find any suitably damp mud and I give them a helping hand by creating a soggy soil and water mix in an old wheelbarrow. The bees then stock their nests with a loose pile of pollen that they collect among the soft hairs on their tummy (they don't have the pollen baskets on their legs used by honeybees and bumblebees). They then lay a single egg, which looks like a tiny white sausage, seal that section of the tunnel off with a wall of mud, and start again. In a deep tunnel they may end up with fifteen or more brood cells, finally sealing up the mouth of the tunnel with a sturdy plug of hardened mud. The eggs hatch swiftly and the ensuing white grubs quickly fatten up on their store of pollen. After just a month or so they are fully grown and spin a brown cocoon in which to pupate. Mason bees have just one generation per year, so they then sit tight for perhaps nine months, right through the summer, autumn and winter, before emerging as adults the following spring. I presume that mason bees don't suffer from claustrophobia since the oldest bees are stuck beneath a dozen or more siblings with no chance of escape. If any of the bees nearer to the entrance die, those beneath them are also doomed unless they can somehow burrow out through the corpses of their brethren.

Mason bees are on the wing early in the year, mainly from April to June, and are great pollinators of spring fruit trees such as my apples, handsomely repaying the effort of providing them with a home. A little later in the year, any unoccupied holes may be taken up by leafcutter bees, relatives of the mason bees but named from their practice of using leaf discs to line their nests rather than mud. These are lovely bees which, like the mason bees, also collect pollen on their hairy tummies, and have the endearing but peculiar habit of waggling their abdomen in the air while feeding on flowers. The males of some leafcutter species have hairy front legs that they use to cover the eyes of their partner while mating. The females snip neat semicircles of leaf, being particularly fond of roses and lilacs in my garden, which they then carry back in their jaws to the nest, before gluing them together with silk.

As with many insects, the males of mason and leafcutter bees emerge before the females, giving themselves a few days to find their bearings before the young virgin females come out. Hence the mother bee always ensures that the first eggs she lays, at the bottom of the tunnel, are female, and then she lays the males on top[30]. She also gives the females more food to eat as they need to get bigger so that they themselves can produce lots of eggs (another common feature of insects, which contrasts with many mammals, is that females tend to be larger than males). Being near the entrance may sound more pleasant to us, but it actually places the young males in great danger. In my garden many of my mason bees are eaten by greater spotted woodpeckers, which have long ago learned the locations of most of my various bee hotels. To them, a bee hotel is like a tube of Smarties, a delicious snack at any time of year but particularly in winter when times are hard. Woodpeckers are specialists in winkling insects out of deep holes. They can chip away at the wood with their beaks if necessary, their skulls being specially designed to absorb the impact and prevent them from damaging their brains. But to get to male mason or leafcutter bees they don't need to do this, because they also have extraordinarily long tongues, armed with barbs at the tip. Unlike ours, the tongues of birds are semi-rigid structures containing cartilage and bone; in woodpeckers the tongue is so long that it curves from the back of the mouth right round the outside of the skull, down between the eyes and into the nasal cavity. I had read about this but recently got the chance

---

[30] If an egg is fertilised it becomes a female, if not it is destined to be a male. Once they have mated, female bees can control whether each egg is fertilized with the sperm they have stored inside them, and so can decide the sex of each offspring.

to examine it first hand, for one of our greater spotted woodpeckers committed hara-kiri by flying straight into our bedroom window (clearly the shock-proofing in the skull is not infallible). It needed a pair of pliers to pull its spiky tongue out fully, which extended to about three times the length of the beak, about six centimetres, which means that the outermost five or six mason bees in a hole stand no chance if they are discovered. Where I have made mason bee holes in softwood or other soft materials, the birds peck away to enlarge the holes and get in deeper to reach the juicier female offspring. They are surprisingly powerful beasts; I have had home-made hotels sturdily constructed of bamboo completely disman-tled by hungry woodpeckers. Chicken wire over the hotels helps to some extent, but doesn't foil them completely.

I must admit I don't try too hard to prevent them. I love bees, but woodpeckers are magnificent creatures too, and they need to eat. I try to make the tunnels as deep as possible, and many of my hotels are drilled into hard oak; so long as most of the females survive, it only requires one or two lucky surviving males to mate with them all, and the population will remain strong. In any case, the woodpeckers don't find every hole. George's bee hotel with the viewing windows has revealed that the mason bees have a tactic to improve their offspring's chances of survival. As well as making nests stocked with juicy grubs, it turns out that the bees often block up the entrance to tunnels they haven't used. It isn't clear why they do this; it may be that they are simply reserving the hole for later use, but then die before they get around to using it, or it may be that they are deliberately trying to deter woodpeckers and other predators. From the outside it is impossible to tell which plugged hole has larvae behind, so woodpeckers may often drill through the hardened mud plug only to find it empty. Perhaps they give up at this point, disheartened by their lack of success, allowing some bees to survive.

For me, the same laissez-faire approach goes for the other all-too-numerous enemies of my mason and leafcutter bees. If you are lucky, you may spot a ruby-tailed wasp scampering nervously about your bee hotel. These small creatures, less than one centimetre long, are among the most beautiful of all insects, with an emerald-green metallic head and thorax and a ruby-coloured abdomen; in direct sunshine they gleam like jewels. They wait for the female mason bee to be out foraging and then they dash in, using a telescopic egg-laying tube to inject an egg into the outermost cell. The resulting offspring bides its time, waiting for the host grub to fatten up on its pollen store before slowly consuming it alive. If the mason bee should return and catch the ruby-tailed wasp in the act, the wasp simply rolls up. Its abdomen has a concave underside into which its head and thorax fit, thus making a neat ball. The wasp's back is also heavily armoured so there isn't much the outraged host can do other than throw the unharmed intruder out of her nest, there being every chance that it will scurry back in as soon as another opportunity arises.

The leafcutters are also attacked by sharp-tailed bees, a type of cuckoo bee which uses its pointed tail to slice through the leaf plug and insert an egg into a recently completed host cell. Unlike the ruby-tailed wasp, which is a carnivore as most wasps are, the offspring of the sharp-tailed bee is more interested in the host's food stores. The egg hatches quickly, and the resulting tiny larva is equipped with long curved jaws that are used to kill the host grub. It then helps itself to the host's food, losing the enlarged jaws (which it no longer needs) as it grows. Sharp-tailed bees are rather scarce, and ruby-tailed wasps are breathtakingly handsome; surely neither should be begrudged their place in the garden because of their nefarious life cycles? But if you accept this argument, then what are we to make of the tiny mites, relatives of ticks, that often infest mason bee nests? There are many species of mites that are found on different types of bees, some so tiny that they cannot be seen with the naked eye. Under a microscope these squat, spider-like beasts are, to most humans, quite revolting to behold. The most common ones on mason bees are pollen mites, which hitch a ride on the adult bees and then jump off into the pollen stores in the nest. Sometimes bees can be heavily infested, their bodies smothered in thousands of tiny mites, so that they spend much time trying to groom them off. Although it makes my skin crawl to see them, the mites do not actually feed upon or directly harm the bee, other than by weighing it down. Once in the pollen store, it is a race between the bee grub and the mites to eat the food. If there aren't too many mites, the grub usually gets most of the food and grows big enough to pupate successfully. In a heavy mite infestation, or if the bee grub is diseased or doesn't develop due to other reasons, the mites proliferate and fill the mud-lined cell with tens of thousands of offspring. In a bee hotel with viewing windows, these cells are obvious in autumn – instead of a chocolate-brown cocoon, the cell appears to contain a dense mass of pinkish-brown spores, each a dormant mite waiting for its chance to infest a new mason bee nest. Any bee emerging from beneath in the spring has to crawl through this mass of tiny parasites and inevitably becomes heavily infested, continuing the cycle.

It is more or less impossible to stop pollen mites from infesting your bee hotels. The mites jump from bee to bee during mating, and will also jump off onto flowers and then wait for another bee to come along, so most mason bees have some mites on them. A large bee hotel left *in situ* for a few years will inevitably contain many mites, and they can sometimes reach the point where few bee offspring survive and the bee population collapses. If the mites don't get them, outbreaks of parasitic wasps probably will. Life is fraught with danger for mason bees, as it is for most wild creatures.

Some have questioned whether bee hotels may do more harm than good, by concentrating large numbers of bee nests in one place and thus providing perfect conditions for outbreaks of parasites and diseases. J. Scott MacIvor of York University, Toronto, found that bee hotels put out in suburban areas tended to encourage non-native (and hence undesirable) bee and wasp species as well as the native ones.[31] So should we all be eagerly building bee hotels and encouraging others to do the same? The truth is we do not know for sure what the net effect of them is on our wild bees. It is certainly something that needs more study. In the meantime, there are a couple of strategies one might use to maximise the benefits and minimise the risks. Firstly, you could wage war on the natural enemies of your bees. George Pilkington is almost fanatically obsessed with looking after his mason bees, and anyone purchasing one of his solitary bee hotels gets extensive advice on how to minimise the risks of the bees being eaten by woodpeckers, attacked by parasitic wasps or infested with mites. A design feature of some bee hotels such as George's is that they can be dismantled once the bee grubs have pupated inside the silken cocoons they spin, and the cocoons removed and gently cleaned of mites before storing them somewhere safe for the winter (he has a special technique for removing the mites available to those who buy his hotels – I am sworn to secrecy). The hotel itself can then be sterilised to kill any mites or pathogens. That way, you stop pests from building up year on year, and by so doing it is possible to build up a huge

[31] In the twentieth century, at least ten different European and Asian solitary bees, mainly leafcutter and mason bees, were deliberately introduced to the Americas with the intention of boosting crop pollination. Given that North America has 4,000 or so native bee species, one might reasonably have thought that, between them, these would have been able to do the job without further assistance.

population of mason bees. This is fine and dandy but seems to me to be a tiny bit obsessive (sorry, George). Mites, parasitic wasps, cuckoo bees, even pathogenic fungi all have their place, and mason bees do not naturally occur in very large numbers in one place precisely because these creatures keep them in check. An alternative approach is to simply not build or buy very large bee hotels, but to scatter small ones around your garden. I opportunistically drill a few holes of varying sizes in any lump of wood I come across, I tie bundles of old bamboo lengths and hang them up here and there, I stuff old tin cans with lengths of dry, hollow hogweed stems, and I occasionally buy or am given a bee hotel. I even have a 'bee brick', a brick cast with holes in it, intended to be built into a wall, which I am trying out. George's hotel I clean out and sterilise every year, storing the mason bees in my shed where they are safe from woodpeckers (I don't think he'd forgive me if I didn't), but the rest I leave to nature. The woodpeckers take their toll on these, and sometimes mites are common, but the mason bees seem to be thriving. Of course I have only had the garden for five years so it is early days. But I take heart from a solitary bee hotel in southern France that has been in continual habitation for nearly forty years without care or maintenance.

My instinct is that nesting places for mason and leafcutter bees are in short supply – dead trees full of holes are not common in the modern, tidy world – and thus that providing them probably does more good than harm. It would be nice to find out for sure, but in the meantime I plan to carry on making them and hanging them up. In any case, there is a quite different argument in favour of putting up bee hotels, for they provide wonderful opportunities for people to encounter and learn about bees, and more generally about nature, close up. As I mentioned, my kids love to look through the viewing windows on my Nurturing Nature box to watch the bee grubs, mites or wasps developing, and outside the bee flight season I often take the entire box with me to display at public events and invariably find that people are fascinated. Even without a viewing window many people get great pleasure from sitting on their patios and watching the little reddish mason bees going about their business, the females trying to stock their nests, the males hanging about in the hope of swift sex, and later they may be lucky enough to enjoy watching leafcutter bees dragging their leaf snippets into the holes. The same argument may be made for keeping honeybees in cities. In ecological terms there may be too many of them, but they provide a fantastic tool for catching the attention of people who might not otherwise spend much, or indeed any, time thinking about nature. St Ermin's Hotel in Westminster has both honeybee hives and a large solitary bee hotel perched high up on a roof terrace, just outside a plate-glass window, so hotel guests can see the comings and goings of the diligent bees from just a metre or so away without any risk of getting stung. To many guests it is an incongruous and unexpected sight, and they will often stop and watch for a little while before they are drawn back to their busy city life.

Charlton Manor Primary School in Greenwich also has honeybee hives (alongside chickens and a vegetable patch), despite having little outside space and being in a densely urban area. The idea to keep them came about when a swarm[32] of honeybees descended on the school, and headmaster Tim Baker noticed that the pupils

[32] To beekeepers, the term 'swarm' refers specifically to a group of several thousand worker honeybees with a queen that have split off from their old colony (usually due to overcrowding) and are looking for a new home. The swarm typically hangs as a mass of bees from a tree branch or other solid object, while sending out scouts to locate a new permanent nest site, which might naturally be in a cave or hollow tree. Swarms can be an intimidating sight but the bees are stuffed with their honey stores and not at all inclined to sting.

were not frightened but both fascinated and calm. He went on a beekeeping training course and, once he knew what he was doing, he installed the first hive. When I paid a visit, it was wonderful to see the children, some of them just seven or eight years old, in diminutive bee suits looking after the hives. Bees and beekeeping have been integrated into the school curriculum, with the pupils practising their own waggle dances in PE lessons, using their own honey in cooking, learning about bees around the world in geography, and setting up a business to market their honey. Tim says that the bees have even helped improve the behaviour of difficult children, who have finally found something at school that they enjoy and are good at. One particularly aggressive child has really taken to the practical aspects of beekeeping and his behaviour has improved enormously. As Jo Sparkes, the school gardener, said: 'We think it is the scale of the responsibility he has been given that he is responding positively to. He can't kick off around the hives because we, and the bees, need to trust him.' Now wouldn't it be wonderful if every school had a beehive and a bee hotel or two, and some patches of bee-friendly flowers for them to feed on, and perhaps a vegetable patch where the pupils could watch the crops being pollinated and harvest the growing fruits? Maybe then all children could grow up appreciating the link between these little creatures and our own well-being.

We do not need robot bees. We have bumblebees, carpenter bees, cuckoo bees, flower bees, mason bees, honeybees, sweat bees, mining bees, longhorn bees and many more. We should welcome and encourage these irreplaceable little creatures into our schools, gardens and parks, and into our hearts.

6

Moth Mayhem

To make goat's cheese

Ingredients: 5 litres goat's milk, 1 sachet mesophilic starter, 4 drops rennet

1. *Warm milk to 29°C, then add starter.*
2. *After 30 minutes, add rennet, stir and cover.*
3. *When curds have set, ladle into muslin-lined cheese moulds, leave overnight.*
4. *Sprinkle cheeses with salt, leave for 24 hours.*

The bacterial starter and rennet can be readily purchased online, and you can modify this simple cheese by adding herbs, or by spraying with spores of Penicillium candidum *mould which gives it a furry white coat and alters the flavour. This may all sound complicated, but it really is a piece of cake. Cheesy cake.*

In September 2016 I received a rather odd email request from a Belgian named Bart Van Camp, asking whether he could visit and catch moths in my garden. He explained that he had spent the last few years trapping moths in the gardens of an assortment of Belgian scientists, journalists, politicians and TV personalities. He was on a mission to highlight the beauty and wonder of this largely unloved group of insects, and bring them to the attention of people who might be in a position to help champion their cause. By sampling in gardens, he also hoped to draw attention to just how much biodiversity lives unnoticed all around us. Bart wanted to expand his horizons beyond Belgium, and was planning a short tour of the UK in 2017.

As you might guess, I bit his hand off. I knew he would be wasting his time in the sense that I needed no convincing that moths are wonderful, but I refrained from telling him that. To many people, moths are drab, brownish creatures of the night, annoying or sinister little beasts that flap into the house on a summer's evening and bash themselves to dusty pieces on the light fittings. Worse, some will infest our wardrobes and secretively nibble holes in a prized cashmere jersey or silk scarf (clothes moths have a taste for the fancy stuff). These stereotypes do moths a great disservice, for in reality they are a hugely diverse, beautiful and fascinating group of creatures, with more than 2,500 different species known just from the UK. Although quite a few are indeed largely brown, others such as the garden tiger or burnet moth are spectacularly colourful, and can rival any butterfly. Even the brownish ones are, under close inspection, often breathtakingly pretty, with blotches, streaks and whorls of chocolate, rusty orange, cream and buff in delicate symmetry. Many moths are wonderfully camouflaged, their wings resembling a folded leaf, or a blade of grass dried and bleached by the summer sun, or lichen-covered bark, so that while they sleep through the day they are unlikely to be spotted by a hungry bird. For example, the angle shades moth has wings patterned in triangles of olive green and brown, and to enhance the appearance of a drying leaf the wings are curled and twisted when at rest so that the creature becomes all but invisible when sitting still among leaf litter. Emerald moths and silver-lines resemble fresh green leaves, streaked with cream lines to match the leaf veins. Some moths appear drab when sleeping, their forewings mottled and patterned in greys and browns, but when disturbed they flash their coloured hindwings, which may be bright crimson, orange, yellow or even blue, the intention being to startle any potential predator while they make good their escape. Others, such as the cinnabar, eschew camouflage in favour of advertising their invulnerability; this species is magenta and black to warn predators that it is poisonous, having sequestered in its body the toxic alkaloids from its larval food plant, ragwort. Burnet moths use the same colours to advertise that they are packed with hydrogen cyanide, and both burnet moths and cinnabars are active in the day because they need have no fear of predatory birds. Other moths go for bluff; the hornet moth, as you might guess from the name, pulls off a striking impression of a hornet (a large and fierce-looking wasp species) by having a yellow-and-black-striped body and slender, scale-less and hence transparent wings. It is not poisonous and neither does it have a sting, but being a scarce creature it relies on birds mistaking it for a hornet and never cottoning on to its secret.

I used to run a home-made moth trap as a child, but it was many years since I had done so and I had no idea what moths might be lurking in my Sussex garden. The prospect of having an expert to help me identify them was very enticing (with so many species, moth identification can be tricky). And so it was that Bart turned up one Thursday afternoon in mid-June 2017 with his photographer friend Rollin, and a camper van jam-packed with moth traps, generators, spools of electrical cable, nets, pots, and other paraphernalia of the entomologist. The biggest and best moth traps use a mercury vapour bulb, which throws out a blinding white light but also a lot of ultraviolet light that we cannot see but which is visible to insects. Bart had no less than three of these big traps, which he placed out in my garden in a rough triangle with about fifty paces between them. The traps themselves work more or less like a lobster pot: the lamp sits above a funnel, which opens into a large chamber filled with egg boxes. In theory the moths crash into the light bulb, fall down the funnel and then, finding themselves unable to easily escape, settle down for the rest of the night on the egg boxes which provide them with a textured surface to cling on to and dark, secluded crannies where they can sleep. The lobster pot arrangement is far from 100 per cent effective, with many moths not falling in, so Bart placed the traps on old white bed sheets that he had spread over the lawn, and then piled extra egg boxes onto the sheets so that any moths that didn't get caught by the traps might hopefully settle down outside them until morning, and would be easy to spot on the sheets and cardboard.

You may have wondered why it is that moths are attracted to lights at all. I would love to be able to tell you but the truth is that no one knows for sure. Of course there are theories, but none of them quite seem to add up. One intriguing one was put forward in the 1970s by US entomologist Philip Callahan. He had discovered that the pheromones of some female moths are luminescent, producing a faint infrared light that helps to attract males. Callahan noted that candle flames (to which moths are notoriously drawn) produce light of a similar wavelength, so perhaps lights are attracting randy male moths looking for a mate? It is an interesting idea, but seems implausible or at least inadequate. Firstly, although the moths attracted to a trap do tend to be disproportionately male, many females are also caught. Maybe these are gay moths? More critically to the theory, moths are attracted most to ultraviolet light, at the opposite end of their spectrum to the infrared produced by females. In any case, most moths produce pheromones that do not luminesce at all, yet these moth species are still attracted. Sorry, Philip, but I don't think this theory quite cuts the mustard.

A second explanation that has been put forward is that disturbed or frightened moths might try to fly upwards to escape, and use the moon as a cue to which way is up. Mistaking the light for the moon, the moths throw themselves at it in their attempts to escape. I don't buy this one either, for I have watched perfectly calm and undisturbed moths slowly warm up by shivering and then fly into the nearest light. Also, flying upwards might be the worst thing a moth can do when attacked, for out in the open it is likely to be easy prey to a bat. In daytime, disturbed moths tend to fly along horizontally and then dive down into the vegetation to hide.

The most popular and convincing explanation is based on the notion that moths navigate using the moon when migrating. A moth intending to travel a long distance in a straight line might fly at a fixed angle to the moon, gently adjusting the angle as the night progresses and the moon moves across the night sky by using some sort of internal clock. Bees use the sun in a similar way when navigating to and from patches of flowers. The theory is that moths mistake a bright light for the moon, but because it is close to them rather than thousands of miles away, their angle to the light shifts very rapidly if they fly in a straight line. To compensate, they curve towards the light, flying in a decreasing spiral until they crash into the lamp. If you don't follow the geometry, try it out; you don't need to use a lamp, any stationary object will do. Find a large, open area such as your local park and place an object in the middle – let's say a football. Then stand a distance away, perhaps fifty metres, and walk slowly while keeping the ball at forty-five degrees to the right of straight ahead. You will find yourself curving right towards the ball and circling it briefly before bumping into it. This works for any angle less than ninety degrees, though at angles approaching ninety degrees you will circle the ball many times before you get to it. On second thoughts, if you *do* want to try this out you might want to do it in a park further from home where you won't be recognised. Apologies for this laboured explanation, but after all that I'm afraid this theory too has a flaw. So far as we know, the majority of moths don't migrate at all, particularly many of the really small species, some of which probably never go more than a few metres from where they are born. Such species would have no need of using the moon to navigate, yet they still pile into moth traps with enthusiasm. Perhaps they use the moon even when just travelling short distances; in any case this seems to be the most plausible theory we have at present, but do let me know if you have a better one.

It was a calm summer's evening, though a little cool. Bart and Rollin turned out to be unusual Belgians in that neither of them drinks beer or any other form of alcohol, so we sat outside in camp chairs drinking apple juice and chatting while waiting for darkness to fall. Luckily they did adhere to one Belgian stereotype and had brought some fabulous chocolate.

At about 10 p.m. the first few moths started to appear. I tried to see what they were but the blinding light from the lamps made it very difficult to see anything other than silhouettes as the confused moths circled the lamp. Bart suggested that it might be wise to get to bed and then make an early start. It was evident that he doesn't like to be far from his precious traps when they are running, as he had set up a small tent in the midst of them all. He had explained that new European regulations now prevent the importation of mercury vapour bulbs from where they are made in China as they are not energy-efficient. He had recently broken his last spare bulb so was understandably concerned for the remaining three. What he will do when they break he did not know, for there is nothing else available that is anywhere near as effective at attracting moths (this presumably not being a major factor under consideration when new light bulb regulations are being considered). Perhaps following Brexit I will be able to import some for him.

I awoke just before 5 a.m. and rushed out in my pyjamas to see what we had caught, soaking my slippers on the dewy lawn. Bart and Rollin, being seasoned moth trappers, had been up since first light an hour earlier but had kindly waited for me to get there before doing more than having a cursory inspection of the moths outside the traps. Opening a moth trap brings back the excitement I used to feel as a child when opening Christmas presents. The sense of anticipation and of having absolutely no idea what might turn up is delicious. We were not disappointed. There were moths everywhere, all over the sheet and egg boxes outside the traps, and hundreds more inside. Rollin busied himself taking pictures of every different moth type. Between them, Bart and Rollin could identify most of the different species by eye, but they like to keep a photographic record from every site. Any moths they cannot identify with certainty on the spot they send photographs of to other experts for verification. A few species cannot be identified accurately without killing them and inspecting their nether regions under a microscope, but Bart and Rollin refuse to kill a single insect so these must remain a mystery. Once photographed and catalogued, each moth was carefully placed into the undergrowth where it would be fairly safe until nightfall. I discovered long ago that running a moth trap regularly in the same place is best avoided as the local insect-eating birds such as wrens and blue tits soon learn where to find a daily breakfast bonanza, and quickly hoover up almost everything, leaving only sad piles of moth wings. Wrens are small enough to actually climb into the trap, and despite their diminutive size they can consume a startling number of moths at one sitting.

While Bart and Rollin busied themselves, I did nothing more useful than gawp and point excitedly. My eyes were first drawn to the hawk moths. As someone who tries to champion the little creatures, I am always slightly annoyed with myself for immediately being drawn to the biggest of them. We humans are innately sizeist, a form of discrimination that has yet to make it into the statute books. But, let's face it, hawk moths are simply wonderful. In case you are unfortunate enough to have never seen one, hawk moths are among the largest of moths,[33] with sturdy, bullet-shaped furry bodies, large eyes and slender pointed wings. They are very fast flyers, and some undertake regular migrations from as far away as North Africa to visit the UK. On these journeys they stop to feed on deep flowers such as honeysuckle, lavender and verbena, hovering in front of the flower and unfurling their long coiled proboscis to probe deep into the nectaries. If one of these beasts flies into your house at night it sounds as if a small helicopter is coming in to land.

In the first trap there was a poplar hawk, a handsome grey creature with scalloped wing margins and an awkward way of sitting with its hindwings in front of its forewings that helps it to resemble a piece of broken bark. There were also no less than five elephant hawk moths. These are not enormous as you might have inferred from the name,[34] but are elegantly shaded in magenta and olive green trimmed with white edging. Few creatures are more beautiful. As I coaxed one to sit on my hand my youngest son Seth, aged

[33] The atlas moth, a giant silk moth from Asia, was long thought to be the biggest moth in the world with a wingspan of 25cm, but it has recently emerged that its close relative the Hercules moth of New Guinea and northern Australia is slightly bigger at an absolutely enormous 27cm. The biggest moth in the UK is the convolvulus hawk moth, a rare migrant from southern Europe with a 10cm wingspan.

[34] The name actually comes from the caterpillars, which are large brown creatures with a long, tapering front section that vaguely resembles the trunk of an elephant. They have large false eyes, so also bear a passing similarity to a small snake. I remember reading in our local newspaper many years ago about an unfortunate incident involving these odd-looking insects. The caterpillars naturally feed on willowherbs, but also find garden fuchsias to their liking. A lady with extremely limited knowledge of wildlife spotted some of these caterpillars feeding on

seven and still an early riser, came running out of the house to see what we had caught. Seth still has that unbridled enthusiasm for bugs that most older children somehow lose, and like me he was transfixed by the array of colourful creatures on display. Sizeist like his father, he soon had an elephant hawk moth on each hand and the poplar hawk perched on his shoulder.

Once I had got over the hawk moth-induced excitement I started looking more carefully at the other moths, and even though I have moth-trapped before I was overwhelmed by the diversity. There were moths in greens, creams, browns, greys, pinks, yellows and shades of orange, tiny frail creatures, sturdy powerful moths, elegant slender creatures with broad, trembling wings, moths that resembled bird droppings, others such as the plume moths whose wings resemble tiny white feathers. Some were starting to fly about, landing in our hair and scampering over our clothing. Bart and Rollin became more frantic in their efforts not to miss recording anything before it escaped.

Bart hurriedly pointed out a tiny silver-coloured moth with a delicate fringe of hairs lining the margins of its wings – a water veneer. I had heard of these but had no idea that they were living in my garden. There were several in the trap, all males, and for good reason as the females of the water veneer are generally wingless and aquatic. The caterpillars live under the water, using silk to glue together a shelter of leaf fragments and feeding by boring through

---

the fuchsia bush in her garden and thought that she had an infestation of snakes. In a spectacular overreaction to the presence of these entirely harmless creatures, she poured a gallon of petrol from her lawnmower can onto the shrub and ignited it. In the ensuing conflagration the poor caterpillars were of course incinerated but she also managed to burn down her garage.

the stems of various aquatic plants. They spin an underwater co-coon filled with air in which to pupate, although I have not been able to find out how they obtain the air bubble. When the adult emerges, the males scramble out of the water, pulling themselves up a plant stem to dry their wings, but the wingless females stay in the water, crawling about in vegetation at or beneath the surface. They mate at the water surface, and then descend down a plant stem to lay their eggs. Fascinatingly, a small proportion of females do have wings and can fly; if they did not, the species would never be able to colonise new ponds. Quite what triggers them to grow wings is not known; it may happen when the population becomes too crowded.

I searched through the trap, the names of moths I had not seen for forty years flooding back into my mind: the leopard moth, a fluffy white creature with black spots; the rosy footman, a gorgeous little orange-and-pink moth with delicate black loops embroidered on its wings; the swallow-tailed moth, straw yellow with short tail streamers; the buff-tip, with an orange hairy crown that looks for all the world like the end of a broken twig. And then a lobster moth, hidden among the egg boxes. I recognised it immediately, though I had never seen one except in books. I had longed to catch one as a child. The moth itself is not especially remarkable to look at, its rather furry grey-and-silver wings camouflaging it perfectly when sitting on the trunk of a beech tree, but the caterpillars are nightmarishly weird creatures. They have a very odd posture when alarmed, bending their tail forward and their head back so that the two almost meet. They have what look like antennae on their tail, and bizarrely long front legs for a caterpillar which they waggle in the air. When newly hatched from their egg they are dark reddish brown and somehow manage to resemble a wood ant. Until their first moult they eat only their egg shell, which they guard jealous-ly against other lobster moth caterpillars. Later they graze on the foliage of various trees, and develop the rich rusty orange colour of autumn beech leaves, but they retain their contortionist's flexibility and as they grow plump they begin to resemble some sort of giant spider (however hard I try I can't see much resemblance to a lobster). Whatever they look like, it most certainly isn't a fat, juicy and harmless caterpillar, which presumably is the point.

Eventually all the moths in the first trap were identified and we moved on. There were more delights in the second and third traps: a pine hawk moth, a scorched wing, a maiden's blush, a ruby tiger, several peach blossom moths, a common lutestring. Writing this, months after the event, reciting the names feels like poetry or perhaps a witch's incantation, and it brings back the excitement all over again. There were more, so many more, but I do not wish to bore you. In total, we caught 864 individual moths belonging to 151 different species. Bart and Rollin then packed up the traps and headed off towards Oxford to spend Friday night catching moths in the journalist George Monbiot's garden, and then the night after to trap in Michael McCarthy's small London garden.[35] Their plan was to come back to my garden for a second time on the way back to the Channel ports for the final night of their short UK tour.

On the Friday afternoon I had a call out of the blue from Michael; he'd completely forgotten that Bart was coming to his house until it popped up in his diary and was a little concerned that this visiting Belgian moth trapper might not be quite sane. I reassured him that Bart was of course as mad as a box of frogs but in the nicest possible

---

[35] Michael was the long-time environment editor for the *Independent*, and is the author of many books on wildlife and the environment including the excellent *The Moth Snowstorm*. I've owed him a debt ever since he helped launch the Bumblebee Conservation Trust in 2006 by putting us on the front page of his paper.

way, and his worries seemed to be allayed. I gather that they had a very pleasant evening, though when Bart and Rollin returned on Sunday I was quietly pleased to find that my garden had produced more moths than either George's or Michael's. Not that I am in any way competitive.[36]

On that final night we caught an extra eighteen species, capped off by a brace of privet hawk moths, the biggest breeding moth species in the UK. These are drab greyish beasts at rest, resembling a heavy flint arrowhead, but with pink-and-black-striped bodies revealed by a flick of the wings if disturbed. I may have a very long way to go to match the 2,673 species Jennifer Owen found in her garden, but 169 moths from just two nights of trapping has certainly helped.

Sadly, moths are in decline. No less than sixty-two British species have become extinct since I started running a moth trap as a child. Others that were once common are now rare; for example, the garden tiger has declined in number by 92 per cent since 1968. Bart and Rollin caught none in my garden. The V-moth has declined by 99 per cent in the same period. Counts from a national network of moth traps reveal that, in the south of England, total numbers of all species have fallen by about 40 per cent since 1968 (while over the same period numbers have remained close to stable in northern Britain). More detailed figures are available for a subset of 337 formerly common and widespread species; for these, 37 per cent of them have declined by more than half. I apologise for bombarding you with statistics, but these numbers are important. In the insect world, it is declines of bees and butterflies that tend to

---

[36] If I'm absolutely honest, this may not be entirely true. At this year's annual summer sports day at Seth's primary school, I ripped my hamstring while winning the dads' sprint by a whisker. I fell over the finishing line and couldn't walk properly for over a month, but didn't regret it for one moment.

get the lion's share of the attention, but clearly we should be just as worried about our moths.

The ongoing demise of many moth species is of course a tragedy in itself, but has knock-on effects for other wildlife, for moths are an integral part of our ecosystems. They are pollinators of some plants, and the adults are a major food source for bats, nocturnal birds such as owls and nightjars (though you'll be very lucky if you get the latter in your garden), small mammals, and also for day-hunting birds that chance upon them. Their caterpillars are a vital food for the chicks of many birds in the spring, providing much needed protein without which they will not fledge successfully. Moth caterpillars are the main food for cuckoos, and their reduced abundance is thought to be the most likely explanation for the dramatic decline in cuckoo numbers. Moths are also hosts to innumerable species of parasitic wasp and fly, which are themselves food for other creatures.

As with bees and butterflies, the causes of moth declines are debated and probably complex. Depending on your particular penchant, you might blame habitat loss, urbanisation, light pollution, intensive farming, insecticides, herbicides, or geo-engineering (chemicals said to be added to vapour trails for nefarious purposes). All but the last are very likely to be playing their part. All are likely to be much worse in the south of England, where most moth declines are occurring. Light pollution may confuse migrating moths, and draw some to their doom. Modern herbicides effectively remove almost all weeds which might otherwise have provided food for caterpillars. Recent research in my lab has found that neonicotinoid insecticides routinely turn up in the foliage of field margin and hedgerow plants, shrubs and trees, so any caterpillar eating their leaves is likely to be receiving a chronic dose of potent neurotoxin. We've made life pretty tough for moths in our modern world.

Luckily, many of the things you might do to help other wildlife in your garden are also likely to help moths. Avoiding use of insecticides will obviously be a good start. Nectar-rich plants such as valerian, buddleia and catmint, which you might already be growing to attract bees or butterflies, are often also visited by moths. If you can, squeeze in a few evening- and night-scented flowers too, such as evening primrose, sweet rocket, jasmine and honeysuckle, since moths love all of these. The more different native plants you have, and the more foliage in general, the more moth caterpillars will be able to find something to eat. Mixed hedgerows are fantastic in this respect, for you can have many woody plant species in a short stretch of hedgeline, and each will support several different types of moth. Hawthorn and blackthorn are both great hedging plants, but you can also include rose, ash, oak, lime, field maple, willow, birch, poplar, privet, hornbeam, or almost any other native tree or shrub you fancy. If you are planning a new hedge, many of these will take simply by pushing a cutting straight into the ground, so planting a hedge need not be an expensive venture. Full-grown trees themselves are also wonderful of course, but not practical in small gardens.

Moths don't need much else beyond sustenance for caterpillars and adults, but one further measure will help some of them. If you can avoid cutting back dead herbaceous growth at the end of the season, it will provide protection and hibernation sites for caterpillars and moth pupae, along with spiders and all sorts of other creepy crawlies. Cut it back in spring just as the new growth is starting, and ideally leave some a little later, and you will have done your bit for our underappreciated creatures of the night.

7

Dive into the Pond

To make rabbit/squirrel/venison pie

Ingredients: one rabbit or three grey squirrels, jointed, or about 800g diced venison; 50g butter; large finely chopped onion; 1 cooking apple, peeled, cored and cubed; 550ml cider; 40g flour; lots of black pepper
   For the pastry: 200g plain flour; 150g frozen butter; pinch of salt

1. *Place flour and salt in a bowl, and grate on the frozen butter. Stir well with a spoon, then mix with your hands while adding a sprinkle of cold water, until the dough holds together in a ball. Place in a Tupperware box in the fridge.*
2. *Brown the meat and onion in the butter, then sprinkle on the flour, add the apple, pepper and cider and simmer for one hour. Pour into a pie dish.*
3. *Roll out the pastry and put over the pie dish, sealing round the edges and making a small hole in the middle to let out steam. Cook at 220°C for 30 minutes or until golden brown.*

I have long held that there is at least a grain of truth in the aquatic ape hypothesis, and that one unlikely line of evidence in support of it comes from house prices. In case you are unfamiliar with it, the aquatic ape hypothesis argues that humans evolved to live on the seashore, feeding heavily on fish and shellfish, and that this explains our hairlessness and upright posture (the latter for wading), among other things. The more evangelical proponents of the theory suggest that our ancestors spent most of their time in the water, even mating while floating about. The idea has been around for nearly sixty years, and is either ignored or derided by much of the scientific community, but I would argue that ancestral humans who chose to live near water may well have had a better chance of survival, and hence that this preference may have been selected in our past. Seas and lakes offer sources of protein-rich food that may be much harder to obtain inland, and they provide a means of transport. When our ancestors spread out of Africa, the evidence suggests that they spread mostly along the coasts of Europe and Asia, and that it was hundreds or perhaps thousands of years before they eventually headed far inland. An evolved, innate preference for being by water is the best explanation I can come up with as to why people are prepared to pay an extra £100,000 for a sea view, even though the majority of the people that do so do not catch fish, own a boat, or actually swim in the sea. Why otherwise do retirees flood to Bexhill so that they can see out their days with a distant view of the greyish-brown, chilly and windswept English Channel? How else do we explain why almost all holiday destinations are coastal, even though many holidaymakers prefer to swim in the hotel pool? Why indeed are we so taken with spending our holidays sitting on plastic loungers next to a blue-tiled hole filled with diluted urine and chlorine? Somehow our soul is soothed by the sight and sound of water.

Whatever the underlying cause of our predilection for water, any view of it pushes up house prices, be it a river, canal or lake, but sadly most of us do not live in sight of an expanse of water. As a substitute, many of us have a pond instead, perhaps with a fountain or pump providing the sound of trickling water to enhance the effect. On the face of it, our fondness for ponds is as hard to explain as our desire for a view of the sea. Garden ponds are expensive to create, provide a potential death trap for small children, are often a bit smelly and can be a breeding ground for mosquitoes, so why are there roughly three million of them in UK, amounting to about one in every seventh garden? Again, I think the primary reason is simply our innate longing for proximity to water. We like the look of ponds, or at the very least we like the look of the magnificent demonstration ponds on display in garden centres and the splendid ornamental ponds that almost inevitably grace the grounds of stately homes, and we optimistically imagine creating something similar in our own garden.

Please don't misunderstand, I love ponds, and if I were prime minister one of the first things I would do would be to make ponds compulsory in every garden (along with the death sentence for people who collect their dog's excrement and then hang the filled bag on a tree like a Christmas bauble). For me, the magic of a pond is in the extra life it brings. I spent much of my childhood pond-dipping, and to this day I love the excitement and anticipation of scooping a net through the water to see what one might catch; perhaps a squat brown dragonfly nymph, a fearsome sickle-fanged great diving beetle larvae, or an orange-bellied smooth newt? If there wasn't one there to start with, I have dug a pond in the garden of every house I have lived in, starting at age seven.

The first one I made was lined with waterproofed concrete, which works well enough but can be a bit ugly and using concrete isn't great for the environment (its creation releases a lot of carbon dioxide). Rigid plastic or fibreglass liners or flexible butyl liners are generally the most practical option, although again not ideal as they too can be ugly and in twenty or thirty years at most they will have degraded and end up in landfill. If you have the time and enthusiasm, a puddled clay pond is best; you may be able to dig clay from your own garden, or puddling clay is quite cheap to buy. In essence all you need to do is dig a hole and line it with a twenty-centimetre depth of clay. To remove any air pockets from the clay it must be puddled, which means trampling it underfoot, or bashing it with the end of a fence post, all the while keeping it wet. It is an enormously messy job, but quite fun, and more so if you invite family and friends to join in. The South Downs used to have many such ponds, known as dew ponds, which were made by shepherds to provide water for their flocks. They would bring carts of clay up from the Weald, dig out a hollow and line it with clay, and then corral a small flock of sheep overnight in the pond to perform the puddling for them.

Whatever method you use, it is simply astonishing how quickly wildlife will arrive in a new pond. The first arrivals are usually insects, such as water boatmen, pond skaters and water beetles. The explanation for this is simple: they can fly. Insects comprise the majority of life on Earth, but are largely confined to land and fresh water, being more or less absent from the oceans. There is good reason for this: the first insects evolved on land, about 400 million years ago, at a time when the oceans were already teeming with a myriad of other invertebrates, including numerous crustaceans, molluscs, trilobites and so on. The key innovation that made insects successful on land was being able to fly, a power which brings many advantages, such as swift escape from predators, and ease in finding a mate or somewhere new to live. Being able to fly is of little use in the sea, and with every available niche in the oceans already crammed full, insects have never been able to invade. In contrast, being able to fly is enormously useful if you live in ponds, particularly ephemeral ponds that dry up in summer. Water shrimps, leeches, fish, frogs or pond snails have no easy or rapid way of getting from pond to pond, whereas for a dragonfly, able to fly at up to 35mph (they are the fastest of all flying insects), travelling to a pond to lay its eggs is simple. Nonetheless, it is rarely long before these other non-flying creatures start to arrive, perhaps hitching a lift on the feet of birds, or crawling laboriously through the damp grass at night. Miraculously, an empty pond will develop a diverse community of life within just a few weeks.

The UK National Pond Survey, which sampled 156 ponds, found a total of 398 different species of invertebrates (insects, snails, crustaceans, etc.), plus nearly as many plant species. A network of forty ponds created in 1990 near Oxford by the charity Pond Conservation is now home to 165 different invertebrate species and 85 species of wetland plants. Ponds support some of Britain's rarest animals, such as the tadpole shrimp (related to the *Triops* that are sometimes reared as pets) and the glutinous snail (the tiny, jelly-like creature known from just one pond in Wales). The reason for the rarity of some of these animals is that the number of rural ponds has been in decline for more than one hundred years. Britain is a damp, cloudy island, and would naturally have had innumerable natural ponds. In 1890 there are estimated to have been about 1.25 million rural ponds, comprising a mix of natural ponds and those such as the dew ponds on the Downs that were deliberately created and maintained by farmers to provide water for livestock. Today there are estimated to be about 400,000; about 70 per cent of our rural ponds have been lost. Sadly, as many as four-fifths of those that remain are estimated to be polluted with agricultural run-off – a mixture of fertilisers and pesticides – or with salty run-off from roads, and so they are in poor condition.

This is exactly why garden ponds are so important. They may be smaller than most rural ponds, but there are many of them, and in large suburban areas the density of ponds today is probably higher than it has ever been. They are providing a network of habitat in which at least our more adaptable pond creatures are thriving.

I was lucky to inherit a decent-sized pond in my Sussex garden, roughly circular and about ten feet across, although infested with invasive South American parrot's feather and overrun with Asian goldfish. Fish are best avoided in a garden pond as they tend to depredate much of the other life. Goldfish are gluttonous omnivores, hoovering up tadpoles and efts (young newts), and to my mind if it is a choice between newts and goldfish then the newts win every time. I've been trying to catch and remove all of the goldfish, but they breed fast amid the dense weedy vegetation and I seem to be making little headway. In the meantime, to provide somewhere for the amphibians to breed in safety, I have sunk an old bath into a quiet corner of the garden where to my delight it has been swiftly adopted as home by several common frogs.

Among the first, and the most beautiful and spectacular, insects that will seek out your pond are the swift-flying dragonflies and their more slender and weak-flying relatives the damselflies. At my larger pond, and despite the goldfish, I have a good breeding population of large red damselflies, dozens of which can be seen throughout spring and summer sunning themselves on the flag iris, attached in mating pairs, or laying eggs on the waterside vegetation. I often also have a male broad-bodied chaser stake out the pond as his territory for a week or two in summer. Chasers are sturdy, fast-flying insects with a powder-blue body chased with yellow spots along the sides. Occasionally a golden-ringed dragonfly swoops by to catch prey, magnificent green-eyed creatures with wasp-striped yellow-and-black bodies. A well-established pond can easily support ten or more types of dragonfly and damselfly.

I am aware of no scientific study of this, but it is my strong impression that ponds with lots of aquatic vegetation are much more attractive to dragonflies and generally support more life that those than are more bare, neat and tidy. Plants oxygenate the water, provide food for herbivores such as caddis fly larvae, snails and tadpoles, and hiding places from predators, and emergent plants are a useful means for dragonfly nymphs to haul themselves out when they are ready to turn into an adult. Your local garden centre will sell you a selection of water and waterside plants from around the world, but when it comes to ponds I prefer to go for natives such as cuckoo flower, yellow flag, water mint, purple loosestrife, hornwort and marsh marigold. With larger ponds, leaving at least some open water may encourage swallows to skim the surface for a drink, and swallows, martins and bats will regularly visit to pick off the midges and dance flies that often cloud the air above the water. At least one shallow margin will allow other birds and small mammals to get to the water to drink, and also help animals to escape if they fall in (I am still slightly traumatised by the childhood memory of finding the bloated corpse of a drowned hedgehog in a small but steep-sided pond at my grandmother's house). The rich life within a pond may attract other predators too; I have seen a grass snake hunting for amphibians along the bank of my pond, and very occasionally a heron comes by to eat the fish (if only she would take more). If you are spectacularly lucky and live near a river it is just possible that you might even be visited by an otter. These elusive mammals are slowly spreading back into our countryside, and they are partial to the fish or frogs that can be more easily caught within the confines of a pond than in a river.

Ponds do not have to be large to attract wildlife. Some aquatic creatures actually prefer very small bodies of water, too small to qualify as a pond (ponds are sometimes defined as any body of water between 1 metre square and two hectares). In particular, a whole suite of organisms have evolved to live and breed in tiny pockets of water which form in the forks of gnarled old trees where rainwater might puddle, in holes where a branch has snapped off, or in the shattered stumps of such trees when they eventually crash to the ground in an autumn storm. In any hollow or crevice in the wood where water collects a miniature microcosm begins to take form. Leaves and other organic matter fall in, and bacteria flourish. Fungi begin the long slow process of digesting the old timber. Moisture-loving plants such as liverworts, mosses and lichens colonise the damp margins of the holes. Mosquitoes lay their eggs, and their twitching larvae filter the water for bacteria and algae. Beetles, tardigrades, earthworms, springtails, booklice, silverfish and earwigs find homes and food in the stagnant water itself or in the damp, mossy margin. A miniature ecosystem has formed, and may last for many years until the timber rots away completely and the water escapes. Of course, really big old trees are rare these days, and any with signs of rot are usually swiftly dispatched since they are regarded as a hazard to passers-by, or a source of disease for other trees. Our modern, tidy world has no place for decay, and hence rot holes are not as common as they once were, though this is not widely appreciated or lamented.

Now, you may well be thinking that this is not such a bad thing. After all, almost no one cares about booklice or silverfish (a great shame in my opinion),[37] and mosquitoes are definitely not something that most of us wish to encourage in the garden. But perhaps you might be more interested if I told you that some of the UK's rarest and most beautiful insects also live in these holes. Some insects only live in these rot holes, some only in rot holes formed in particular species of tree. Such specialism is a foolhardy strategy

[37] Silverfish are an ancient lineage of flightless insects that have been wriggling about in the damper corners of our Earth for nearly 400 million years, and aside from rot holes can also be found under damp carpets in our homes. They have an elaborate courtship dance in which the male and female entwine quivering antennae, playfully chase one another, and finally press their vibrating bodies together. All of this wonderful romance may take place beneath the stained linoleum on your downstairs cloakroom floor.

ill-suited to a rapidly changing world, and the demise of old, rotting trees has led to the decline of these insects. Indeed, a good candidate for the UK's rarest insect is the pine hoverfly, a handsome shiny black insect with a bright red tail which appears to mimic the red-tailed bumblebee. The pine hoverfly, as you might have guessed from the name, breeds in rot holes in Scots pine, holes in which a particular fungus with the tongue-twisting name *Phaeolus schweinitzii* thrives. Anecdotal accounts suggest that the pine hoverfly was once common in the Caledonian pine forests of Scotland, but modern forestry practices were its downfall and this lovely fly now survives in just one tiny population in the Spey Valley. When I was based at Stirling University I had a student, Ellie Rotheray, who spent her PhD studying this elusive beast and its slightly less endangered cousin the aspen hoverfly. Opinion differs as to the aesthetic appeal of the larvae of the pine hoverfly (which is to say that there is Ellie's opinion, and then there is everybody else's). They are large, cream-coloured, legless, cigar-shaped maggots that sport a slender, telescopic tail which they use as a snorkel. The larvae lurk an inch or so down in the murky soup of the rot hole, too deep to be spotted and eaten by birds, and extend their long tails up to the surface to obtain air. Other less rare hoverflies have similar larvae and they are collectively known as rat-tailed maggots. Most people are at least a little revolted if not utterly repulsed when they first encounter these beasts lurking in a puddle of stagnant water, but Ellie loves them, and has attempted to rebrand them as 'long-tailed larvae'. She spent countless hours working out how to rear them in captivity, using water-filled glass jars to which she added various combinations of sawdust, woodchips and wooden strips to act as ladders for the larvae (they can drown if they sink too deep in the water and have nothing to clamber up). Strangely, in captivity the pine hoverfly larvae didn't seem to care if they were given spruce wood rather than pine, although in the wild they are only found in pine. The fact that they only occur in pine rot holes is presumably because this is where the females lay their eggs, begging the question as to why they are so fussy if their offspring aren't. It is most likely simply because spruce trees are not native to Scotland and hence the mothers have not yet adapted to take advantage of this new resource.

The larvae grew slowly, some of them taking two years to reach full size, but they seemed to do fairly well in Ellie's jars and many pupated (climbing out of the water to do so). The Royal Society for the Protection of Birds was keen to see the pine hoverfly back at its Abernethy Forest reserve, a place where it used to be found. To create breeding habitat for it the RSPB felled one hundred pine trees, the stumps of which Ellie then used to create artificial rot holes by digging into their heart with the tip of a chainsaw blade. She reared many larvae and released hundreds into the new holes, where they seemed to fare well. She also freed dozens of captive-reared adults in the summer, but sadly to little avail. Ellie finished her PhD in 2011 (and subsequently moved to Sussex University) and in her absence numbers of the fly appear to have dwindled, and the introduced population at Abernethy has fizzled out. There are plans afoot to bring in a fresh bloodline from Finland where the fly remains widespread, based on concerns that the tiny surviving Scottish population is highly inbred. The fate of this beautiful creature in the UK hangs in the balance.

Based on her experience with the pine hoverfly, Ellie has devised a simple means to create one's very own artificial rot holes, or, as Ellie calls them with her passion for making hoverflies more appealing to the public, 'hoverfly lagoons'. All you need is a waterproof container, some organic matter, such as lawn clippings or fallen leaves, and a few small sticks. You place the organic matter in the container, fill it with water, shove in the sticks so that they protrude from the top (allowing the full-grown larvae to climb out), and place the whole lot in a quiet corner of the garden. Of course nothing you can do will entice pine hoverflies to your garden unless you live on Speyside – and even then it is a thousand-to-one shot – but Ellie has found that her lagoons seem to work well at attracting some of the more widespread hoverflies that breed in rot holes. Inspired by her success, Ellie asked me and other friends and colleagues at Sussex University to try it for ourselves.

I am not a hoverfly expert, but I have found making and observing my own lagoons to be brilliant fun, and engaging for my kids. When we moved to our two-acre patch in Sussex, we inherited, scattered among the overgrown nettles and brambles, a selection of battered old containers suitable for making a fine array of lagoons. Ellie uses the bottom half of four-pint plastic milk bottles, but I improvised with a couple of plastic plant-pot trays, a long, deep plastic window box, a galvanised metal dustbin, and a large metal jam-making pot. I have to admit they aren't beautiful, and they are much larger than the lagoons that Ellie has experimented with, but I figured the bigger they were, the more hoverflies I would get. In the winter of early 2016 I set two up with wood shavings, two with grass cuttings from the lawn, and one with grass cuttings plus some well-rotted compost from the bottom of my compost heap, all topped up with rainwater (though Ellie says that tap water seems to be fine). Every month since, I've been searching through the smelly gloop for hoverfly larvae.

The ones with wood shavings have been useless so far – nothing has gone near them, and the wood shavings appear to be unchanged. I will leave them a year or two more as perhaps when the shavings eventually start to rot they will attract something. These aquatic hoverfly larvae feed on bacteria so they need the substrate to be actively decomposing. I had high hopes for my grass-cuttings and compost lagoon, but it has also been a bit of a disappointment; it smells rather ripe, much more so than the others, and has attracted a dozen or so handsome ginger dung flies (*Scathophaga stercoraria*). These are territorial and so are constantly fighting, which is entertaining to watch. They are also predators of small insects, so that may well be putting off female hoverflies looking for somewhere to lay their eggs; so far I have had no hoverfly larvae in this lagoon. I've nothing against dung flies, but they weren't what I was aiming for. Luckily my two grass-cutting lagoons have been rather better; in April, just a couple of months after setting them up, I saw clusters of white, elongate eggs, a little like miniature grains of basmati rice. By May both lagoons had dozens of tiny long-tailed larvae. By June some of them were quite large, perhaps three centimetres plus their tail.

Just as with the pine hoverfly, once fully grown the larvae climb out of their lagoon and drop down to the ground. My lagoons were amid long grass and it proved impossible to find where the larvae had gone. Ellie advised placing the lagoon on a tray containing woodchips or dry leaves, which would provide secluded nooks and crannies in which the larvae were content to turn into pupae. I tried this, and a few days later found half a dozen pupae; brown, barrel-shaped objects which still retain the long tail and also have two breathing holes which look a little like a pair of ears. The overall appearance is that of a tiny mouse. I placed them in a jam jar on a north-facing windowsill and a couple of weeks later was delighted to find that they had hatched into adults of 'the footballer' (*Helophilus pendulus*), a handsome hoverfly named after its yellow-and-black stripes that clearly reminded somebody of a football jersey. Ellie and other volunteers have between them found a range of different types of hoverfly using their lagoons, and over time we hope to learn more about which designs and types of organic material are preferred by the different species.[38]

---

[38] At the time of writing we are running a citizen science project in which we are asking people to report the success of their home-made hoverfly lagoons. If you are interested, go to www.buzzclub.uk.

Installing some kind of pond, or at the very least a hoverfly lagoon, may or may not placate your ancestral urge to live within sight of water, but it is the single measure you can take in a garden that will do most for biodiversity while occupying only a small space. If you want something to distract your children from watching screens, in my experience getting them dipping in the pond is one of few things that wins out over Minecraft, at least for a while. The *Oxford Junior Dictionary* recently removed the word 'newt' (along with acorn, minnow, kingfisher and dandelion, among others) after deciding the word was no longer relevant to children. What better way to ensure that newts are not just relevant but are loved by your children than to give them a chance to catch them, feel them wriggle in their wet hands, and gaze into their golden eyes? Go on, grab a spade, and get digging ...

8

Ants in my Plants

To make elderberry wine

Ingredients: 1.3kg ripe elderberries, 1.6kg sugar, wine yeast

1. *Crush elderberries, add 4 litres of water and yeast, cover with cloth and leave for 2 days.*
2. *Strain liquid through muslin cloth, add sugar.*
3. *Place in 5-litre container (e.g. demijohn) with airlock, wait until bubbling ceases.*
4. *Siphon off residue, seal in bottles.*
5. *Wait 6 months or more if you have the patience.*
6. *Drink (not all at once).*

Making wine at home is a dying art, but it is so easy and cheap and the results can be delicious. This recipe makes a rich, port-like red wine; I have kept some for twenty years and it gets better and better. Many other fruits also work well, for example blackberries and blackcurrants, or gooseberries for a white wine.

You probably do not realise it, but there is an army of diminutive farmers living in your garden. They have livestock which they 'milk' regularly as their major source of food, and which they care for, and will fight to the death to protect. These creatures live in complex societies comprising thousands and sometimes millions of individuals, almost all female, and each is allocated a particular job. There are very approximately 10,000 trillion of these creatures on Earth, which means that they outnumber us by more than one million to one, but most of us scarcely ever notice them. In terms of biomass, they make up about one-quarter of the total biomass of all land-based animals (with humans making up another quarter). Of course I'm talking about ants, arguably the most successful creatures on the planet, though they don't tend to boast about it. It often seems to me that humans dominate the modern world, that there are people everywhere, but if you lower your gaze to the millimetre or so just above the ground surface, or stare closely at the trunk of any tree, the first living thing you will usually see is an ant.

In my garden, and in most British gardens, the ant most frequently encountered is the common black ant, *Lasius niger*, one of the most abundant and widespread ants in Europe; if you have a garden of almost any size, you will have these ants. Even if you have no garden at all they may well invade your home in the summer months looking for food. As is the case with most ants, common black ants are aggressive towards other ants, fiercely defending their territory and their food. They are predatory on small creatures, which they hunt for in the soil, on the soil surface, and among herbaceous vegetation. They have no fear of heights,[39] and will travel high into the canopy of the tallest tree in my garden, a sycamore, in

---

[39] Of course vertigo would make no sense in ants as they could fall from a mile above the ground and would land without the slightest harm befalling them in the impact. Such tiny creatures fall very slowly due to their small weight and relatively large surface area; the terminal velocity of an ant is about four miles per hour, no more than our walking speed. In comparison, the terminal velocity of a man is about two

search of their prey. Multiple busy ant trails wend their way up the trunk every day through spring and summer.

In contrast to the common black ant, its close relative the yellow meadow ant *Lasius flavus* is a much less adventurous creature. It is also common in my garden, but it never seems to enter my house, and it never climbs trees. In fact this species rarely pokes its head above the soil surface, though it does sometimes build large mounds in tussocky grass into which it moves its brood to warm in the sunshine on summer days.

Both of these ant species are opportunistic predators, but much of their food comes from their livestock: aphids. Aphids feed on the sap of plants, which is what makes some of them such troublesome pests. They have mouthparts shaped into a pointed tube which they carefully stab into the tissue of the plant until the tip locates the phloem, the arteries of the plant that carry sugar-rich sap to wherever it is needed. The whole process is very similar to the blood-sucking behaviour of a mosquito, which has independently evolved rather similar apparatus for tapping into our circulatory system. Plant sap may be rich in sugar but it is very low in the amino acids and proteins that a hungry aphid needs to grow and to produce its offspring, so each aphid ingests huge volumes of sap, absorbs the protein, and then excretes the sugar as an unwanted by-product: honeydew. Ants have latched onto this ready supply of waste sugar, and for many species it is the main source of carbohydrate that fuels their activities. Aphids usually live in large groups, and the ants tend them just as a dairy farmer might look

---

hundred miles per hour. The so-called glider ants which live in the rainforest canopy of the Amazon are even able to steer their fall so that they crash into the nearest trunk, saving themselves a long fall and a long and perilous walk back up the tree.

after his herd of Friesians, protecting them from predators such as ladybirds, milking them, and meticulously grooming them with their mandibles to prevent any fungal growths (admittedly a few human farmers might not indulge in the last activity). Some aphid-tending ants will carry their charges down into their own nests at night for shelter and protection from predators. Aphids may switch to a winged phase and fly away if they detect that their population has become overcrowded and that their host plant is weakening, but some species of ant will bite the aphids' wings off to keep them captive. Others will carry the aphids from the stricken plant to a healthy, uninfested one to avoid them developing wings in the first place, managing their stock as a farmer might move his cows to a fresh field of grass. If the ants get the urge for more protein, or the aphids become unproductive, the ants will cull and eat their erstwhile charges in the same way that a farmer will dispose of an ageing herd of dairy cows. Just as in industrial farming, there is no room for sentiment in the world of insects.

Ants do not restrict themselves to farming aphids. As I write, on the windowsill behind my laptop a trail of common black ants is winding its way out of a crack next to the old window frame, and marching up the side of a plant pot and onto the Kaffir lime plant that I have been trying to nurture these last three years. The lime plant is infested with scale insects, flattened, limpet-like brown insects that suck the sap from the plant and in so doing also sap the strength of the plant, so that my Kaffir lime looks rather pale and regularly drops its leaves. Much like their aphid relatives, the scale insects exude honeydew, and so the ants that live in my wall tend them and prevent predators or parasites from attacking them. The ants appear to be thriving on their sugary diet, for every night they excavate a bit more mortar from my wall to make more nursery chambers for their expanding brood, leaving a pile of grains of crumbled cement on the windowsill for me to vacuum up.

Common black ants mainly tend above-ground livestock, but the agoraphobic yellow meadow ant necessarily sticks to aphids below the ground. You may not have realised that many aphids live underground – most likely, you never gave the subject a moment's thought – but there are many different types of subterranean aphid, each species preferring to suck on the roots of a particular plant species. Dandelions, for example, have their very own species of root aphid, as do lettuce, docks and many grasses. Some feed on the base of the root just at soil level, and their ant protectors carefully pile up grains of soil around them to provide a defensive corral. Aphids themselves are surprisingly diverse and underappreciated creatures. There are nearly six hundred species in the UK, with just a handful being significant pests of our crops and ornamental plants, while most of them live out their lives unnoticed by man, quietly feeding on the roots or leaves of wild plants in our hedgerows, grasslands and woodlands. Much of the success of these diminutive insects results from the assistance of their ant guardians.

There are not many types of creature of which the UK can claim to have the biggest. In fact I can only think of one, and it is an aphid, the giant oak aphid, *Stomaphis quercus*, which is the size and colour of a pale-roast coffee bean. It is the world's largest known aphid, but is now only found at five sites in the UK, though one imagines it might easily have been overlooked at other sites as, despite being the world's largest, it is of course still pretty small and inconspicuous in the grand scheme of things. It seems to be tended almost exclusively by the jet black ant, *Lasius fuliginosus*, and to be unable to survive without them. The jet black ant lives up to its name, being a very shiny black, almost as if it has just been dipped in gloss paint. Clusters of the shiny black ants are said to be the best indication of the presence of the giant oak aphids, which are themselves rather well camouflaged. The ants act like alpine shepherds, carrying the aphids up the tree to the more tender shoots in spring and then back down to crevices low on the trunk for autumn. The bark of oak is of course pretty thick, so this aphid has evolved extraordinarily elongated mouthparts, more than twice the body length in young aphids, which can be inserted deep into the bark to reach the sap. Unlike smaller aphids, the giant oak aphid breeds quite slowly and is thus poorly suited to life in the fast-changing, modern world. It was once common in the forests of the East Anglia Breckland, but almost all of these have been felled to create farmland.

Although I have a lovely half-grown oak on my boundary, I guess I'm not ever going to find this particular aphid in my garden. The nearest to me that the giant oak aphid has been recorded in recent years is Colchester, which would be quite a long journey for a pea-sized aphid. In any case, I don't have the right ant species in my garden. Although the jet black ant is found in Sussex, it seems to be quite scarce and I can find none locally. It has a peculiar biology, for it is a semi-social parasite of a semi-social parasite. That is to say, to get a colony of the jet black ant you first have to start with a common black ant colony. This then has to be attacked by a queen of *Lasius umbratus*, who enters the nest and kills the resident common black ant queen and enslaves the workforce. She produces her own workers, and eventually the old workforce of common black ants die off, leaving a *L. umbratus* nest. Unlike the semi-arboreal common black ant hosts, the parasitic *L. umbratus* are yellowish, subterranean ants, superficially similar to *L. flavus*. They are relatively uncommon and rarely noticed, so they have never been given a common English name. Next, the *L. umbratus* nest has to be invaded by the queen of the jet black ants, which in turn kills the *L. umbratus* queen (no less than her just deserts, you might think) and once again slowly replaces the workforce with its own. Finally, the giant oak aphid has its essential bodyguards in place.

Quite why any species would evolve to depend upon such an unlikely sequence of events taking place to provide it with the conditions it needs to survive is a good question, but it certainly explains why the giant oak aphid is uncommon. Like the bamboo-eating giant panda, the giant oak aphid seems to have painted itself into an evolutionary corner from which there is no easy escape.

The giant oak aphid is not the only rare insect that has an obligate association with ants. The caterpillars of many of our blue butterflies have a special gland on their back from which they exude sugar- and amino acid-rich drops of liquid, by which payment they enlist the protection of ant bodyguards. Both the holly blue butterfly and the common blue butterfly can sometimes be found in gardens, and both are tended by a range of ant species. Their exceedingly scarce relative the large blue butterfly has accomplished an audacious coup, subverting this uneasy mutualistic relationship with ants to further its own advantage. The large blue female lays her eggs on wild thyme or marjoram, which the tiny caterpillars feed on for a few days before dropping to the ground. Ordinarily, this would be a suicidal thing for a caterpillar to do, for once on the ground it is at the mercy of any passing predator such as a mouse or ground beetle, but the caterpillar is gambling that it will be found first by an ant. It needs not just any old ant, but an ant of one particular species, the red ant, *Myrmica sabuleti*. If a red ant finds the caterpillar, she picks it up and carefully carries it back to her nest below the ground, placing it inside a brood chamber. She does so because the caterpillar has evolved to smell like a baby ant, so that the worker ant's natural instinct is to return it to the nest. If that weren't remarkable enough, the large blue caterpillar then begins to quietly consume the real ant grubs in the brood chamber. Almost all butterfly caterpillars are herbivores, but after a brief vegetarian phase the large blue caterpillar turns into a carnivore, and spends the next ten months snacking on its adopted siblings.[40] The adult ants would be perfectly capable of intervening, and could easily kill the defenceless butterfly caterpillar even though it grows much larger than them, but they do not. Instead, they ignore the slaughter and continue to care for the giant alien grub in their midst. In late spring the large blue pupates, and after a couple of weeks the adult butterfly hatches within the ant nest. At this point the young butterfly has to scramble out through the narrow ant tunnels to daylight while her wings are still soft and folded. Sadly, as a result of habitat loss and perhaps also because of this rather complicated life cycle, the large blue became extinct in Britain in 1979. The details of the life cycle were worked out by Professor Jeremy Thomas, but just too late to inform a conservation strategy and so prevent its extinction. It has since been reintroduced from Sweden with some success, and several healthy populations of this remarkable creature can now be found in the south-west of England.

Much more recently, Jeremy's research group made another fascinating discovery. Female large blue butterflies are apparently able to tell which marjoram plants have red ant nests beneath them simply by sniffing the leaves, and hence by selectively laying their eggs on these plants they can improve the chances of their offspring being picked up swiftly by an ant of the correct species. It is even conceivable that the marjoram plants have evolved to use scent to call the butterfly to their aid; the ants damage the roots of the plant, and the butterfly gets rid of some of the ants, so it pays the plant to signal to the butterfly that it has ants beneath it.

---

[40] There are a handful of other carnivorous caterpillars in Hawaii. Most depredate flies, which they catch with elongate and claw-tipped forelegs, but one truly odd species (*Hyposmocoma molluscivora*) spins webs in which to catch snails.

You are exceedingly unlikely ever to see a large blue butterfly in your garden, but you will most certainly have a range of types of ants. From a gardener's perspective, ants are an unavoidable and mixed blessing. You will always have them and it is pointless and, frankly, dumb to try to get rid of them. You may easily have one nest per square metre in your garden, sometimes more, and to stand any chance of eradicating them you would have to turn your garden into a toxic wasteland. You may wonder why I feel the need to say this, but the sad truth is that many people do try to get rid of them. I have seen folk pour boiling water onto the nests, particularly when they are producing winged queens and males in the swarming season. Your local garden centre will sell you ant killer, sweet liquid baits loaded with neurotoxic neonicotinoid insecticides that are intended to kill the queen and hence destroy the entire nest. They may well do so, but you can be quite sure that the nest will be swiftly replaced by another one, for ants are tough, adaptable creatures, and every time they swarm thousands of new queens are produced, enough so that almost every suitable site is soon likely to be reoccupied. All you will have succeeded in doing is contaminating your garden with a pretty nasty chemical.

Putting the futility of trying to wipe out ants to one side, it is also probably counterproductive. On the downside, the help that ants provide to aphids can greatly elevate aphid populations on broad beans or apple trees by preventing other natural enemies such as ladybirds from doing their job. The flying reproductive stages of ants can be mildly irritating if they decide to swarm from between the patio slabs while you're having a barbecue, but they don't actually do any harm. The pile of crumbled mortar on my windowsill every morning is a bit annoying. But that's about it. Think yourself lucky; if you lived in other parts of the world you might have to contend with fire ants, the sting of which I can say from first-hand experience is exceedingly painful and similar to being jabbed with a burning match head. Worse still you could be living alongside bullet ants, regarded as delivering one of the most painful stings in the entire animal kingdom.[41] In comparison, a few common black ant queens landing in your hair once or twice a year is really no big deal. On the plus side, ants do lots of positive things; for example, when not tending aphids they depredate many small insect pests such as moth caterpillars on our vegetables and fruit trees. Ants were perhaps the first biocontrol agents actively managed by man; for 1,700 years orange growers in China have been hanging nests of the citrus ant in their orchards. These are voracious predators of pest insects and this species of ant shows no interest in tending aphids. Ground-nesting ants are also said to help the worms in keeping the soil healthy and aerated with their tunnelling activities, and to increase nutrient levels in the soil by carrying food below ground. All in all, these little creatures probably do a lot more good than harm.

The success of ants, the explanation for their extraordinary abundance on Earth, is largely linked to their social lifestyle. Like their cousins the bees and wasps, ant colonies comprise a large group of sisters working to help their mother. In some tropical ant species, the colony can comprise as many as 10 million workers, though common black ant colonies in the UK rarely exceed 10,000 in number. Nevertheless that is still a lot of sisters in a small space, and one might anticipate the potential for considerable sibling rivalry, but for most of the time life within an ant nest is relatively

---

[41]   Bullet ant stings contain a potent neurotoxin, so it is no surprise that it smarts. The chemical constituents of ant stings are highly variable, variously containing formic acid, acetylcholine, noradrenaline, alkaloids and so on – chemicals that the ants have evolved with the express purpose of inflicting maximum pain.

harmonious.[42] Each ant tends to specialise in a particular task, and learns to perform it efficiently; younger ants usually stay in the nest, caring for the brood or repairing tunnels, older ones may forage for food or defend the nest against invaders. In the honeypot ants (a range of ant species found in arid regions of the USA, Africa and Australia), some workers become living jam jars, being fed by their sisters with so much nectar that their abdomen becomes enormously distended and transparent, forming a grape-sized balloon of honey. They are the larder of the nest, serving the same purpose as the wax cells that honeybees fill with honey. These individual ants may spend their whole life clinging to the ceiling of an underground chamber, too heavy to move and in any case too fat to easily fit through the nest's tunnels. The aboriginal people of Australia greatly prize these ants as providing a rare and valuable source of sweet liquid in the arid outback.

The queen has by far the most challenging job, for she has to found the nest, usually alone. In the common black ant the young queen mates once or twice on her nuptial flight, and then contorts her body to chew off her wings before burrowing into the soil. She blocks up her burrow entrance to keep predators out, and there in peaceful, dark isolation she lays her eggs. The queen does not leave her brood or eat for several months, managing to support both herself and her growing brood by living off her fat reserves and by absorbing her redundant flight muscles. When her offspring become adult workers they break open the nest entrance and begin to

[42] This is not to say that there are no conflicts. Worker ants of some species can lay eggs, and they may fight each other over the right to do so, and fight with their queen over who produces male offspring. If you would like to know more, do read Bert Hölldobler and Edward O. Wilson's superb book *Journey to the Ants*.

forage. The queen at this point may have lost half her body weight, so her daughters need to find food quickly to revive her health; if she dies they are all doomed. From this point on the queen's task is simple: her sole job is to manufacture eggs, fertilising them with the sperm of her long-dead mates.

In some ants, including the common black, two or three young queens will sometimes occupy the same cavity, maintaining an uneasy truce. They may even provide each other with food via 'trophallaxis' – the unsavoury habit of exchanging vomit, mouth to mouth. These nests with multiple queens have a higher survival rate in their early stages, and because each queen produces offspring they collectively produce a larger batch of workers so that the nest has a better chance of success when it breaks open to the outside world. It might seem like a wise strategy, but there is a major cost: at the point where the nest is opened up, the young queens fight to the death. The winner inherits the nest and all the workers.

Given how many young queens are produced each year, inevitably most must fail. Either trying single-handedly to found a nest or founding one with a small coalition and then fighting to the death to inherit it are clearly both high-risk gambits. This presumably explains why queens of some ants, such as *Lasius umbratus*, resort to the alternative strategy of invading an existing nest of another species, killing the queen and enslaving her workforce.

While the young queens, whatever strategy they choose, face a challenging and complex early life, the males have a simple but short one. They are rather feeble and tiny-winged creatures that have just one purpose, to mate, and regardless of whether or not they find a mate during the swarming season, they live but a day or two.

The workers, which comprise the vast majority of the population for most of the year, divide up all the other jobs that must be done between them, although they can switch between tasks if necessary. This division of labour is clearly a successful strategy. While a butterfly or a grasshopper has to do everything for itself – find food, evade predators, find and court a mate, lay eggs and so on – for the most part each ant has to be good at just one thing. The queen has a swollen abdomen for producing thousands of eggs, and wings to help her find a good nest site, while the males are lightweight and winged to aid them in the task of finding a mate. Workers have dispensed with wings entirely since they never need to disperse from their natal nest. In some ants, such as the tropical leafcutter ants, the workers' size relates to their task, with tiny workers specialising in within-nest jobs, medium-sized ants gathering leaves, and the biggest workers defending the nest against large predators such as anteaters. The actions of the tens of thousands to millions of individual ants within a colony are coordinated by communication, usually achieved using chemicals secreted by a variety of glands but also by vibrations and physical signals such as waving antennae or legs, or modifying their body posture. This communication enables ants to recruit nest-mates to a good food supply, indicate that the nest is under attack, ask for food or assistance, or coordinate complex tasks such as nest construction or aggressive raids on other nests. Working as a team in this way is clearly a very successful strategy, and enables ants to thrive in diverse habitats from the most arid deserts to steamy rainforests and from a suburban English garden to well inside the Arctic Circle.

Communication may be key to the successful coordination of the activities of the multitude of ants within a colony, a code of chemicals, visual and audible signals, but codes can be cracked. The large blue butterfly has done so; by mimicking the scent of a larval ant, it fools its host into caring for it. Many other creatures have evolved similar tricks. A minuscule reddish-brown wasp, *Paralipsis enervis*, is a parasitoid of aphids and so has to evade the guarding ants to lay its eggs in its target host. This would ordinarily be a dangerous task, for it is much smaller than the well-armed ants, but it has evolved to mimic the smell of the common black ant, so it is ignored. What's more, it actually solicits food from the guarding ants, so that it can wander about among the aphid colony at will, snacking on sugary ant vomit and parasitising the ant's aphid herd to its heart's content. However, it has only cracked the code of the black ant. Other species of ant will either ignore it or kill it, depending on the type of ant.

There are many other creatures, including various beetles, true bugs and spiders that deceive ants, either simply so that they can live safely within the ants' nest, or so that they can eat the ants or the ants' food. This infiltration of ant colonies by their enemies illustrates an important point. Ants may, collectively, behave in complex and remarkable ways – such as fire ants which in times of flooding can form a raft and carry their queen and brood to safety – but individually they are hard-wired automatons. Although they are capable of limited learning they cannot work out that they are being duped. Their only response is an evolutionary one; if the infiltrators become too abundant and take a heavy toll on the ants, natural selection will eventually favour the ants switching to a different signal. It is a very slow version of the battle between wartime code makers and code breakers, taking place over millennia.

Code-breaking butterflies, wasps and beetles must have some impact on ant populations, but by far the most serious enemy that ants face are other ants. Ant wars, violent and bloody struggles between colonies, are common. Because of their abundance, ant workers regularly encounter ants from other colonies, both of their own and other species, and the colonies themselves may often be close together. Most ants are generalist omnivores and hence nearby colonies, even of different species, are likely to be in direct competition for food. In addition, ants are partial to eating ants of other species, or indeed cannibalising members of their own species – the young larvae are particularly juicy – so neighbouring colonies are both rivals for food and potential food themselves. This makes for uneasy relationships at best. As Hölldobler and Wilson ominously put it: 'The foreign policy of ants can be summed up as follows: restless aggression, territorial conquest, and genocidal annihilation of neighboring colonies whenever possible. If ants had nuclear weapons, they would probably end the world in a week.' So much for any residual notions you may have had that nature is harmonious.

Most ants are armed with sharp jaws and a sting or poison spray, and so they are well equipped for combat. Ants appear to weigh up the strength of rival colonies; if their armies are of similar size then outright war is usually avoided, presumably because both colonies would suffer terrible losses, the equivalent of our concept of 'mutually assured destruction'. However, if one is markedly weaker than the other then their neighbour will launch an all-out assault, ganging up to spreadeagle their opponents and then snip off their limbs and heads, or spraying them with acid or other poisons. Once the workers have been dispatched the queen and her young are slaughtered, or in some cases larvae and pupae may be taken home and adopted by the new colony as their own. When they become adults the adopted ants are presumably unaware that they are now working for the colony that murdered their mother and sisters. In honeypot ants, the swollen, honey-filled adults themselves may be kidnapped, dragged out of their home nest by an invading force and suborned into service in a neighbouring colony. As you might guess, young colonies are particularly vulnerable to attacks; if they are too close to an established colony, they will almost certainly be overrun and exterminated. Of the countless millions of young queen ants born every summer, a great many will be killed by other ants.

In some types of ant, such as the appropriately named big-headed ants of Mexico, there are supersized workers with large heads packed with muscles which drive their formidable jaws; these workers specialise in combat, particularly against raids by army ants, either fighting invaders near the nest entrance or, if severely pressed, withdrawing into their colony entrance and using their heads to provide a snug-fitting and near-impassable plug to prevent ingress by the raiders. When fighting against honeypot ants, *Conomyrma* ants of the south-western deserts of the USA will drop pebbles down the vertical entrance tunnels of their enemies, a rare example of tool use in an insect. Some Malaysian *Camponotus* ants possess huge glands which run the length of their bodies, and are packed with toxic secretions. Under severe duress, such as when being overwhelmed by a superior force of ants or being attacked by some larger predator, they contract muscles in their abdomens so violently that they explode, killing themselves but spraying their adversaries with sticky poison. It seems that ants evolved both farming and suicide bombers long before we did.

Given their psychotic tendencies, it is paradoxical that ants can be unexpectedly long-lived for such tiny creatures. Common black ant queens, for example, can easily survive for fifteen years, with unverified reports of them lasting up to thirty years. Perhaps even more remarkably, since they only mate during their nuptial flight at the beginning of their adult life but continue to produce offspring throughout it, they are somehow storing viable sperm inside themselves for decades. The workers can survive for four or so years, and make interesting and very cheap to maintain 'pets'. There are various commercial designs of formicarium or 'ant farm' on the market, typically consisting of two sheet of glass or Perspex fixed about two centimetres apart in a frame, which one fills with damp sand or soil. These are great fun to set up with kids; all of my boys have kept ants, just as I did when I was about nine or ten years old. Introduce a dozen or so worker ants to the chamber (easily found under a stone or paving slab in the garden) and they will busily burrow about, creating a network of chambers and tunnels. If you collect a few of the creamy white larvae when gathering the adults they will tend to these too, usually constructing a 'brood chamber' to house them in. So long as every now and again you add a few crumbs of food and a drop or two of sugar water in a small dish they will survive for years.

Whatever we do to the planet, I have a strong hunch that ants will be here long after we are gone. They have been around for 100 million years, originating in an age when dinosaurs stalked the Earth. These diminutive insects are relentless and merciless, the tiny terminators of the backyard. They couldn't care less whether they have it or not, but nonetheless they deserve our respect.

9

The Wriggling Worms

To make Sussex honey & apple pudding

Ingredients: 450g Bramley apples, 4 tbsp honey, 2 tbsp water, 50g breadcrumbs, ¼ tsp cinnamon, 50g ground almonds, 100g caster sugar, 1 free-range egg, 75g butter

1. *Cook peeled and sliced apples in honey and water until soft.*
2. *Mix in breadcrumbs and cinnamon, place in shallow ovenproof dish.*
3. *Melt butter, add almonds, sugar and beaten egg, then spread over apple mix.*
4. *Bake at 190°C for 45 minutes until browning on top.*

Absolutely delicious with custard or vanilla ice cream, my favourite hot pudding.

I'm worried about the worms. This may seem to be an odd concern, but it seems to me that they don't get enough attention, that they are being neglected. Are they doing OK? Is anyone keeping an eye out for them? Troublingly, the answers are a) we don't know, and b) no, not really. This is something that should bother all of us, for few if any creatures on Earth (or perhaps I should say 'in earth') are quite so important.

I should clarify that I'm not talking about any old worms; I'm talking specifically about earthworms, the wriggly beasts that, regrettably, get cut in half almost every time a gardener puts their spade into the soil. There are many other types of worms – flatworms, tapeworms, roundworms, spoon worms and even penis worms, for example – but let's leave them for another day (though in case you and any male earwigs reading this book are concerned I should reassure you that the penis worm does not live in penises, or eat penises, but rather it resembles a penis). You may be wondering what is so important about earthworms that I should be lying awake in the depths of the night worrying about them. The answer is of course that these lowly creatures perform an unglamorous but vital job in keeping our soils healthy and recycling dead organic matter; without them, crops and wild plants would grow much more slowly, and ultimately there would be less food both for humans and everything else with which we share the planet. Arguably, worms may be more important to the health of our ecosystems and to human well-being than are bees (and you probably know how I feel about bees).

Charles Darwin wrote a whole book about worms, with the snappy title *The Formation of Vegetable Mould, Through the Action of Worms, With Observations on their Habits*. He wrote: 'It may be doubted whether there are many other animals which have played so important a part in the history of the world, as have these lowly organized creatures.' In Christopher Lloyd's entertaining book *What on Earth Evolved*, he lists the hundred most important wild creatures on the planet, and by his reckoning the earthworm is number one. As Lloyd says: 'Wherever earthworms plough, people thrive. When worms perish, societies collapse.' Perhaps now my worries seem a little less foolish.

So what exactly are earthworms, and how do they accomplish so much? Technically, earthworms belong to the huge and ancient phylum the annelids, a group of segmented, tubular creatures that includes ragworms and leeches, and which have been slithering around in the ooze at the bottom of the oceans for at least half a billion years. The ancestors of earthworms were probably among the first animals to crawl out of the seas onto land, although as you might guess they don't tend to fossilise very often (having no bones) and so we know little about their ancestry. Earthworms are simple, soft-bodied creatures, little more than a muscular tube connecting a mouth at one end to an anus at the other, with a linear gut connecting the two. They don't bother with lungs or gills; they just breathe through their skin, which means they are prone to drying out and can only live in damp, humid places. They have a rudimentary nervous system with only a minimalist and superfluous brain at the front end near their mouth, and they have no eyes, just a few specialised photosensitive cells along their back which tell them if they have foolishly crawled out into the daylight and are in imminent danger of becoming lunch for a bird.

Earthworms are so simple that, unlike French aristocrats, they are only very mildly inconvenienced by having their head sliced off; most species of earthworm can grow their head back after it has been removed without any great difficulty. You might think that cutting worms in two is the preserve of revolting little boys, but the American scientist G.E. Gates spent the best part of forty years from the late 1920s to the 1960s studying the regenerative abilities of earthworms. To be fair to him, he didn't just slice them in two. His specialism was taxonomy – the naming and classification of species – and he went on several expeditions to Burma and India on which he discovered many new species of earthworm. I imagine him as an intrepid explorer, wearing a pith helmet and laden with trowels and jam jars, hacking his way through the jungle in search of new and wonderful worms. When he wasn't on expeditions to exotic climes he filled in the intervening time chopping various bits off different species of earthworm to see whether they could grow them back. Gates justified this obsession with dismembering worms as being 'because little interest was shown by others', though I'm not sure that this in itself is a fantastic justification for a lifetime's work. His legacy is a handful of scientific papers containing painfully detailed descriptions of his amputation experiments. He found that types of earthworms were very different in their responses to bodily disunion. Many, such as the common lob worm (*Lumbricus terrestris*), known in America as the nightcrawler, could readily grow back their head but not their tail, while a few can regenerate the tail but not the head. He found that just one species, the reddish-coloured brandling worm (*Eisenia fetida*) that is very commonly found in compost heaps, could regenerate both halves, but only if cut in exactly the right place – between segments 20 and 24, counting from the head end. Thus he was able to clone a worm, creating two genetically identical, entire worms from one. Not perhaps the most useful discovery, but strangely fascinating.

Despite their name, not all earthworms live in the earth. Some inhabit tidal mudflats, some live in the bottoms of streams and ponds, some in the carcasses of long-dead rotting tree trunks, and a few adventurous species are arboreal, living amid the leaf litter and debris caught in the forks of large trees, sometimes dipping into rot holes. Even among those that live in earth, their habits are very variable. Some, such as the brandling worm, live in the leaf litter on the soil surface. Others, such as the grey worm,[43] make mainly horizontal burrows within the top 30cm or so of soil, while the lob worm makes deep, vertical burrows that may go down a metre or more, coming to the surface at night to grab dead leaves and then dragging them down deep into their subterranean lairs.

[43] Grey worm is also the unlikely name of a fierce warrior eunuch in the hit TV series *Game of Thrones*.

Let's take a look at what it is that makes worms so essential. Their most important role is in the creation of fertile soil. Worms eat decaying organic matter, such as compost, fallen leaves, the bodies of small animals and fungal material, which they suck into their pharynx at the front of their body. This then gets ground up in their crop, with the help of mineral particles ingested along with the food, and digestive enzymes are also added. Worms absorb some nutrients but the bulk of the rotting plant material and the mineral particles are ground together into a fine paste which is eventually excreted, in some species as a cast at the soil surface. Studies have found that fresh earthworm casts are five times richer in available nitrogen, seven times richer in available phosphates, and eleven times richer in available potassium than the surrounding upper six inches (150mm) of soil. Each individual worm is capable of producing up to 4.5kg of nutrient-rich casts each year.[44] In a healthy garden full of worms that adds up to a lot of prime compost for your plants to grow in.

On top of this, worms also do a grand job of aerating the soil, allowing oxygen to penetrate down to the roots of plants, preventing soil from becoming compacted, and helping water to penetrate the surface, so reducing run-off in heavy rain and hence reducing flooding downstream. Having no rigid skeleton, worms move via a simple hydraulic system. The body is a tube of liquid encased within both circular muscles that run round each segment and longitudinal muscles that run lengthways along the worm. If the circular muscles contract the worm gets narrower, and because the liquid

---

[44] Worm casts are considered unsightly by some, and undesirable on golf greens, so it used to be common practice to pour pesticides such as the organochloride lindane or carbamate insecticides onto ornamental lawns to kill all the worms. Fortunately this is now outlawed in most developed countries.

has to go somewhere it necessarily gets longer – think of it like squeezing a long thin balloon. Conversely, if the longitudinal muscles contract the worm becomes short and fat. To move, a worm alternates contracting these two sets of muscles. The contractions in themselves would not get the worm anywhere, but in addition it has retractable bristles that poke out of its sides and anchor part of the worm in place. Hence if it anchors its tail and squeezes its circular muscles, its head pushes forwards. It then anchors the head and the longitudinal muscles pull up the tail. As you might imagine, this is not a speedy process. A large lob worm has a top speed of about one centimetre per second if it really pulls out all the stops (about two-hundredths of one mile per hour), while smaller worm species are much slower. Some slugs are quicker.

Hydraulic locomotion may not make for speed but, just like the hydraulics of a tractor or digger, it is powerful. A worm can exert more than one hundred times its own body weight in pressure to force open crevices in the soil, enabling it to penetrate through compacted ground if it has to. It facilitates this by secreting a slimy liquid which helps to lubricate its passage. All this burrowing about does not just provide tunnels for air to diffuse through, it actually pumps air up and down, for the body of the worm acts like a piston while it moves through its tunnels. As a lob worm burrows upwards from deep underground to feed at night it sucks stale air up behind it, and then as it goes back down, towing a bundle of leaves, it pushes fresh air deep into the soil. Of course worms don't do any of this deliberately. Just as a bee does not set out to pollinate flowers – its goal is to gather food – so a worm does not intend to create compost and aerate and drain the soil, but nonetheless it does so remarkably well. Aristotle obviously recognised their worth, aptly describing worms as 'the intestines of the earth'. Cleopatra is not famed for her environmental credentials but it seems that she was very protective of worms, for she declared them to be sacred, to be honoured and protected by all her subjects. The ancient Egyptians identified the link between worms and soil fertility, and by Cleopatra's somewhat heavy-handed but laudable royal decree anyone caught taking worms out of Egypt was to be put to death. Records do not reveal whether worm smuggling was in fact a significant issue at the time or if any executions for this crime actually took place.

Aside from their long-recognised and vital role in maintaining soil health, worms provide an additional benefit to the wildlife gardener, for they are a major source of food (again, not something the worms actively seek to participate in). Worms form a significant part of the diet of numerous garden birds, such as blackbirds, starlings, crows, owls and robins, and in the countryside provide important food for rare and declining species such as curlew and lapwing. They are also among the preferred snacks of many mammals, from shrews and hedgehogs to foxes, badgers and bears.

Precisely because so many creatures wish to eat them, all earthworms spend the very large majority of their time tucked well out of sight in their burrows. This is just as well, because they are hopelessly ill-equipped to survive out in the open for long. They may be strong, but at two-hundredths of one mile per hour they have little chance of outrunning a predator (if indeed 'run' is the correct term). For obvious reasons when they do come to the surface they tend to stay close to their burrow. In most earthworm species their only defence against a hungry bird is to retract into the burrow as quickly as possible. Darwin was fascinated by this response and explored what sounds caused worms to retreat by placing pots of worms on his piano and striking different keys. According to him, when he played a C on the bass clef the worms 'dashed like rabbits into their burrows', though given what we know about worm speeds this seems like a rare occasion on which Darwin may have been exaggerating.

If their dash for cover is too slow and their head is grabbed by the bill of a hungry blackbird, earthworms fatten the part of their body that is in the burrow by contracting their longitudinal muscles, and they push out the retractable bristles from their sides into the walls of their burrow to lock themselves in place. Usually the outcome is that the worm gets snapped in two, but as we have seen this is not always disastrous, depending on where it breaks.

A few worm species have other tricks up their sleeves when attacked. The brandling worm earned its specific name, '*fetida*', because it squirts a foul-smelling liquid from tiny pores along its side when it is attacked. This doesn't seem to be entirely effective because these worms are popularly used as fishing bait, but perhaps the liquid is more successful at repelling birds or moles than it is fish. One type of worm, the delightfully named Australian blue squirter worm, *Didymogaster sylvaticus*, has a more impressive defence. When under attack, this slightly obscene frankfurter-sized bluish-purple worm can squirt its own hydraulic body fluids out through pores in its back. The resulting fine jets of slimy liquid spray nearly 30cm into the air, presumably enough to give a hungry kookaburra pause for thought if the appearance of this worm were not enough to put it off in the first place.

Many types of earthworm have to come to the surface to find a mate, and sometimes they do so in large numbers on wet, warm nights in the summer. When it comes to sex, earthworms have the advantage over most other animals in that they are hermaphrodites, both male and female at the same time. This does not mean that they can mate with themselves – this would be a pointless endeavour, since the benefit of sexual reproduction is to shuffle one's genes with those of another individual to produce unique combinations of genes in one's offspring. But it does mean that they can mate with any other adult individual of the same species, each donating sperm to the other as they lie head to tail alongside one another in the dewy grass. The sperm are stored for a few days or even weeks, during which time the saddle (the swollen, paler band visible on any adult earthworm) secretes a slimy ring of tissue, a little like a tiny elastic band. The worm then delicately backs out of this, sliding the band forward over its female parts, which attach twenty or so eggs as the band passes, and then over the segment which stores its partner's sperm, which is duly allowed to fertilise the eggs. Finally the worm slips out of the band completely, leaving the eggs behind inside the slimy ring which dries and shrinks around them to produce an object that is the shape of a tiny lemon, and which is oddly known as a cocoon (the word cocoon more usually being used to describe the silken protective case which a moth caterpillar spins to protect itself when it is about to pupate). When the baby worms hatch two to three months later they look very much like miniature versions of the parents, but without the saddle, which only develops when they are sexually mature.

Thanks to the efforts of G.E. Gates and his like, we know that there are at least 6,000 species of earthworm in the world. The lob worm is the largest British earthworm, living for eight years or more if they are lucky or wise enough to avoid one of their many predators for so long. The biggest known specimen was found in Widnes in 2016, and was a magnificent 40cm long and weighed in at 26 grams. He was named Dave by the boy that found him; sadly he is now pickled in a jar at the Natural History Museum in London, with the label bearing the legend '*Lumbricus terrestris*; known as Dave'. However, Dave was a minnow compared to the python-sized giant Gippsland earthworm found in Victoria, southern Australia. This monstrous beast can grow to three metres in length, with a girth of about 9cm, but even the Gippsland is a tiddler compared to the African giant earthworm. One of these found by the side of the road in South Africa in 1967 was claimed to be nearly seven metres long, and weighing 1.5 kilos. At the other end of the spectrum, the smallest earthworm species are barely 1cm long. It would be a safe bet that there are many more of these lowly creatures to be found if someone were to take up the challenge of being the next G.E. Gates.

The biological importance of worms is largely a function of their numbers. Their role in creating compost, aerating soil and providing food for hungry animals would not be particularly significant if it were not for the fact that worms can be staggeringly abundant. A 2004 survey of the worms in the kitchen garden at Down House, Darwin's home for most of his life, found a little over seven hundred worms per square metre. This equates to seven million worms per hectare, a mass of worms with a total weight of two and a half tonnes. Recent surveys of pastures typically find in the region of two to three million worms per hectare, in total weighing over one tonne. The weight of worms in some farm soils may easily exceed the weight of the farmer's livestock. In some habitats, worms may weigh more than all the other animals put together. This is why they are so important; a few worms would do almost nothing, but millions of worms together can transform soil health.

Given the huge value of worms to us, we would be wise to look after them, but in truth we have very little idea as to how well they are faring, and as to how their numbers may have changed. The last hundred years have seen huge changes to farming practices, including the introduction of tractor-powered ploughing, synthetic fertilisers and all sorts of new pesticides. We know that other wildlife has tended to decline over this period, some of it dramatically so. Given that, at least since Aristotle's time, the importance of earthworms has been well recognised, you'd think we would have some sort of long-term worm-monitoring scheme in place, to tell us if they are increasing or declining.

Surprisingly, until very recently there seems to have been no such scheme in place anywhere in the world. In the UK there is now a 'citizen science' scheme for worm recording run by OPAL (Open Air Laboratories based at Imperial College London), which encourages members of the public to count and identify the common worm species in their garden or local area, but since this is new it cannot tell us how things have changed over time.

I was interested to discover how many worms were in my garden soil. OPAL have a useful website and provide a simple protocol for counting worms, along with a colour-identification guide to the common species. So long as you don't mind getting down on your hands and knees and getting muddy it is a fun and easy thing to do, involving digging a small rectangular pit and searching through the soil and roots carefully for worms. My son Seth loved it, and between us one Sunday morning in early autumn we dug half a dozen pits and tried to identify the worms we found. We counted and discarded immature worms (ones without a saddle) as they cannot be identified. It turns out that even adult worm identification is a bit tricky for the novice, there being about thirty different UK species, so we put the worms into a shallow white plastic tray and took them into the kitchen so that we could compare them to the pictures in the identification key on my laptop. Two-hundredths of one mile an hour may not sound fast, but when you have fifty worms all heading in different directions at the same time it is quite hard to keep an eye on them all while also looking for subtle identification features, and we soon had worms slithering all over the table and dropping onto the floor. Nonetheless it was entertaining, and we managed to identify at least six different types: lob worms, brandling worms, redhead worms, grey worms, green worms and black-headed worms. To be honest, the names are a bit misleading and I think the person that coined them must have had a vivid imagination. Despite the names, all of the worms were in reality a mix of greys and reddish purples. The heads of black-headed worms aren't black, and green worms have only the faintest tinge of green. We may also have had an octagonal-tailed worm, but so far as I could see its tail was not octagonal (the guide unhelpfully explained that this feature is 'very difficult to see in live earthworms'). Numbers varied a bit across the garden, with most in a pit we dug next to the compost heap. Overall, we averaged 511 worms per square metre, the majority immature but with a good smattering of adults and one whopping 20cm lob worm (nothing to rival Dave of course). At a rough calculation, that means my garden, which is about one hectare in size, contains about five million worms, all quietly burrowing away and defecating compost; not quite up to the standards of Down House, but I was pretty pleased.

I was intrigued to see how this compared to an arable field. About three hundred metres from my house, on exactly the same heavy clay soil as my own, is a very large field (about twenty hectares), the edge of a large farmed estate, with a footpath along the side. The week after my garden survey I snuck in, armed with a bucket, trowel and notebook, to see what I could find. There are no houses within sight and it is a quiet area, but nonetheless I felt very conspicuous and guilty to be digging small holes on someone else's land. I guess I should have asked for permission but I had no idea who to ask, and anyway I wasn't taking anything away. The field had been under wheat earlier in the year, with just the stubble now left, so there was little vegetation to obstruct my excavations. Although the digging was easy, the resulting worm haul was disappointing; an average of thirty-two per square metre (about 300,000 per hectare), equivalent to six per cent of the worm density in my garden.

Of course this doesn't tell us too much in itself as to what is happening with our worms. If one could sample dozens or better still hundreds of garden and farmed sites with different management, then one might be able to tease apart what factors determine worm abundance. Ideally, if we had a long-running national earthworm-monitoring scheme, where multiple sites scattered across the country were surveyed every year for decades using a standard protocol, then we would know exactly what is going on. Given the long-understood importance of worms, it is surprising that no one ever thought to set this up. Searching through the scientific literature, I can find a scattering of measures of worm density in different habitats, locations and years. Recent surveys of arable soils mostly found even fewer worms than in the field I surveyed, often no more than twenty per square metre. Older studies of arable land in the 1950s tend to have more, in the region of 150 to 300 per square metre. When I was growing up in the sixties and seventies I vividly remember seeing huge flocks of gulls following ploughing tractors to scavenge the upturned worms, but this is something I scarcely ever see any more. Perhaps this is because there are fewer worms, or fewer gulls, or because farmers plough less, or perhaps my memory is just playing tricks. Worm numbers are very variable, and the history of management of every field is different. All we might tentatively conclude is that gardens seem to be very good places for worms, that arable farmland is not so good, and that numbers in arable farmland might have declined over the last fifty years or so.

Why might arable farmland be less worm-friendly compared to garden soils? Pesticides are likely to have had some impact. Arable crops in the UK are routinely treated with about twenty different pesticides per year, including insecticides, fungicides, molluscicides and herbicides. Although short-term toxicity tests are commonly carried out on earthworms, we have little idea what chronic exposure to this barrage of chemicals does to worm populations, just as we don't know what it does to bees or to us. Applying multiple pesticides to crop seeds before they are sown in the ground is often thought to be a safer way of using them than spraying them from the back of a tractor, but from a worm's perspective (if a blind creature can have a perspective) this provides little packages of concentrated pesticide that they might bump into on their subterranean travels. Copper, often used as a fungicide on horticultural crops (and with limited use allowed on organic farms), is highly toxic to worms, and can accumulate in soil. In the past, some pesticides such as the fungicide Benomyl were widely used before it became apparent that they were highly toxic to earthworms. Benomyl was used to control apple scab in commercial orchards until it was discovered that it was decimating worm populations, all but eradicating lob worms. In an unanticipated side effect, it turned out that the absence of worms to pull the fallen leaves beneath the surface made the scab fungus problem much worse, for the fungus overwinters on these leaves before producing spores to infect young growth in spring.

In addition to pesticides, one might imagine that the low numbers of worms in arable soils might relate to mechanical cultivation, ploughing, harrowing and so on, which must smash up their burrows, chop up some of the worms, and expose others for birds to eat. In contrast, although gardeners dig their soils and no doubt chop up some worms (and a bold robin will usually grab the odd one or two), they usually only dig over a small portion of their vegetable patch each year, and one would guess that hand-digging would be less violent and harmful to the worms. However, counter-intuitively, short-term trials over two years suggest that worm numbers can actually be increased by ploughing of grassland, particularly those worm species that live near the surface and burrow horizontally. This may be because the ploughing loosens the soil and hence makes it easier for the worms to burrow about, or because the burying of the grass provides organic matter for them to eat. On the other hand, in recent years some farmers have moved towards using 'no-till' techniques in which the soil is not ploughed and seeds are sown using a special drill that cuts slots into the soil surface, and there is clear evidence that this too increases worm numbers, particularly those of deep-burrowing worms such as the lob worm, providing a seeming contradiction. The explanation seems to be that it is actually all about organic matter, and has little to do with the direct effect of ploughing (or not ploughing). As G.E. Gates so thoroughly demonstrated, worms cope pretty well with being chopped up. What is really important is how much food they have; how much organic matter there is in the soil. Cultivation exposes the soil to erosion and exposes organic matter to oxidation, so arable soils tend to slowly lose their organic matter over time, becoming gradually less fertile and less hospitable to worms. This process can be halted or reversed by no-till farming, or by adding manure, or by leaving the land fallow for a year and then ploughing in the vegetation. Growing leguminous crops – peas and beans – also seems to help. So long as the farmer makes sure that there is plenty of organic material the worms will have the basics they need to thrive, and in return they will do their best to give the farmer healthy, well-drained and fertile soils.

One threat to worms which seems to have proved to be more of a damp squib than a serious menace is the New Zealand flatworm. This 20cm-long shiny purplish-black slimy beast arrived in the UK in the 1960s, thought to have been brought in by accident with potted plants. They've since spread all over the UK, again probably by us, and they are now common in wetter parts of the country, primarily the west and Scotland. I often used to find them under flowerpots in my garden in Dunblane in Scotland. The flatworm feeds exclusively on earthworms, wrapping itself around its un-suspecting prey and then secreting a mucus containing powerful digestive enzymes which liquidises the hapless worm. The flatworm then sucks up the pool of nutritious worm smoothie. When this creature was first discovered in the UK there was widespread dismay and speculation that this might be the end of our worms. Although its dining habits are not endearing, the flatworm-induced worm apocalypse seems not to have materialised; earthworms remain reasonably abundant in northern and western Britain, and were plentiful in my Dunblane garden, although of course without a worm-monitoring scheme we can't say more than that.

The only worms we know of that appear to be in serious trouble are the really big ones.[45] The Oregon giant earthworm, a one-metre-long worm species found in woodlands, has not been seen since 2008, with much of its former habitat now converted to housing estates or farmland. The giant Palouse earthworm from Washington State was thought to be extinct by the 1980s. Fortunately it was rediscovered in 2010, but it remains very rare and its future is uncertain. In Australia, the Gippsland giant earthworm is also now very scarce and is considered to be in danger of extinction. It seems to have been adversely affected by the introduction of superphosphate fertilisers and ploughing; being three metres long, they would be chopped into many pieces by a passing plough. G.E. Gates never got his hands on them so we don't know for sure, but it would be a good guess that this would be terminal. Like many other endangered species, the Gippsland giant earthworms are slow to mature, taking five years to reach reproductive age, and the odds of them surviving so long have diminished. It is difficult to ascertain how many are left as they rarely come to the surface and they live at such low density that they are near impossible to find by hand digging. In wet weather they can apparently be heard in their deep tunnels

---

[45] With one exception: the Lake Pedder earthworm. This tiddly 5cm worm was known from only one site, a beach on the edge of Lake Pedder in Tasmania. Unluckily for the worm the beach now lies several metres below the surface of a huge new lake constructed as part of a highly controversial hydroelectric power scheme which flooded 242 square kilometres of pristine native forest. The worm is presumably extinct, unless it has a very long snorkel.

as they make sucking and gurgling sounds as they move about, but I guess this isn't much of a basis for a systematic monitoring scheme. Until 2012 this species had its own 'Giant Earthworm Museum', near the town of Bass in Victoria, in which visitors could crawl through an oversized replica of a worm burrow and even through a worm's stomach. I can't imagine that it was ever a huge draw for tourists, but it seems sad that this unique opportunity no longer exists.

In the UK at least, a new champion has emerged for the lowly worm. The Earthworm Society of Britain was created in 2012 by Emma Sherlock, a worm specialist at the Natural History Museum. Emma hopes that the society can promote an appreciation of the importance of worms among the general public. So far it has attracted 215 members; it seems unlikely that the society will ever rival the Royal Society for the Protection of Birds, with its million-plus members, but it is a great start. They offer training courses to enable volunteers to learn how to identify all of our native earthworms, going beyond those included in the OPAL scheme, and they are trying to get a national survey of worm abundance and distribution up and running.

For me, one of the joys of living in Britain is that it is possible to have a viable society devoted to earthworms; no other country can boast half as many esoteric societies obsessively devoted to obscure creatures. Delightfully, Britain is also home to both the World Worm Charming Championship and its fierce rival the International Festival of Worm Charming. The former first took place at the Willaston County Primary School fete in Cheshire in 1980, and has run annually ever since. Worm charming, also sometimes known as worm grunting or worm fiddling, is the arcane art of coaxing worms out of the ground. There are many techniques, but most involve some method of vibrating the soil. Quite why this brings worms to the surface remains the subject of much debate in certain circles. One theory is that the vibrations resemble heavy rain, and that the worms come up to avoid drowning. This seems implausible as, in my garden at least, worms do not come up in large numbers when it actually rains, and as I discovered many years ago when feeding worms to my pet great diving beetles in a fish tank, worms can live quite happily under water for several days. As is so often the case, it appears that Darwin may have been the first to provide the correct explanation. He suggested that the vibrations convince the worms that a mole is digging close by, and so they surface as part of evasive manoeuvres. Recent research by Kenneth Catania of Vanderbilt University, Tennessee, has shown that the introduction of a mole to tanks filled with soil and worms does indeed cause the worms to surface, while playing back the recorded sound of digging moles straight into the soil also causes them to pop up.

Whatever the explanation, gulls have long used this to their advantage; most days there are two or three herring gulls on the lawn outside my office at Sussex University, hopping rapidly from one foot to the other in what appears to be an avian performance of *Riverdance*, their keen yellow eyes focused on the grass in front of them where they hope a worm will pop up. In Florida, wood turtles do the same, stamping their stubby feet to lure up their prey. Human worm charmers have devised various techniques; worm grunters drive a wooden stake known as a 'stob' into the ground, and then rub the top of the stob with a flat piece of metal called a 'rooping iron'. Worm fiddlers also use a wooden stake driven into the ground but then vibrate it by drawing a blunt saw over the protruding end. Other techniques include pouring water, beer or tea onto the ground, twanging a garden fork, singing and chanting, beating the ground with cricket bats, or blasting loud music of various genres into the earth. Darwin tried beating the ground with a spade but no worms emerged for him, and he concluded that 'perhaps it was beaten too violently'.

Strict rules for competitive worm charming have now been drawn up by an august body known as the British and European Federation of Worm Charmers, including that any liquid used must first be drunk by the contestants to prove that they aren't going to poison the worms. Each team must consist of a charmer, catcher and counter, and there is a five-minute 'worm-up' period to prevent pulled muscles. All worms must be returned to the ground at the end of the competition. The current world record-holding charmer is Sophie Smith who, aged ten at the time in 2009, coaxed no less than 567 worms to pop out of her three-by-three-metre plot.

The rival International Festival of Worm Charming was set up in 1984, and has since attracted teams from as far afield as New Zealand to the small village of Blackawton in Devon where it takes place. It is distinctly less serious than the (not terribly serious) World Worm Charming Championship, with the teams wearing fancy dress and starting with refreshments in a local pub before processing to the competition ground, accompanied by morris dancers. Once the excitement is over, 'worming down' also takes place in the pub.

To me, these light-hearted and slightly daft festivals hark back to the ancient pagan festivals, when people were infinitely more connected to nature than they are today, and celebrated the passing of the seasons, fertility, growth, harvests and death. They seem like great ways to encourage people of all ages to re-engage with nature; honouring the humble worm is surely a good place to start.

10

Garden Invaders

<u>*To make Jerusalem artichoke & squash soup*</u>

Ingredients: 1 tbsp olive oil; 1 tbsp cumin seeds; 1 onion, diced; 400g Jerusalem artichokes; 400g squash or pumpkin, peeled and diced; 100g red split lentils; 600ml water; 2 stock cubes; 1 tbsp harissa paste; 1 tbsp Worcestershire sauce; handful of thyme and/or marjoram; black pepper

1. *Fry the cumin seeds in the oil for 1 minute, then brown the onion.*
2. *Add everything else, and simmer for 30 minutes or until lentils and squash are both cooked. Blend.*
3. *Can be served with a dash of cream or yogurt and pepper.*

Jerusalem artichoke is incredibly easy to grow in the garden, giving a large yield of pest-free tubers. It is also delicious simply roasted with oil or butter and a sprinkle of salt.

In November 2007 I received an unexpected parcel in the post. At the time I was living in Muthill, a small village in rural Perthshire, having moved up to Scotland some six months previously from Southampton at the other end of the country. The parcel had been sent from Southampton by our former neighbour, a lovely lady named Mary who was in her late eighties at the time. Inside was a matchbox, carefully sealed with tape, and a short letter which rather mysteriously said that she had found a ball of these insects clinging to her curtain pole and wondered what they were. Intrigued, I sliced open the tape and popped open the box, whereupon three or four dozen multicoloured beetles stampeded out, running in all directions across the kitchen table. This was my first encounter with harlequin ladybirds, and luckily I recognised them from pictures I had seen and realised that I had a potential catastrophe on my hands. Shouting to my family for help, I gathered up as many as I could, my young boys helping to search under the table and on the floor for any that had got away. The ladybirds were rather beautiful, some red, some orange, many of them with variable numbers of black spots, and a few of them black with red spots. It was with some regret, and much protest from the boys, that I popped them in the freezer so that soon they were dead.

The tale of the harlequin ladybird is an interesting one. It is a species native to Asia, where it is of no great consequence but plays a minor role in controlling aphid pests. It is a species that is quite easy to breed in captivity, and so it was thought that it might be a useful species to breed and release as a biological control agent. Many batches were reared up and released at sites all over the world, particularly in the USA, from 1916 onwards. They were considered to be moderately effective for short periods immediately after release, but they seemed to die out quickly and none became established in the wild. Something then happened to the harlequin in Louisiana in the late 1980s, some sort of evolutionary shift that is not understood. The colourful but innocuous little beetle somehow became turbo-charged and turned into an invasive pest. Suddenly, large numbers started turning up in the wild in Louisiana and then shortly after in the surrounding states. Within twenty years it had colonised almost every state of the USA.

The story is similar in Europe. Harlequins had been imported and released many times, and by the mid-1990s were being bred and sold on a large scale by some of the big biocontrol companies based in northern Europe. These companies specialise in breeding predatory mites, parasitic wasps and other predators of crop pests, particularly for use in control of glasshouse pests. They also breed buff-tailed bumblebees for pollination of glasshouse crops. One might question why they did not breed and sell European ladybirds, of which there are many species, but then these are the same companies that were happy to sell buff-tailed bumblebees to Chile,[46] many thousands of miles outside their native range, so why should they worry about shipping Asian ladybirds around the globe?

The history of shipments of such insects is difficult to reconstruct, but genetic studies suggest that some of the superharlequins were brought from the USA to Europe. By the turn of the millennium harlequins started turning up in the wild in Europe, just as they had in North America. They have now colonised at least twenty countries in Europe, from Spain and Ireland in the west to Ukraine in the east, and from Greece in the south to Norway in the north. Elsewhere in the world it has recently turned up in South America, Egypt, Mexico and South Africa. Extrapolation of its potential distribution from the range of climates it has so far occupied suggests that it is very adaptable. Apart from the Arctic Circle, very hot and arid regions such as the Sahara, and possibly very wet lowland tropical areas such as Amazonia, it can live more or less anywhere, and seems intent on doing so as quickly as possible. The harlequin looks set to become the world's most abundant ladybird.

[46] The sad consequences of introducing buff-tailed bumblebees to South America are recounted in my book *Bee Quest*.

Harlequins arrived in Britain by unknown means in 2004. They prefer to hibernate in dense clusters, using a pheromone to find each other as autumn sets in, and these aggregations often form in crevices in houses, sometimes in furniture. If disturbed, the beetles leak poisonous alkaloid-laden secretions as a defence (like most ladybirds, their bright colours are a warning that they are poisonous). There is plenty of trade between the Continent and the UK and many thousands of cars travel across on the Channel ferries, so it is easy to imagine a cluster of harlequins being accidentally shipped over in a consignment of antique furniture or perhaps stowed away among a shipment of ornamental plants. However they got across the Channel, it then took them just three years to spread across most of southern and central England and Wales, pretty speedy for a beetle that is not a great flyer, but once again they probably hitched rides. Which brings us to my first encounter with them in 2007. At the time, our house in Muthill was about 200 miles north of any recorded sighting of the beetle. If they had escaped from my kitchen, this would have opened up a new invasion front and certainly accelerated their colonisation of Scotland.

You may well be wondering why having an extra ladybird species in the UK should be a cause for flapping about in a panic in my kitchen. Ladybirds are beneficial insects, so surely the more the merrier? The problem is that, like other ladybirds, harlequins don't just eat aphids. Aphids are their preferred food, but once they have eaten all of those in their patch they will switch to other insects such as caterpillars, or other ladybirds, including their own kind. The UK has forty-six native species of ladybird, and the harlequin is doing its best to eat its way through them. A national ladybird-monitoring scheme coordinated by Dr Helen Roy at the Centre for Ecology & Hydrology in Oxfordshire, and based on records sent in by members of the public, shows significant declines in seven of the eight commonest UK ladybirds since the harlequin arrived. Most hard-hit seems to be the two-spot ladybird, one of our most abundant ladybirds until the harlequin arrived, but now rather scarce. Similar declines seem to be affecting native ladybirds across Europe and North America.

There is an interesting similarity between the harlequin ladybird and a much more ancient invasion – that of the UK by rabbits. Rabbits are native to Iberia and North Africa, but have been introduced all over the world, most famously in Australia, where they have become a pest of enormous importance. I may not have rabbit problems on the scale of the Australians, but they are probably the most troublesome pest in my garden, laying waste to my vegetable crops and gnawing through the bark of my fruit trees in winter. I occasionally shoot one for supper, but it seems to make little difference to their numbers, so I have to fence in any plants I value. It was long thought that rabbits were introduced to the UK by the Normans about 800 years ago, but recent archaeological finds of rabbit bones in Norfolk from 2,000 years ago make it clear that the rabbit should be added to the lengthy list of things that 'the Romans have done for us'. Rabbits were regarded as a delicacy by the Romans, and subsequently by the Normans, who nurtured them in protected enclosures, even building artificial burrows for them. They seem to have been delicate creatures, not able to cope well with our winters. Henry III is said to have been particularly partial to them, and had them served up on special occasions. Although rabbits must have escaped from these enclosures, and there are some records of them in the wild, they remained relatively rare and prized animals for about 1,700 years, from their introduction until the eighteenth century when they started to be regarded as a pest. By 1950 there were about 100 million of them in the UK.

As with the harlequin ladybird, we don't know what happened. Perhaps some sort of evolutionary event, an adaptation to the cold, took place. The onset of persecution of predators such as foxes and buzzards by gamekeepers in the 1700s must have helped, though of course the rabbits were trapped and shot too. Whatever it was, it enabled rabbits to become enormously troublesome pests. In an attempt to curb their numbers, myxoma virus, a non-lethal disease of related rabbit species in the Americas, was introduced to the UK in 1952, and rapidly killed 99 per cent of the population (about 99 million rabbits), many of them suffering a painful and lingering death. I have vivid childhood memories of country walks in the sixties and seventies in which we would all too often stumble upon a diseased, blinded rabbit sitting helpless in the open. My father would invariably do it the kindness of bashing it over the head with a stick. Since then the rabbits have evolved some resistance, and the virus seems to have itself become less virulent, for the rabbit population has partially recovered. More recently, in 1992, a new virus, rabbit haemorrhagic disease from China, was accidentally brought into the UK with domestic rabbits, and has caused some devastating local epidemics and the deaths of many pet rabbits. This doesn't appear to have made a huge impact on the wild rabbit population, certainly not if my garden is anything to go by. Currently, UK rabbit populations are thought to be about half of their peak 1950 level.

We are currently not very good at predicting which species are likely to become invasive and which are not. There seem to be no hard-and-fast rules, and so any species that we bring into the UK might become an unwanted pest in the future. Aware of this threat, some countries such as Australia and New Zealand now have stringent biosecurity measures in place to prevent further escapes of non-native species. In the UK we are rather more relaxed about this threat, particularly when it comes to our garden plants. For 250 years we have deliberately sought out unusual and exotic plants from every corner of the globe, and attempted to grow them in our gardens. The numerous plant specimens brought back by Joseph Banks from his round-the-world expedition with Captain Cook on the *Endeavour* (1768–1771) sparked a mania for novel plants, with wealthy patrons sponsoring expeditions so that they could show off their latest acquisitions to their friends. Adventurous plant hunters risked their lives staging expeditions to far-flung lands throughout the eighteenth and nineteenth centuries. This demand from gardeners for novel and beautiful plants never waned, and today most gardens are jam-packed with exotic specimens from every corner of the globe. Imagine our gardens without magnolia, rhododendron, the monkey puzzle tree, azalea, bamboo, camellia, philadelphus, clematis, mahonia and buddleia, to name but a few. While I cannot find it in my heart to wish away these wonderful plants, there is no doubt that our zeal for growing foreign plants poses a threat to our native flora and fauna, and has already led to some environmental disasters. Vast tracts of western Britain are covered in thickets of the purple-flowered *Rhododendron ponticum*, smothering native plants and displacing whole ecosystems. The River Uck and its tributaries that wind near my house in East Sussex are lined along both banks every summer with a dense stand of head-high Himalayan balsam, loved by bumblebees but squeezing out the native plants that used to thrive there. Spreading stands of giant hogweed, the flowers standing three metres tall, are swamping native meadow and hedgerow plants in many parts of central and northern Britain, while the dreaded Japanese knotweed is so hard to remove that house sales regularly fall through if it is detected in the garden (on one two-hectare development site it cost £2 million to remove the weed before any building work could start). These were all once specimen plants, often purchased for a premium price from a garden centre and nurtured by their proud owners. Any of the 14,000 introduced plants that we grow in the UK could possibly become invasive weeds in the future.

It is not just plants that we have deliberately introduced for their ornamental value, only for them to become unwanted pests. Grey squirrels were brought from North America in 1876 and released in the grounds of country estates, where they were initially regarded as an attractive addition to our native fauna. That they might impact upon the native red squirrel was presumably not considered, but sadly they have. There are now about two and a half million grey squirrels in Britain, compared to around 100,000 of the native red (less than 10 per cent of their former population), and the greys are still spreading northwards. The greys are bigger, stronger, produce more offspring, and crucially they are carriers of squirrel pox virus, a disease that does not naturally occur in Europe but was brought in with the greys. The disease seems to do little harm to the grey squirrels but has a devastating impact on the reds, causing facial ulcers, scabbing and swelling of the head, lethargy and, eventually, death. So far as we know, not a single red squirrel that has become infected with the virus has ever survived. Once the disease gets into a red squirrel population an epidemic spreads swiftly among them, and soon they are gone. Most British people have never seen our native red, a dainty species with delightful tufts of hairs on its ear tips, for they have long been wiped out in southern and central UK (apart from on Brownsea Island and the Isle of Wight, where the greys have not arrived).

In the 1930s recognition that the grey squirrels were causing the red to disappear finally dawned and led to bounty schemes whereby children could earn a shilling by handing in a grey squirrel tail at their local police station. It had no appreciable effect, and the greys continued to multiply and spread, despite further sporadic attempts to control them throughout the twentieth century. Much more recently, the ongoing demise of our native squirrel has led to grassroots efforts to stem the spread of the grey in Cumbria. Former gymnast Julie Bailey had watched the red squirrels disappear from her garden in 2009, and took to shooting and eating the greys.[47] Her passion for saving the reds led her to become a major player in pulling together groups of volunteers across northern Britain, and eventually led to the formation of Red Squirrels United, a National Lottery- and European Union-funded programme to eliminate the grey in the north, which has the prominent support of Prince Charles. So far, the ongoing culls have resulted in some local stabilisation of red squirrel numbers, and have been most successful on Anglesey, where 6,000 greys have been dispatched so far, and where numbers of reds have recovered to 700 or so from being on the brink of extinction.

These last-ditch attempts to save our red squirrels are highly controversial. More than 95,000 people have signed a petition against the cull, mostly people who live in the south and are accustomed to seeing grey squirrels. Invasive or not, greys are loved, and many people cannot bear the thought of them being slaughtered. They reasonably point out that it is not the squirrels' fault that we brought them here, and that after 140 years they should now be considered part of our fauna. To these people, the grey squirrel is endearing, one of few wild mammals that we regularly see scampering in our parks and gardens in the daytime, a charming, mischievous and entertaining garden acrobat.

[47] Carcasses of red squirrels were commonly sold for eating on London markets in the days when they were still common. I can confirm that greys are good eating, but I must confess to having been put off the meat when one of my PhD students, Steph O'Connor, kindly offered me some squirrel casserole that she had cooked. The first mouthful was delicious but on the second I hit a lump of fur. As I was spitting and pulling hair from between my teeth she explained that she had used a frozen squirrel which she'd shot some months earlier, and not having time to thaw it properly she had cooked it in chunks with the skin still on.

The Garden Jungle

In contrast, to their detractors the greys are nothing more than fluffy-tailed rats, carriers of disease, predators of baby birds, and pests of forest trees.

It is fascinating that we humans can arrive at such different opinions of the same creature. It is also worth noting that we were not so keen on the native squirrel before it was endangered. Just as greys do damage to trees, so red squirrels can strip the bark from young trees in forestry plantations. To prevent this, in the first thirty years of the twentieth century 85,000 reds were slaughtered by the Highland Squirrel Club. One wonders what members of the club would make of today's Red Squirrels United.

Our confusion and inconsistency with regard to grey squirrels is also highlighted by two recent court cases. In 2010 a man named Raymond Eliot was ordered to pay a hefty fine for catching and drowning a grey squirrel that kept raiding his bird table, his offence being that drowning is considered cruelty under the Animal Welfare Act. Not long afterwards, a former Welsh Guardsman was successfully prosecuted when, in an attempt to protect the birds in his garden, he caught several grey squirrels and released them a few miles from his home. His offence was releasing an invasive species, which is illegal. In the event that one somehow catches a grey squirrel, it must be killed, but in a way that is deemed to be humane – shooting it is fine, and whacking it over the head (euphemistically known as 'cranial dispatch') is also acceptable if you do not have a gun to hand. Drowning it is not acceptable, and that seems fair enough, I guess.

To recap, we used to eat and persecute red squirrels as pests. We introduced grey squirrels because we thought they were cute. Then they spread and the reds started to decline, so we reversed our opinion, deciding that the reds were now cute and the greys should be killed. Except in the meantime some people had grown to love the greys.

So what next in this confusing saga? I guess the culls will continue despite the protests, but without some major scientific breakthrough such as an easily administered pox vaccine for reds or some new clever way of killing greys, or sterilising them, it is a war that will go on forever. It would be impossible to eradicate the greys in much of England (and there would be huge opposition), but they might be kept at low levels in certain areas in the north so that the reds can survive. An alternative strategy would be to stop interfering and see what happens. One could certainly argue that the money would be better spent on other conservation issues; looking globally, red squirrels are abundant across much of Europe and Siberia. If they did become extinct in the UK it would not be a significant event in a world where thousands of species are in imminent danger of global extinction. Perhaps the reds will eventually evolve some resistance to the pox. Perhaps the slowly recovering pine marten population in northern Britain might offer some hope for the squirrels. Pine martens eat both red and grey squirrels, but, being lighter, the reds can evade capture by climbing onto slender twigs which do not carry the weight of a grey. Hence the greys tend to be selectively depredated. The martens are recovering from centuries of persecution by landowners wishing to protect their gamebirds (which the martens also eat) so they could shoot the birds themselves. Sadly this persecution continues in some places.

There are some interesting parallels with *Rhododendron ponticum*. Controlling *R. ponticum* is enormously expensive and difficult to do, usually involving heavy use of herbicides. There is no chance of ever getting rid of this species, so attempting to control it is to enter into an expensive war that can never be won; as with the squirrels, and the trench warfare of the Great War, stalemate is the best outcome one can hope for. Unlike either squirrel species, *R. ponticum* is a rare species in its native range, being found only in small areas of Portugal and Bulgaria. Climate change threatens to snuff out both populations. Imagine for a moment that *R. ponticum* had not been introduced to the UK back in 1763 and had not gone on to become a major pest. In such circumstances one might well argue for deliberate introduction to the UK to prevent the extinction of what is undoubtedly a magnificent plant. Bear in mind also that *Rhododendron* species naturally occurred in the UK about 20,000 years ago (along with rabbits). They and the rabbits were wiped out during the last ice age but failed to make a return under their own steam. Had their seeds been accidentally transported back to the UK sometime in the last 10,000 years on, say, the feet of a migrating goose, it would be a prized native species. Although *R. ponticum* shades our native vegetation in woodland, it is a great source of nectar for our native bumblebees, and recent studies from Imperial College have shown that native wood mice compete fiercely to live under the protection of *R. ponticum*, which provides great shelter from owls and hawks.

The line between native and non-native, good and bad, is sometimes not as clear as one might expect. Almost all Britain's flora and fauna arrived in the last 10,000 years, for most of Britain was scraped clean of life by a great sheet of ice during the last ice age. What should we make of the house mouse, which seems to have arrived in Neolithic times, about 3,000 years ago? What about the many species, such as the rabbit, brown hare, edible dormouse, pheasants, sycamore, fallow deer and nettles that were probably introduced by the Romans about 2,000 years ago? How long should something be here before we accept it as belonging? Were it possible, would it be desirable to eradicate these species? If we were to remove nettles, we would wipe out the peacock and small tortoiseshell butterflies that feed on them, and which presumably only arrived once the Romans introduced their host. Most of us would not want to lose these species, but then where do we draw the line? Should it be with the Canada goose (introduced in the 1600s), muntjac deer (1838), ring-necked parakeet (1855), sika deer (1860), grey squirrel (1876), midwife toad (1890s), American mink (1929) or signal crayfish (1975)? In reality, most of us base our opinion of each species on entirely subjective criteria: do we like the creature, or find it attractive, or think it might be doing harm to other creatures that we value? The American mink is a beautiful animal, but is reviled because it loves to eat our water voles, themselves enormously endearing and valued all the more for providing the inspiration for the much-loved character Ratty in *Wind in the Willows*. If instead mink preferred to eat rats (incidentally both black and brown rats are also non-natives, having invaded Britain via ships in about 1200 and 1728, respectively), then I'm sure we would welcome them.

What about species that arrive under their own steam? We have embraced the tree bumblebee (first recorded in the UK in 2001), a European species that may or may not have crossed the Channel unaided, but which has set up camp in our gardens and nests in our tit boxes. In contrast, the potential establishment of the Asian hornet (*Vespa velutina*) in Britain has led to media hysteria, with phrases such as 'Asian killer hornet' and 'deadly Asian hornet' suggesting that this beast might threaten human lives. One broadsheet newspaper claimed that a university student in Devon had been 'lucky to escape with his life' after encountering an Asian hornet in his bedroom. The plucky student had survived by beating the offending insect to death with a rolled-up magazine. The accompanying photograph showed a slightly squashed common wasp.

There sometimes seems to be a tinge of xenophobia in these accounts. Indeed, in 2009, the British National Party branded the signal crayfish 'the Mike Tyson of crayfish ... a diseased, psychotic, evil, illegal immigrant colonist ... [that] totally devastates the indigenous environment'. I'm not here to defend the signal crayfish, rhododendron or Asian hornet, but perhaps we need to try to keep things in proportion. In the case of the Asian hornet, this species was accidentally introduced to Bordeaux in 2004, purportedly in a consignment of pottery from China. It has since spread as far as Spain and Portugal in the south, Italy in the east and to the English Channel in the north, and the first genuine sightings in the UK were made in 2016, when a nest was found (and destroyed) in Gloucestershire. It is a general predator of larger insects, and there are genuine concerns that it depredates honeybees and may contribute to the problems beekeepers face. On the other hand, much of the newspaper coverage has claimed that we are faced with an invasion of the 'giant Asian hornet' (which technically refers to *Vespa mandarinia*), a truly formidable creature, but in fact the giant Asian hornet is still safely in Asia. The Asian hornet is little bigger than the common wasp, smaller than our native hornet, and no more of a threat to human health than a wasp or honeybee. The giant Asian hornet stages all-out assaults on honeybee hives, wiping out entire colonies, but in contrast the Asian hornet is a solitary hunter, taking adult honeybees one at a time. The hornet will return to a hive over and over again to take bees, and if a large hornet nest is close to a honeybee hive this might eventually result in the hive weakening and collapsing. On the other hand, on my farm in France, situated only about one hundred and fifty kilometres from Bordeaux, the Asian hornets have been in residence for ten years yet honeybees remain abundant.

There is no doubt that, at a global scale, invasive species are a major problem. There is a danger that we end up with homogenisation of our fauna and flora, just as town centres around the world now all have McDonald's and Starbucks. If we are not careful, every climatically similar region of the world will end up with the same selection of tough, adaptable species: creeping thistles and nettles, harlequin ladybirds and American cockroaches, houseflies and buff-tailed bumblebees, house sparrows and house mice, brown rats, rabbits, foxes and feral cats. That would be terribly sad, because of course it would mean we would have lost the unique, indigenous species in each region. Conversely, we have to accept change. We are profoundly altering our climate, and so the pool of plants and animals that can thrive in our gardens, woods and meadows is going to change, yet much conservation effort is devoted to trying to preserve exactly what we have. We currently spend about £2 billion a year on controlling invasive species, with Japanese knotweed and *Rhododendron ponticum* the worst culprits, and neither of these being battles that will ever be won.

Perhaps that money could be better spent. Let me highlight one alternative possibility: the 3,500-acre 'rewilding' project at the Knepp Estate[48] in West Sussex is supported by £250,000 of taxpayers' money per year. £2 billion could support 8,000 Knepps, which would cover roughly half of the UK. Of course that would not be practical – not least because we need room for growing food – but it illustrates that £2 billion could go a very long way in the world of conservation. Maybe we should rethink our priorities.

If we were to abandon attempts to control it, *R. ponticum* would undoubtedly spread beyond its current extent, particularly in West Wales and Scotland, but I suspect that in the end some kind of balance would be reached. In any case much of our uplands are already blighted by vast monocultures: tracts of heather moorland managed for grouse, impoverished grasslands overgrazed by sheep and red deer, and dark forestry plantations of non-native spruce. I'm not convinced that larger areas of *R. ponticum* would not be better than these dismal habitats that we have deliberately created.

---

[48] You can read more about the rich wildlife community developing at Knepp in *Bee Quest*. Knepp was intensive farmland until the year 2000, but is now stocked with large herbivores (cattle, deer, ponies and pigs) and otherwise is left for nature to do its thing. It is a magical place.

I sometimes wonder whether, with the inevitability of significant climate change looming, we shouldn't be more willing to accept the invasions that are already under way, and perhaps even encourage invasions by European species better adapted to the climate we will soon have.

In the meantime, in my own garden I have a few decisions to make. The non-native rats, mice, rabbits, grey squirrels, nettles and sycamore will no doubt continue to thrive, all of them mixed blessings but certainly not worth waging war against so far as I am concerned. No doubt new species will arrive. In 2017 I had a visit from my first rose-ringed parakeet, a noisy blighter but with beautiful emerald-green plumage. They've been spreading from populations established in south-west London, and I wouldn't be upset if they came to stay. I'll carry on pulling up the Himalayan balsam seedlings that keep popping up by my pond, but I'm not sure what to do with the pond itself. The pond has a bit of an infestation of parrot's feather, an invasive aquatic weed from South America that can block ditches and streams, leading to flooding. I could, and perhaps should, rip it all out and compost it, but it is home to the native water veneer moths, and I'd be very sorry to lose them. For the moment I think I'll leave nature to take its course.

11

The Cycle of Life

To make Jew's ear tagliatelle

Ingredients: a handful or two of Jew's ear fungus, washed and sliced into strips; 1 bulb of garlic, peeled and chopped; 30g butter; 360g fresh tagliatelle; olive oil; black pepper

1. *Put tagliatelle on to cook in a pan of boiling water.*
2. *Melt butter in a large pan, fry garlic for 2 minutes, then add fungus for 2 minutes.*
3. *Mix in cooked tagliatelle, add a splash of olive oil and plenty of black pepper (serves 4).*

Jew's ear is a very common and distinctive fungus, and one of the best to eat – it grows almost exclusively on dead elder wood. The odd name derives from the close resemblance to a reddish-brown human ear, and the belief that Judas hanged himself from an elder tree (which seems unlikely to me as they are small and frail trees, ill-suited for hanging).

We modern humans have developed a strange attitude to food. We buy shiny, waxed apples from the supermarket while allowing those on the garden tree to fall and rot. We ignore tasty mushrooms that sprout in our pastures and woodland for fear of poisoning ourselves, when many are tasty and easily identified. Few bother to pick the glistening ripe blackberries that droop from our hedgerows in September. We prefer our food to be as detached from its origins as possible, processed, packaged and uniform. Our ancestors from just a few generations ago would think us mad.

Our lack of connection with where food comes from is apparent in our squeamishness when it comes to roadkill. For millennia our ancestors have exerted huge efforts in hunting animals of all sizes to provide them with valuable protein. Catching a pigeon or rat would probably have been considered a successful outing for a Stone Age hunter. Snaffling a larger animal such as a deer would have been cause for jubilation, and would have fed the family for weeks. Yet today, most of us will leave a rabbit or pheasant killed in a traffic collision to slowly rot by the roadside rather than picking it up for dinner. Looking online, I see that Waitrose will currently sell you a rack of venison ribs for £60.74 (£45 per kilo), neatly vacuum-packed in polystyrene and plastic film. You might well drive past a fresh deer carcass on your way to pick it up.

Part of me is thankful for the squeamishness of others; it would be hard to get fresh roadkill if everybody stopped to pick it up. As it is, I often seem to be able to top up the freezer with tasty, healthy wild meat. This has on occasion got me some funny looks and enhanced my reputation for eccentricity. One cold winter morning when I was based at Stirling University, on the way in to work I spotted a plump female roe deer, recently deceased, lying on the fresh snow by the roadside. I was driving a small hatchback with nowhere near enough room for her to fit in the boot so I squeezed the carcass onto the passenger seat, and put the seat belt on to keep her from flopping about (much easier and less dangerous than on another occasion when I put an injured but very much alive and kicking fallow deer in my car). The dead deer sat there all day in the car park at work, apparently peering inquisitively out of the window, and attracting some confused looks from my colleagues. The next day was Saturday, and so first thing in the morning I butchered her on the back lawn, which was still covered in snow. I must confess that I've no great expertise in this and it always takes me quite a while to skin the carcass and joint all the meat. It is surprising how much blood a deer contains. By the time I had finished, my chest freezer was nearly full and the sloping, snow-covered lawn was running with rivers of crimson, reminding me of the infamous scene from the movie *Fargo*. The snow didn't melt for a fortnight so the bloody spectacle was preserved for a while, but my neighbours never said a word.

Most roadkill is good to eat, so long as it is fresh; almost any bird bigger than the size of a collared dove is worth having; crows and rooks are very tasty, and pigeons are delicious (if sometimes a bit dungy to my taste). I'm told that gulls can be good, although the only one I've had was rather too fishy for me. Woodpecker is supposed to be pretty nice; I've never tried one, but a friend had a green woodpecker fly into his window and break its neck (I'm starting to wonder if this isn't something of a woodpecker speciality), so he cooked it up for lunch. Squirrels and rabbits are of course excellent. Wild animals tend to have much less fat on them than farmed meat, and are likely to be largely free of pesticides and antibiotics, so are very healthy. You can eat them knowing that the animal had a happy life, or at the least that it wasn't kept in a cage or pen, and that they were dead anyway, so your action in eating them has zero impact on the environment (in stark contrast to eating farmed meat). So next time you see a corpse by the roadside, check it out. Don't drive by a free and tasty meal for your family – unless you live near the village of Blackboys in East Sussex, in which case please leave it for me.

Nature recycles everything. Life could not have survived for nearly four billion years if it relied on depletion of finite resources, and if we humans are to survive many more years we need to learn this lesson. For me, part of the fun and satisfaction of gardening is trying to ensure that nothing goes to waste, and at the heart of this is the compost heap. There is nothing glamorous about decomposition, the recycling of dead plants and animals, but without recycling of nutrients there can be no spring flush of leaves, no blossom, no buzzing of the bees or blackbird song at dawn. The energy for virtually all life comes from the sun, which plants catch and use to build complex molecules, sugars, proteins and so on, but they also need the basic building blocks of these molecules, the elements carbon, oxygen, nitrogen, potassium etc., in usable forms. In nature, the growth of plants is more often limited by the supply of nutrients such as nitrogen and phosphorus than it is by a lack of sunlight. For a supply of these nutrients, plants depend upon a myriad of tiny creatures, including worms, woodlice, millipedes, maggots, mites, springtails, fungi and bacteria, which together break down leaves, twigs and branches, faeces, animal corpses and indeed anything organic, and release the nutrients within. Without these creatures, leaves would pile up on the ground, dung would accumulate, plants would stop growing, and life on Earth would cease.

Decomposition goes on all the time in soils and on the soil surface, but accelerates in late summer and early autumn as leaves and fruits begin to fall, and before temperatures become too low late in the year and slow things down. A good gardener can manipulate this process to his or her own ends, moving organic material around the garden to mulch and fertilise vegetables and flower beds, to create compost for growing seeds and potting up plants, and to take nutrients away from wildflower meadow areas.

Creating compost is incredibly easy. Whole books have been written on how to do it properly, but at its most basic any pile of organic matter will eventually become compost. Of course it looks tidier if the composting matter is contained within something;

plastic, barrel-shaped composters are available at a subsidised price from most local authorities, and work reasonably well. The textbooks will tell you that, for effective and rapid composting, you need to optimise the carbon to nitrogen (C:N) ratio of the material you include, aiming for about twenty-five to thirty parts carbon to one part nitrogen. It is a bit like balancing your own diet; we instinctively tend to balance our intake of carbohydrates and protein (which approximately correspond to carbon and nitrogen). Knowing the optimum ratio isn't in itself very helpful, though, since you then need to know the C:N ratio of the materials you might be throwing in your heap. Wood, paper, cardboard, sawdust and twigs are all carbon and very little nitrogen (their C:N is about 300:1), so a heap comprised only of these will compost very slowly because the decomposing organisms will not have enough nitrogenous material to thrive. At the other end of the spectrum, kitchen waste, lawn clippings and weeds have a C:N ratio of 15:1. A heap made exclusively of those initially starts to decompose quickly but collapses into a wet sticky mass in which the oxygen is used up and decomposition then slows right down. Anaerobic bacteria take over, and as well as being rather slow these have the unfortunate disadvantage of producing smelly gases such as ammonia and hydrogen sulphide (which smells of rotten eggs). Hence a compost heap comprising mainly kitchen scraps is likely to become a smelly, gloopy mess.[49]

The obvious solution is to mix up the two types a bit, avoiding heaps that consist entirely of grass clippings or twigs or kitchen waste if possible. The fallen leaves of deciduous trees have a near-perfect C:N ratio and make a wonderful leaf-mould compost all on their own.

---

[49] If you have a small garden and hence most of your compostable material comprises kitchen scraps, consider having a wormery instead of a compost heap. Instructions can be found at the end of this book.

If you get the mix anywhere near right a new compost heap quickly warms up, the heat created by the metabolic activity of trillions of aerobic bacteria. The first ones to thrive are those adapted to cool temperatures, proliferating at about 12°C, but they engineer their own demise by warming the heap up too much, so that warmth-loving bacteria take over. In just a few days successive waves of bacteria adapted to ever higher temperatures take over from one another, the earlier colonists being killed by the heat, until the centre of a large heap may reach 70°C or more. Shove your hand into the centre of the pile and you'll find that it is literally too hot to keep it there. At this temperature weed seeds cannot survive, and nor indeed can any animal life. This only lasts a few days, and then the temperature gradually drops. Actinomycete bacteria move in, organisms that are able to break down lignin and other highly indigestible (to most of us) compounds found in woody material. They release many of the delicious earthy smells we associate with a healthy heap, much the same as the smell you get when you kick your boots through the leaf mould on the woodland floor.

Perceived wisdom has it that it is best to turn the compost heap at this stage, move less composted material from the edges into the centre, but it's quite a chore and I rarely bother. This is the stage at which animals start to colonise. Millipedes and woodlice wander in, and begin chewing away at decaying vegetable matter, breaking it up and increasing the surface area for attack by bacteria and fungi. Worms burrow up from the soil below and begin ingesting and grinding up fragments of leaf. Springtails[50] and mites arrive in vast

---

[50] Springtails are delightful little creatures, when fully grown no bigger than a full stop. Primitive and ancient animals, they used to be classed as insects but are now placed in their own separate group. They are named for their prodigious leaps effected by a spring-loaded lever on their belly that fires them upwards in times of peril. They can leap

numbers to graze upon the fungi. Hair-like nematode worms suck up the countless bacteria. The nematodes, springtails and mites are food for ants, pseudoscorpions, centipedes, rove and ground beetles and spiders. In winter, voles and mice will nest in the heap, enjoying the residual warmth. In spring, the small hair- and grass-lined hollows made by the overwintering rodents may be occupied by bumblebees. If you are really lucky, slow-worms might turn up to feed on slugs and woodlice. Wrens and robins will clamber about the edges looking for prey. A compost heap is an entire world in itself, an interacting web of life built on decay.

I have eight compost heaps dotted about my garden, three plastic composters I inherited and five big cubic ones I made by crudely screwing old wooden pallets together. I much prefer wood to plastic, and unwanted pallets are pretty easy to come by. Having lots of compost heaps means it is never far for me to walk to the nearest one with an armful of leaves or weeds, and because I only dig out one or two each year the waste in each one gets a good four years or more to break down. I try to mix up the material in each heap, but I don't worry about it too much and there always seems to be at least one bin full of musty, crumbly black compost ready to use in the garden. I know I'm lucky in having a big garden, but nonetheless

---

15cm into the air, the equivalent of a man leaping over the Eiffel Tower. They also possess a peculiar telescopic trunk-like appendage under their head which they use to groom themselves. Being so tiny, they are hard to count. The best method is to collect up compost or leaf mould and put it into a funnel under a warm lamp; the heat drives the small creatures to drop out of the funnel into a waiting receptacle. I estimate that there are about 120,000 of them in each of my mature compost heaps. There are 250 UK species, but I have not yet attempted the daunting task of working out which species I have in my garden.

anyone with outside space should be composting. National surveys suggest that the number of gardens with compost heaps varies from just 6 per cent in inner cities to about 30 per cent in suburban areas. As an avid composter, I find it bewildering that the large majority of people in suburbia do not compost their waste. Of course many councils collect green waste and compost it, which is a good second-best, but this still requires energy to transport the waste and then to distribute the compost. If you do it yourself, you create a home for millions of tiny creatures, and at the same time you get a ready supply of free compost to fertilise your garden. Mixed with a little sand, it is perfect for potting up container plants and growing tomatoes. For germinating seeds, I use a mix of leaf-mould compost with sand, as this tends to be free of weed seeds. Until the 1970s all keen gardeners made their own compost and very little was sold in sacks at garden centres.

I guess most people these days can't be bothered, or don't want a compost heap cluttering up their garden, and in any case compost can be bought quite cheaply from the garden centre, so why bother making your own? Each year, 3.9 million cubic metres of compost are bought in the UK, with about two-thirds of this purchased by amateur gardeners and the remainder by the horticultural industry. The figure has been rising year on year, for we Brits love our gardens. Unfortunately, more than half of this – about 2.9 million cubic metres – is comprised of peat. My local garden centre sells no less than sixteen different types of compost, and fourteen of them are peat-based. Multi-purpose composts are commonly about 70 per cent peat, but they rarely make this clear on the label. We have been aware that using peat-based compost is harmful to the environment for thirty or more years, so why are we still using it?

You may well be familiar with the arguments against using peat, but since the message doesn't seem to have got through to the majority of people please bear with me while I repeat them. Peat is similar to coal or oil – it is created by the slow accumulation of organic matter over long periods of time. It is created in bogs, areas of land with poor drainage, and specialised plant communities often dominated by sphagnum moss, plants that are adapted to the sodden conditions that prevail. The majority of the UK's peatlands (about one and a half million hectares) are upland blanket bogs, found mainly in Wales, northern England and Scotland. The waterlogging excludes oxygen so that dead plant material decays extremely slowly, and so it gradually builds up over time at a rate of about one millimetre per year, forming a black bed of accumulated organic material that may go down many metres, the lowest layers having been deposited shortly after the last ice age some 10,000 years ago. Peat bogs comprise a unique record of our past, for pollen grains can survive in them for millennia, allowing us a window through which we can see what plants used to grow in Britain. Occasionally human bodies, the remains of unfortunate souls who sank into the bog perhaps thousands of years ago, are also found more or less intact, complete with clothing and their possessions. This very gradual decay of any type of organic matter means that the nutrients trapped within it are released very slowly, and hence the plants that grow in bogs have to be able to cope with this. Some, such as the sundew, butterwort and bladderwort, have evolved an alternative means of gaining vital nutrients, by trapping and digesting insects.

Lowland 'raised bogs' (named because the accumulating peat causes the bog to rise up above surrounding areas) are one of western Europe's rarest and most threatened wildlife habitats, containing a unique assemblage of species, including in the UK about 3,000 species of insect and 800 species of flowering plant. As a butterfly-collecting child growing up in rural Shropshire, I found that the richest habitat within cycling distance was Whixall Moss, a lowland bog straddling the borders with Cheshire and North Wales. It was the first place that I ever encountered the large heath butterfly, a beautiful, fawn-coloured and rather furry butterfly with large eye spots, and also the small pearl-bordered fritillary, a delicate creature with a chequerboard pattern of orange and black chased with silver on its hindwings. Whixall is also home to rarities such as the raft spider, a large chocolate-coloured spider with a cream stripe, which skips across the surface of bog pools in search of prey, and to the diving bell spider. Just as the water veneer is one of very few aquatic moths, the diving bell spider is one of very few spiders that lives most of its life underwater. It creates a dense web underwater which it fills with air by carrying down small bubbles trapped in the water-repellent hairs on its body, so creating an air-filled, silvery bell in which it spends most of its life, and from which it sallies forth to prey on aquatic insects. I did not know it at the time, but no less than 670 species of moth have also been recorded at Whixall, along with very rare insects such as the delightfully named picture-winged bog crane fly.

The UK used to have about 95,000 hectares of lowland raised bogs (about 5 per cent of all our peatlands), but today only 6,000 hectares remain intact, representing a loss of about 94 per cent. This massive loss is primarily due to two factors: drainage to create fertile farmland and peat extraction. Historically, peat was commonly used as a fossil fuel, for once dried it will burn, but it is smoky and releases little heat compared to coal. These days, peat extraction is mainly for the garden trade. Unfortunately, the peat in lowland raised bogs is considered to make a better growing medium than that from upland bogs, so these lowland bogs have been particularly hard hit. As a teenager, I remember watching with dismay the peat extractors using diggers to carve great chunks of peat from Whixall. On average, peat extraction removes about 22cm depth of peat per year, something that will take 220 years to replace. Thankfully, Wixhall was declared a National Nature Reserve in the 1990s, and is now protected from further damage, although not before about one-third of it was destroyed by the peat extractors.

Because the supplies from the UK have dwindled, much of the peat sold in garden centres is now imported from other countries, notably from Ireland, Estonia, Latvia and Finland. Estonia is a wild and unspoiled country where bears and wolves still roam, and it is sad to reflect that great chunks of it are now being dug up so that we can grow begonias.

Loss of a wildlife-rich habitat is just one facet of peat extraction, and one which may not trouble folk who couldn't care less about the picture-winged bog crane fly, even if they were aware of its existence. However, there are two other powerful reasons to look after these bogs. The first is that peat has a fantastic capacity to absorb water, acting as a vast sponge. This is particularly important in our upland bogs, which catch and absorb the high levels of rain that fall on the hills and mountains of Britain, then slowly release a trickle of water. Without its blanket of peat, heavy rain on Dartmoor, for example, quickly becomes a roaring torrent flooding over the banks of rivers in lowland Devon. Given that extreme weather events, including heavy rainfall, are predicted to become more common in the future, we would do well to keep our peat bogs intact. Which brings me to the second and most compelling reason for caring for our peat bogs: they are gigantic stores of carbon, and thus their fate is linked to our future climate.

Over the past 10,000 years, UK peatlands have quietly sequestered 5.5 billion tonnes of carbon – nearly forty times the 150 million tonnes of carbon stored in our woodlands. We think of trees and woodland as helping to combat climate change, but in reality once it is mature a woodland more or less stops sequestering carbon. It becomes carbon neutral, with old trees dying and decaying to release carbon, and new trees growing and absorbing it. In contrast peat bogs continue to lay down ever deeper layers of peat, and so keep absorbing carbon from the atmosphere. Peatlands contain about half of the UK's stored carbon (the rest mainly being in other soils and a bit in trees). Globally, peatlands store about half a trillion tonnes of carbon, twice as much as is estimated to be stored in the world's forests, yet peatlands cover just 3 per cent of the land area of Earth.

At this point you may be thinking that digging up the peat and moving it to your garden does not destroy it, but you would be wrong. As soon as peat is removed from the saturated conditions in a bog and oxygen can get to it, the organic matter it is made of starts to decay, releasing carbon dioxide. It may take decades, but eventually it will all have gone into the atmosphere. In fact the peat does not even need to be removed from the bog for this process to begin. Cutting drainage ditches to lower the water table achieves exactly the same thing, but on a huge scale. The deep peat soils of the Fens have all been drained to create rich farmland, but it is farmland that lives on borrowed time as the peat slowly disappears into thin air – quite literally. Dartmoor and many of the upland bogs of Britain are criss-crossed with drainage ditches, often intended to improve the grazing for cattle or sheep, or to allow planting of blocks of non-native trees for forestry purposes. These ditches are disastrous for the long-term survival of the bogs, for all of their associated wildlife, in exacerbating flooding downstream, and for our climate.

Given all this, one has to wonder why we continue to use peat in our gardens. There are perfectly good alternatives. If making your own is too much trouble, there are some excellent peat-free composts available on the market (for example, I can highly recommend organic SylvaGrow compost, which is endorsed by the Royal Horticultural Society and was named a 'best buy' by *Which?*

Gardening). Of course, one way forward would be if customers re-fused to buy anything other than compost that is peat-free, but sadly it seems that most gardeners are still unaware of this issue, or simply don't care. Perhaps for them the state of their hanging baskets is more important than the state of the planet.

If customers can't be relied upon to change their buying pat-terns, perhaps a solution can be found in the supply chain. Garden centres surely have some responsibility here. I tried asking in my local, independent garden centre why they were still selling most-ly peat-based composts, but the sales assistants were completely unaware of the environmental issues surrounding peat. I even-tually found one more senior member of staff who just said that they sell what customers want to buy. To my mind this is abdicat-ing responsibility, justifying their position based solely on profit. Any of the big garden centre chains such as Wyevale, Notcutts or Dobbies could make a bold decision and lead the way by banning peat, but none of them show any sign of doing so at present. As with pesticides, B&Q seem to be more proactive than most and say they are 'moving to zero peat', although they do not say over what timescale, and for the moment they are cheerfully selling peat-based composts.

Perhaps the Horticultural Trades Association (HTA), which represents the gardening industry, might show some leadership here, or the Royal Horticultural Society? In June 2016 these two organisations launched a pilot 'Responsible Sourcing Scheme for Growing Media', the aim of which is to provide a tool that horticultural companies can – if they choose to do so – use to calculate their environmental impact from using peat. As the HTA website says, 'the pilot scheme is a very gentle first step in understanding what the situation is within the industry'. It smugly goes on to add 'this is a proud moment for everyone in-volved'. So, after thirty years of being aware that extracting peat was really bad for the environment, and at a time when the UK gardening industry is ripping 2.9 million cubic metres of peat every year from wildlife habitats across Europe, they are introducing a voluntary pilot scheme that will simply tell companies what is blindingly obvious: that we need to stop using peat now. Completely. Not think about possibly trying to quantify the impact, not phasing in reductions at some future point if and when it suits us. We are weighing up growing pretty flowers against the devastating impacts of climate change, a process which threatens catastrophe for life on Earth.

As with pesticides, it seems that we cannot rely on the Horticultural Trades Association or the Royal Horticultural Society to show any moral spine or rise above the pursuit of financial gain. Might the UK government step in with protective legislation? In 2011 the government published a White Paper which contained voluntary targets for the end of peat use in horticulture. It aimed for all compost available to amateur gardeners to be peat-free by 2020 – a target which seems highly unlikely to be achieved, since so far as I can see peat-free composts are scarcely more common in garden centres in 2018 than they were in 2011. There is also a voluntary target for all compost used in horticulture to be peat-free by 2030. Nineteen years seems like a very generous adaptation period. There are quite a few small nurseries that are entirely peat-free right now. Given that there are perfectly good alternatives to peat, why should we wait another twelve years for the horticulture industry to finally stop using it?

Interestingly, protecting peat bogs might be one of our most powerful tools in actively combatting climate change, and not simply because they are a massive existing store of carbon. Over the last 10,000 years, rates of carbon sequestration by peat bogs have been higher in relatively warmer periods, presumably because the sphagnum moss and other plants grow a little faster. Given that the global climate is set to get warmer, this may mean that our intact peat bogs sequester carbon at a higher rate than at present, providing a negative feedback mechanism that could go a small way towards mitigating climate change. Of course this can only happen if we leave the bogs in a healthy, undrained state.

You may well be wondering what you can do in your garden to help capture carbon and so do your bit. Luckily, most of the things that you might do are great for wildlife, and also benefit your flowers and vegetables. The aim is to build up as much organic matter as possible. If you have room, grow a tree or two. Although mature forests are carbon neutral, growing a tree where there didn't used to be one locks up carbon every year that the plant is getting larger – up to eight tonnes of carbon is ultimately locked up in a big oak, for example. It will stay there until the tree dies and rots away, which in theory could be 800 years from now. Most gardeners don't have room for large trees, but the basic rule is that the more bulk of vegetation you have the more carbon you are storing, and remember also that Ken Thompson's studies of Sheffield gardens showed that the more vegetation you have the more insect diversity you will have too. Brash piles and log piles also lock up carbon for as long as it takes them to decay, which can be many years. I harvest wood from my garden to feed our wood-burning stove, but I leave some logs in piles to gently rot. Ken's Sheffield studies found that a small pile of birch logs supported an average of ninety different individual creatures after twenty-three months, most common unglamorous creatures such as woodlice, spiders, slugs, snails, springtails, centipedes, fly larvae and mites. My own log piles usually have a resident toad too.

Rather than burning it, I pile some of the twiggy material left over from tree pruning into quiet corners, where it is often nested in by blackbirds and sometimes song thrushes, and provides yet more scope for a variety of other small creatures to find homes. I live in hope that it might provide excellent hibernation possibilities for hedgehogs, but to my sorrow I have yet to see a hedgehog in my Sussex garden.[51]

My brash piles have not always lasted as long as I would hope. My sons decided to make a den out of one particularly large pile I had created when a storm blew down some Norway spruce (former Christmas trees planted by the previous owner). They hollowed out the top of the pile, creating something resembling a giant crow's nest in which they could hide from view. One late-summer afternoon my eldest, Finn, along with his friend Max came up with the idea of creating a secret tunnel out of the den by burrowing diagonally downwards (every den needs a secret entrance). It was hard going cutting through the drying spruce branches, so they hit upon the brilliant idea of pouring white spirit onto the more stubborn branches to burn through them. Half an hour later a team of firemen had just about got the inevitable conflagration under control, which had burned through the hedge and was threatening to set fire to a neighbour's shed. This fire was certainly not what anyone had intended, but it had an unexpected benefit. Had the fire been allowed to burn out, the branches and leaves would have been reduced to ash (which would have been a good source of nutrients for my vegetables). As it was, by its being put out with a jet of water from the firemen's hose, I was left with a large amount of

[51] Our poor hedgehogs are fast disappearing. Although, as with worms, we do not have accurate estimates of past population size, anecdotal evidence suggests they have undergone a massive decline in numbers to their current population of a little below one million. The most recent estimates suggest a fall in numbers of about 50 per cent in the last fifteen years. The causes are likely to include loss of insect and slug prey in intensive farmland, road fatalities, poisoning by slug pellets, and predation by badgers. Urban populations seem to be holding up slightly better than rural ones.

steaming wet charcoal. Charcoal is a remarkably inert substance, similar to coal; mixed into soil it can remain almost unchanged for thousands of years, and there is growing interest in deliberately creating charcoal from wood and then mixing it into soils as a way of locking up carbon. This also improves the soil condition, increasing water retention and reducing leaching away of water-soluble nutrients. James Lovelock, among others, has advocated the planting of fast-growing trees for production of charcoal for long-term storage or incorporation into soils as a powerful weapon against climate change, although there seems to be no large-scale uptake as yet.

In fact there is nothing new about his idea. In Amazonia, an area characterised by generally infertile, thin soils, there are areas of dark, deep soils created by humans between 4,000 and 1,000 years ago. Over generations, these early farmers added charcoal, dung, bones and other organic matter to the soil, building it up to a depth of two metres or so. These soils, known as '*terra preta*' (Portuguese for black soil), may contain up to seventy times as much carbon as surrounding areas, and they remain highly fertile 1,000 years after they were abandoned by collapsing civilisations.

I have a mind to create my own *terra preta*. Charcoal has been produced in the Weald of Sussex for thousands of years, primarily for use in iron manufacture, and it is relatively easy to produce your own without the aid of firemen. Charcoal is normally produced when wood or other organic material burns with limited oxygen. I've been experimenting with setting light to a pile of small branches in a shallow pit, then once the smoke starts to die down shovelling on a thin layer of soil to exclude oxygen (sometimes along with a few baked potatoes wrapped in tinfoil). It is tricky to get it just right, avoiding stopping it too soon and being left with charred but intact sticks or letting it burn too long and ending up with nothing but ash, but I generally produce at least some charcoal to dig into the veggie patch. Perhaps 1,000 years from now archaeologists may muse over how a small patch of deep black earth came to be perched on the dense clay of East Sussex.

In fact the chances are that, even if you do nothing, your garden soil is already quite rich in organic carbon, at least relative to farmland. A recent study by Jill Edmondson from Sheffield University compared the health of soils in allotments, gardens and farmland, and found that allotment soils had 32 per cent more organic carbon when compared to conventional farmland soils, and were also more fertile with 25 per cent higher levels of nitrogen. The allotment soils were also more open, with more air pockets allowing oxygen to the plant roots, compared to the compacted farm soils that are compressed by the wheels of heavy machinery. Garden soils were similar to allotments, with areas beneath trees in gardens having even more organic carbon. Part of the reason for the higher organic carbon content is that allotment and garden soils are never exposed to the devastating erosion that can occur when heavy rain falls on a recently ploughed and bare arable field. Interestingly, Edmondson found that allotmenteers are far more aware of the value of compost than the average gardener; in contrast to suburban gardens, only 30 per cent of which have compost heaps, 95 per cent of the allotments studied by Edmondson had compost heaps.

When it comes to doing our bit to combat climate change, we gardeners face a win–win situation. The more carbon we can store, by adding home-made compost, mulches or charcoal to our soils, the deeper, darker and healthier our soils will become, the more our worms will thrive, the better drained the soil will be, and the faster our plants will grow. Growing plants locks up yet more carbon, and the more bulk of plant material we have the more wildlife we will attract. Perhaps, 1,000 years from now, archaeologists may not be puzzling over a small patch of rich black earth in Sussex, but instead arguing as to how such soils appeared in large patches scattered all across the lowlands of Britain.

12

Gardening to Save the Planet

To make blackberry jam

Ingredients: blackberries (or almost any other fruit), sugar

1. *Mix 450g of fruit with 450g sugar.*
2. *Microwave for 20 mins, stirring halfway through (you may need to adjust the time slightly, depending on the power of your microwave – if the jam doesn't set, give it longer; if it has turned to toffee, cook it less next time!)*
3. *Pour into pre-warmed jam jars, and seal.*

Making your own jam is so easy I have no idea why everybody does not do it. Microwave jam is incredibly quick, and you lose fewer of the vitamins in the fruit because it is not cooked for anywhere near as long as conventional jam. Spread on seedy wholemeal toast, this intensely purple-black gloop is heavenly.

Surely there can be few more 'green' activities than gardening? Growing flowers and vegetables is a wholesome, absorbing and therapeutic activity, which can provide food and lodging for a multitude of wild creatures as well as healthy, nutritious, more or less free, zero-food-miles produce for the kitchen. After a day in the garden, digging, tending and harvesting, one can sleep well,

muscles aching from the exercise, content in the satisfying knowledge that one has done one's bit to save the planet and at the same
time reduced the shopping bill. Unfortunately, it is actually a bit
more complicated than that. While all of these things can be true –
as I shall argue later, gardening may well be part of the answer to
saving the planet – the devil is in the detail. It all depends on how
you garden.[52] To see what I mean, let me take you on an imaginary
weekend trip to my nearest garden centre superchain, which for the
sake of indiscretion we will call Noblier Vale.

It is a warm Sunday morning in late June and the vast car park
is almost full. We squeeze into a space between a Range Rover
and an Audi convertible, half a mile from the main entrance,
and walk over the hot tarmac, weaving between customers pushing trolleys back to their cars, laden with ornamental plants
in a profusion of colours and destined to be planted in neatly
manicured borders across East Sussex. Near the entrance, dozens
of retirees are disembarking creakily and stoop-backed from a
shiny, oversized coach. Inside the automatic sliding entrance
doors the cavernous air-conditioned interior offers a panoply of
delights, a shopper's heaven. Most of the garden plants are of
course out at the back of the main building, but to get to that we
first have to traverse aisles filled with orchids, bonsai trees, gardening equipment and tools, classy garden furniture made from
tropical hardwoods, battalions of pesticide bottles stacked ceil-
ing-high and ironically placed next to an array of garden wildlife
products from bird feeders to the optimistically named 'lacewing
houses', and rotating stands enticingly displaying packs of seeds.

---

[52] I am indebted to John Walker, eco-gardener and quiet eco-warrior,
who opened my eyes to the realities of the modern gardening industry.
His books *Digging Deep in the Garden* and *How to Create an Ecogarden*
are well worth a read.

Of course, these days garden centres do not just sell gardening products; there is an extensive clothing section, a delicatessen offering interestingly pungent cheeses, stuffed olives, game pie, quail's eggs and eye-wateringly expensive shortbread biscuits, there is an aquarium and pet shop, a section filled with china figurines, scented candles and greetings cards, and a cafe selling a bewildering selection of cakes and hand-cut gourmet sand-wiches and serving a three-course roast lunch at weekends. It is hard to think of anything that one can't buy at Noblier Vale – if one's wallet was fat enough, one need shop almost nowhere else. Indeed, the upholstered patio loungers look so comfortable I have wondered if they would notice if I moved in permanently.

We finally make it out of the back of the store to the acres of bright flowers arranged in alphabetical order along serried rows of benches. The first section is devoted to bedding and hanging-basket plants: begonias, busy Lizzies, lobelias, pelargoniums, petunias, tobacco flowers, and many more. Beyond those are the herbaceous perennials, a mouth-watering selection all in perfect bloom. There are plenty of honeybees and bumblebees buzzing about, taking their pick from the gourmet selection, an unsubtle hint as to which ones you might buy for them. Forget the 'Perfect for Pollinators' or 'Bee-friendly' labels, just follow the bees if you want to identify the flowers that they find most attractive. It is hard to resist filling a trolley with these lovely blooms, although the prices are a forceful disincentive. Beyond the flowers are sections for fruit trees, terracotta pots from China, concrete statues, shrubs, plastic pond liners and fountains, and a vast selection of composts and growbags in brightly coloured plastic sacks.

By now you will have probably worked out why I have brought you here. Much as I enjoy visiting Noblier Vale, browsing the plants and having a cappuccino in the cafe, this is an emporium devoted to consumption and profit. Buying most of the goods on sale here is actively harmful to the planet. I know that I am in danger of becoming tiresomely preachy, but bear with me for a moment or two, because I think this is important. Everything on sale here took resources to create. The plants were probably reared in continental Europe, often in heated polytunnels, grown in peat-based compost inside a disposable plastic pot, treated with fertilisers to make them grow quickly and pesticides to keep them looking perfect. They were then shipped hundreds of miles to the UK. Many are annuals, or poorly suited to the local soil or climate, and one way or another will be dead within the year, to be turfed into the bin (or ideally the compost heap) to make way for more next spring. Many of them have been intensively selected for larger blossoms with extra petals, and have lost all appeal to bees.

And that is just the plants. Much of the rest on sale is just as bad: pointless but beautifully presented tat. I'm not suggesting that we should all don a goat-hair shirt and live on home-grown turnips for the rest of our days. Life would be scarcely worth living if we couldn't treat ourselves to a slice of carrot cake and a goji berry smoothie before buying a packet of cucamelon seeds and a statuette of a miniature samurai at the local garden centre every now and again, but we should all be aware of what we are doing, and of our impact on the planet. There are simply too many of us here to do otherwise.

Of course one can still have a beautiful, productive garden, teeming with life, without needing to buy anything much at all. The best sources of plants are neighbours, family and friends. The best way to discover which plants will thrive in your garden is to look in gardens nearby, which necessarily are likely to have very similar conditions, in terms of soil, climate and so on. Most plants are very easily propagated by splitting clumps, collecting and sowing seeds, digging up surplus seedlings, or by taking cuttings, and enthusiastic gardeners are usually very happy to swap or donate bits of plants.[53] This way, you get plants that are free of chemicals (providing that your neighbour hasn't sprayed them), and which have been created with zero impact on the environment. There is absolutely no need for artificial fertilisers or pesticides in the garden, and as we have seen there are great alternatives to peat-based composts (you can even make your own). Aside from some basic gardening tools, which can be picked up for almost nothing at a car boot sale if you want to be really frugal, and some packets of vegetable seeds (many of which you can collect for yourself if particularly keen), there is no need to buy anything. Gardening can be truly green, and I think it might just contain the key to saving the planet. To explain why, let's leave the decadent temptations of Noblier Vale behind and take a brief look at modern farming.

In developed countries, the model of farming which we are used to seeing is one of big monocultures of crops, sown in huge blocks across tens or hundreds of hectares. In the UK, wheat is the single biggest crop, covering about two million hectares, with barley and oilseed rape each covering another 600,000 hectares or so. To keep them 'healthy', these crops are typically treated with a barrage of pesticides and also receive multiple fertiliser applications. The end result is impressive in its way; bright green fields stretching to the horizon, with scarcely a weed, slug or insect pest in sight. Unfortunately this farming system has many drawbacks.

[53] My grandmother on my mother's side was a very keen gardener and had a different, illicit strategy for obtaining new plants for her garden. She would regularly visit ornamental gardens and stately homes armed with a pair of secateurs and a folded umbrella. Snippets of interesting plants would miraculously drop off as she passed, somehow falling into her umbrella, to be potted up as soon as she got home. Of course I couldn't possibly recommend this unlawful approach.

The intensification of farming and the conversion of ever more natural habitat to farmland at a global scale is the biggest driver of biodiversity loss; very little can survive in a modern crop aside from the crop itself. Species are currently disappearing from our planet at the rate of between 1,000 and 10,000 per year (the latter equating to about one per hour), and the rate is accelerating fast. Those creatures that remain are far less common than they were. In the UK, the total number of farmland birds has fallen by 58 per cent since 1970.[54] In Germany, catches of flying insects sampled by amateur entomologists using the aforementioned Malaise traps recently revealed a drop of 76 per cent in the total biomass of insects caught between 1989 and 2014. Older readers may have noticed that, even when driving in the height of summer, you almost never need to stop to clean your car windscreen of bug splats in the way that you once did (though a small part of this can be explained by many cars being more aerodynamic than they used to be). Large arable fields are terribly susceptible to soil erosion, particularly after ploughing, so that we are currently losing about 100 billion tonnes of soil from the surface of the globe every year. The resulting sediments do ecological damage to rivers and coastal waters, while increasing flooding. Soil erosion is worse in the tropics, but there are dramatic examples in the UK. At Holme Fen in East Anglia, a post driven down through the deep peat soil in 1851 now appears to have risen to tower four metres above the landscape, though in fact it is not the post that has risen but the ground that has fallen. Drainage of the surrounding fens to create arable land has led the peat to collapse,

[54] Many surveys of wildlife abundance began around 1970 so declines since then are often quoted, but it should be borne in mind that 1970 was certainly not a pinnacle of wildlife abundance, following as it did at least thirty years of rapid agricultural intensification and the widespread adoption of synthetic pesticides such as DDT.

and now that it is exposed to the air rather than being inundated with water the peat is steadily oxidising to carbon dioxide, contributing to climate change. The surrounding area is now three metres below sea level and still falling at the rate of one centimetre per year. Half of East Anglia's fenland peat has gone, and the rest will eventually disappear if it continues to be farmed in the way it is at present.

Industrial farming is also a major source of pollution. Fertilisers contaminate hedgerows, causing docks, hogweed and nettles – plants that thrive on highly fertile ground – to go berserk at the expense of more delicate flowers that might otherwise live in field margins. The fertilisers contaminate the groundwater as well and leach into our silted streams, rivers and lakes, causing algal blooms that smother and poison aquatic life. Some pesticides are similarly prone to wandering out of the crop they were aimed at; my own research group at Sussex University has found mixtures of neonicotinoids and other pesticides in the pollen, nectar and foliage of hedgerow wild flowers. Neonicotinoids regularly turn up in water samples taken from streams and ponds, and have even been found in drinking water.

You may be surprised to hear that farming activities are one of the biggest contributors to climate change, having an impact roughly the same as energy production. A recent estimate calculated that global farming activities create 12,000 megatonnes of 'carbon dioxide equivalents' per year (some greenhouse gases such as methane are more potent than carbon dioxide and so are weighed accordingly). This is almost a quarter of all greenhouse gas emissions, the combined effect of fertiliser manufacture, carbon dioxide emissions from soil erosion, methane from livestock, fuel costs and so on.

As if all this weren't enough, the modern system of mechanised farming employs very few people, so that rural communities have dwindled, and it is heavily supported by the taxpayer. In the UK, we subsidise farming to the tune of about £3 billion per year, tax-payers' money that is mostly given to large-scale, industrial farmers. The bigger the farm, the more he or she gets. I hate to sound for a moment like a *Daily Mail* columnist, but we pay Saudi Prince Khalid Abdullah al Saud £400,000 per year in farm subsidies to run his estate near Newmarket where he breeds racehorses. We subsidise grouse-moor shooting estates in northern England and Scotland, huge estates owned by very wealthy people and managed for the exclusive benefit of a tiny number of other wealthy folk whose expensive and eccentric hobby is obliterating wildlife while sporting baggy tweed trousers. More typically, we pay farmers to grow large fields of wheat and oilseed rape in a way that harms the environment.

In summary, industrial farming is wiping out wildlife, depleting and polluting our soils, streams and lakes, and acting as a major contributor to climate change which is itself likely to have further devastating consequences for the planet. To add insult to injury, we are expected to subsidise this system through our taxes. Our eighty-year-long flirtation with industrial farming should be regarded as an experiment that has failed badly.

At this point I can imagine that any farmer who has read this far may be getting a little hot under the collar. I know that many farmers feel they are unfairly blamed for the world's ills, and they resent environmentalists such as myself when we raise these issues. They have a point. Industrial farming came about not because farmers planned it that way. It is in large part the result of policies and subsidies introduced by short-sighted, greedy or incompetent politicians. It might also be blamed on agro-industry, the multinational companies that manufacture and peddle pesticides, fertilisers and the machinery that makes industrial farming possible. They benefit hugely from the current system, have come to dominate research and development in the agriculture sector, and employ armies of agronomists to push their latest products onto farmers. It can also be blamed on consumers, who seem to want to buy cheap, un-blemished food without caring that it may be laced with pesticides, rather than buying quality, local produce. If you are only willing to pay £7 per kilo for chicken breasts, don't expect those chickens to have had anything but a brutally short, cramped and unpleasant life. It might be blamed on the supermarkets, who want to sell milk as a loss-leader at £1 for four pints, and use their huge buying power to squeeze farmers' profits and reject even slightly misshapen vege-tables. Of course some of the blame must also lie with the farmers, some of whom have clearly not been the custodians of the country-side that one might have wished them to be. We are all complicit, and farmer-bashing is not going to help. We need farmers, more than any other profession. If lawyers, politicians, bankers, univer-sity academics or salesmen were to somehow disappear tomorrow, I think the world would muddle through pretty well. Some things might even get better. But if farmers were to vanish, most of us would be dead within a year.

One might argue that the changes that have occurred to farm-ing over the last hundred years were necessary; that the human population, seven billion of us and growing, necessitates food pro-duction on a massive scale and that the only way it can be done is via industrial farming. This evening, 228,000 more people will sit down to dinner than did yesterday. Maybe polluted streams and dwindling bird and butterfly populations are simply unavoidable collateral damage in the drive to feed humans. Just as we can try to build robot bees, perhaps in the future we can find ways to grow crops without needing soil or clean water. Perhaps too we can find a technical fix for climate change, by spraying aluminium dust or some other reflective material into the atmosphere. Possibly, but it seems to me that we are asking a lot of the ingenuity of future gen-erations, and that such technical fixes might create more problems than they solve. We will bequeath them a polluted world, depleted of many of its natural resources, and from which most of the natural beauty has been annihilated, and expect them to sort it out and make do. Most parents and grandparents would do almost anything for their offspring, except, it seems, when it comes to leaving them a healthy planet to live on.

The aspect of this that bugs me most is that it really isn't necessary. The collateral damage could all be avoided. There are much better ways of providing sustenance to people, not least because the current system is staggeringly inefficient. Roughly one-third of all the food that is produced in the world is thrown away, with waste being higher in developed countries and running at over 50 per cent in the USA. Of course some food waste is unavoidable; however careful you are, there will always be the last slice of bread that goes mouldy or the bottle of milk that goes off while you are away for the weekend. On the other hand, much food waste is needless; nutritious crops are rejected because they do not conform to strict and arbitrary standards of size or shape, perfectly edible food is discarded on its best-before date in shops, while consumers take little trouble to eat up what they have in the fridge. In the developed world, food is cheap and many people seem not to care that they are wasting money by throwing away food which they paid good money for. In the USA, restaurants often serve vast portions so that diners are accustomed to pushing away their plate while it is half full. I have watched people at all-you-can-eat buffets piling their plates high and then leaving much of the food uneaten. I was brought up differently, by a mother who had lived through the war and loathed waste, and I am upset by this casual discarding of perfectly good food.

If we didn't waste so much food then we could grow it much less intensively, or we could turn vast tracts of land back over to nature. Currently, 49 million square kilometres of the surface of the globe is used to produce food. Theoretically, if food waste were eliminated, about 16 million square kilometres of land – the equivalent of the entire area of the USA plus Australia – could be turned into nature reserves, perhaps in the form of vast rewilding projects. It is a fabulous if fanciful thought. Of course we can never eliminate all food waste, but nonetheless this gives some idea of the scale of the benefits we might gain simply by improving the efficiency of the system even a little.

In addition to the scandalous waste of perfectly good food, there is a second aspect of the current system that is hugely inefficient, and that is our excessive and growing consumption of heavily processed food and sugar. Processing foods and adding refined sugars greatly reduces the nutritional value. While 750 million people in the world regularly go hungry, an estimated two billion are overweight or obese. India has perhaps the most dramatic contrasts; about 200 million Indians are significantly underweight, while at the same time 30 million people in India are obese, the latter figure representing a twentyfold increase since 1975. As a result, diet-related diseases have overtaken infectious diseases as the biggest cause of premature death at a global scale. The cost of treating chronic diseases associated with obesity and poor diet is contributing to the collapse of the UK health service; official government figures suggest that obesity-related health problems cost the economy about £27 billion every year, with diet-related diabetes and the complications associated with it accounting for about half of this figure.

We are also all aware that many of us eat more meat than is good for us. With much of Asia moving towards consuming meat at a rate similar to those of us in the developed West, it is estimated that global meat consumption will double by 2050. I find it slightly hard to believe, but apparently the average USA citizen consumes a grotesque 124kg of meat each year, surely something we do not wish to emulate. Aside from destroying the planet, eating too much meat increases risks of heart disease, cancer, kidney disease, osteoporosis and all sorts of other unpleasantness, many of them also diseases that are exacerbated by obesity. Already about two-thirds of the world's farmland is pasture for grazing animals (most of the remainder being arable crops). On top of that, about one-third of the arable crops grown are fed to livestock, so that in total about 76 per cent of the Earth's farmland is currently being used for meat production, either directly or indirectly. Overall, nearly three-quarters of the greenhouse gases produced by farming activities come from livestock production.

Children learn at school about trophic pyramids; the sun's energy is used by plants to grow. Plants are eaten by grazing animals, but the efficiency with which energy is transmitted up the food chain from one level to the next is usually only about 10 per cent at most. To put it simply, the sunlight falling on one hectare of land might support ten tonnes of vegetation, but that can only support one tonne of munching herbivores, and one-tenth of a tonne of predators that eat herbivores. That is why eagles and lions will always be scarcer than rabbits or antelope. This unavoidable ecological fact points to an obvious conclusion: if we wish to support the growing human population without destroying the planet, we have a much better chance of doing so if we behave as rabbits rather than trying to be eagles.

While this simplistic analogy illustrates the point well enough, the reality is a little more complicated. Not all meats are equal, in terms of the environmental impact of producing them. Poultry convert the food they eat into meat far more efficiently than cows; it takes about two to three kilos of grain to produce a kilo of chicken, while it takes about four kilos of grain per kilo of lamb or pig, and somewhere between seven and twenty kilos per kilo of cow. If we look at the greenhouse gases associated with rearing different types of meat, the contrast is even more dramatic; producing one kilo of chicken protein releases 3.7kg of carbon dioxide equivalent, while producing a kilo of pig protein releases 24kg and producing a kilo of cow protein releases a disturbing 1,000kg. The huge difference is largely down to the chronic flatulence and endless belching which results from cattle fermenting their lunch in their stomachs, a process that produces copious methane. The conclusion is clear: if, like me, you don't want to become vegetarian, and think that meat is both delicious and probably also part of an optimal diet for humans, then eat a little, and eat mainly chicken or roadkill. If you must eat beef (and I love a steak and black-pepper pie more than most), then try to find grass-fed beef, for there are many areas of the globe which are not well suited to arable farming, and where grazing animals may make the best use of the land; some of the wetter, more westerly parts of the UK spring to mind. Better still, although a step too far or not practical for most, rear your own animals. I keep Maran and Light Sussex chickens along with Bourbon Red turkeys, letting them roam the garden during the day so that they can glean their own food. They are a great way of recycling kitchen scraps, they wolf down any leftover apples in the orchard, and peck out the seeds from surplus marrows, all of which means I don't need to buy too much feed for them. Each year I hatch a few new ones, with the males being reared up for Sunday lunch or, in the case of one turkey each year, for Christmas, so we have a steady supply of zero-food-miles, low-carbon eggs and meat. Supplemented with the occasional roadkill butchered on the lawn and stored in chunks in the freezer, we buy very little meat.

Sadly most people don't have room to keep chickens or grow their own veg. Eighty per cent of us in the UK live in cities or the surrounding urban sprawl. Developers squeeze houses onto tiny plots of land to maximise their profit, so modern gardens tend to be small, while many of us live in flats with no outside space at all. One solution to this might be allotments.

Allotments in the UK have an interesting history. They came about in part because of enclosure of the countryside, whereby chunks of common land – which local people had previously had the right to graze or farm – were appropriated and assigned to one landowner, the new boundaries marked with hedges or fences to 'enclose' the land. This began as long ago as the twelfth century, but really gathered pace in the eighteenth and nineteenth centuries when most of the land was taken into private ownership, displacing rural communities and forcing many to move into cities to find work. This process, combined with the gradual introduction of mechanisation, allowed the emergence of large monoculture cropping, a shift from subsistence farming – in which most of the food grown was for local consumption – to growing cash crops for profit. A similar process can be seen in the 'land grabs' going on in many developing countries today, particularly in Africa and South America, where wealthy corporations are acquiring vast tracts of land on which to grow cash crops, often displacing local people from the land they have occupied and farmed for generations but to which they have never been given legal title.[55]

---

[55] Approximately 50 million hectares of land has so far been acquired in land grabs, with the problem at its most severe in Africa, where an estimated 9 per cent of all arable farmland has been purchased so far, but it is rife in South America and parts of Asia as well. Some defend land grabs, arguing that the foreign investment will ultimately benefit the country involved, creating jobs, increasing exports and boosting infrastructure and the economy. I doubt that the peasant farmers who have been evicted from their land would agree. More subtle land grabs are also taking place in Europe, where multinational companies are buying up land to take advantage of lucrative area-based subsidies available through the Common Agricultural Policy.

In the UK, the enclosures led to considerable social unrest. In 1607, revolting peasants in Northamptonshire ripped up the newly planted hedges and filled in ditches. They were brutally suppressed by the landowners, forty or fifty people were killed and the ringleaders were publicly hanged and chopped into quarters to make a messy example of them. Forty years later, Gerrard Winstanley founded the Digger movement, based on the premise that it was man's God-given right to dig the earth to cultivate crops. With a group of like-minded souls he set up a colony of vegetable growers on enclosed land at St George's Hill, Surrey. Of course local landowners saw this as a threat to the status quo and sent a gang of armed men to beat the Diggers, burn down their dwellings and drive them from the land, but at least they avoided being dismembered. The following two centuries saw lots of similar protests and riots from the poor and dispossessed, but with the enclosures enshrined in law by successive Acts of Parliament, they were doomed to failure. Many protesters were hanged or deported to the colonies.

The provision of allotments was seen as a way to appease the landless poor, as a way to keep them out of trouble and out of the pub, and as a way to prevent them starving if they became unemployed. In 1887 the Allotment Act made it compulsory for councils to provide allotments if there was local demand, allotments being restricted to 253 square metres in area and available for a peppercorn rent. Allotments really came to the fore in the Great War, when German blockades prevented food importation, so that fresh food was suddenly in short supply and food prices rocketed. Councils were given the right to appropriate any derelict land for allotments, and railway companies were obliged to give up any of their unused land (rail travellers may have the false impression that Britain is full of allotments because a disproportionate number are next to railway lines). By 1917 there were 1.5 million allotments in the UK, the most there have ever been. Allotmenting slumped a little between the wars, but came into its own once more with the resumption of hostilities in 1939. Newspapers coined the phrase 'dig for victory', a slogan which Gerrard Winstanley would surely have approved of and which was then adopted by the government. Films and adverts promoting growing food were commissioned, tens of millions of leaflets were distributed, and in the spirit of communal endeavour and sacrifice several of London's beautiful royal parks were dug up and planted with vegetables, including Hyde Park and St James's Park. There were even allotments in the dry moat of the Tower of London.

This golden era of home-growing was to fizzle out through the rest of the twentieth century. By the 1960s food had become plentiful and cheap, removing the incentive to grow your own. The population boom led to huge demand for more housing, so allotment sites were sold off to developers. By 1997 there were just 265,000 allotments left, less than one-fifth of the number eighty years earlier.

Today, things are changing once more. Interest in growing your own food is slowly increasing, perhaps fuelled by television programmes such as *River Cottage* which expound the health virtues and satisfaction to be gained from growing your own produce, and perhaps also driven by concerns over animal welfare and the environmental impacts of conventional farming. Allotment numbers are back up to around 330,000.[56] An estimated 90,000 more people are on waiting lists for allotments in the UK. These are people that want to grow their own sustainable, zero-food-miles produce, but can't because the land is locked up under other uses – primarily under intensive farmland.

At this point you might be wondering where I am going with this. Surely I can't be advocating turning highly productive

---

[56] There are estimated to be three million allotments in Europe.

farmland into the chaotic and ramshackle patchwork of make-shift sheds, flapping plastic greenhouses, vegetable rows, fruit trees and overgrown bramble patches that constitute most allotment sites? You might think that this messy shambles couldn't possibly make any significant contribution to feeding the world, but you would be wrong. Allotments can be surprisingly productive. In fact studies by the Royal Horticultural Society and *Which?* magazine, which accord with historical records of food production during the world wars, suggest that a competent allotment holder or gardener can get yields of between thirty-one and forty tonnes per hectare. To put this into context, a farmer gets about three and a half tonnes of oilseed rape or eight tonnes of wheat per year from every hectare of land, and will apply about twenty different pesticides plus fertilisers to achieve this. Thus an allotment holder or gardener can grow between four and eleven times the weight of produce that one might get from an intensively farmed arable field, depending on the skill of the allotment holder and the types of crops that he or she chooses to grow. Bear in mind also that only one-third of the UK wheat crop is good enough to go for human consumption, the remainder going for livestock feed. In contrast, 100 per cent of the allotment food is available for humans to eat.

It is also interesting to consider that the yields obtained from arable crops are the result of decades of investment, billions of dollars spent on research into better crop varieties, the development of new pesticides, optimisation of sowing rates and fertiliser applications, and much more. As a result, wheat yields quadrupled between 1920 and 1990 but, along with those of other major crops, they have remained stubbornly stable for the last twenty years or so. In contrast, food production in gardens and allotments has received negligible investment in research, and is largely based on anecdote, hand-me-down folklore and guesswork. Yet it still outperforms conventional agriculture four- to eleven-fold in terms of the weight of food produced per hectare.

You may question how this can be. On the face of it, it makes little sense. An amateur bumbler with a fork and trowel can produce eleven times the food of a professional farmer using the latest equipment and advised by expert agronomists? In fact the explanation is simple. In a garden or allotment one can pack in lots of different crops to a small area. In my garden I plant lettuce in between the rows of potatoes in spring; they are harvested before the potato foliage gets too large and smothers them. I sow patches of radish between my runner beans' wigwams, and plant out young squash and courgette plants in May among my garlic and onions, which are harvested in June before the squash really get going. Mangetout peas scramble up my purple sprouting cabbages, making it harder for large white butterflies to identify their host plant when looking to lay their eggs. Strawberries and pumpkins grow beneath my blackcurrant bushes. There are enormous advantages to growing multiple crops in close proximity. One can get several harvests per year from one small patch of land, and there are far fewer pests as they have to work harder to find their host plants amid all the other foliage, and even if they do they are more likely to be wolfed down by one of the myriad of natural enemies that thrive in this system: earwigs, ladybirds, hoverflies and parasitic wasps. A garden or allotment vegetable patch mimics a natural ecosystem, where woody plants, herbs and grasses intermingle, each occupying a slightly different ecological niche, so many more can be squeezed in. The ground is rarely bare, meaning that much more of the available sunlight is captured.

In my own garden, I keep a diary of my crop yields each year. As I write it is January 2018 and the harvest for last season is now complete:

Artichoke, 0.5kg	Lettuce, 1kg
Asparagus, 2kg	Loganberry, 2.5kg
Beetroot, 2kg	Mangetout peas, 2kg
Blackberry, 2kg	Marrows, 81kg
Blackcurrant, 2kg	Medlar, 1kg
Blueberry, 0.5kg	Occa, 3kg
Broad bean, 6kg	Onion, 40kg
Broccoli, 2kg	Parsnip, 15kg
Cauliflower, 1kg	Pear, 15kg
Chard, 5kg	Plum, 4kg
Chinese artichoke, 0.5kg	Potato, 95kg
Courgettes, 22kg	Purple sprouting, 3kg
Cucumber, 5kg	Quince, 2kg
Filbert nut, 0.2kg	Redcurrant, 4kg
French beans, 3kg	Rhubarb, 6kg
Garlic, 1kg	Runner bean, 35kg
Gooseberry, 1.5kg	Squash, 36kg
Grape, 4kg	Strawberry, 44kg
Honeyberry, 1kg	Tayberry, 1kg
Japanese spinach, 2kg	Tomato, 2kg
Jerusalem artichoke, 22kg	Yakon, 8kg
Leek, 15kg	

This amounts to just a smidge over 500kg of fruit and vegetables, all produced from an area of about 160 square metres, quite a bit smaller than a standard allotment (I'm not including the much larger area of orchard which produces several tonnes of apples each year, most destined for the cider press). At a rough calculation, based on what it would cost to buy this produce in the supermarket, I reckon I'm saving about £1,600 per year, though given the choice I might not buy quite so many marrows. Scaling this up, this equates to about 31 tonnes per hectare, putting me at the bottom end of the range of yields measured by *Which?*; I am certainly not the most efficient of gardeners.

Aside from yield, there are many other advantages to this kind of food production too. As we have already seen, gardens and allotment soils generally contain more carbon than farmland soils, and have the potential to lock up even more. They support far more wildlife than conventional farmland, and require few or no pesticides. On top of all this, there is one final compelling reason why anyone who does not have their own veg patch should think about getting an allotment: it makes you healthier. A recent study from the Netherlands compared multiple measures of health in people holding allotments with their immediate neighbours. After correcting for extraneous factors, young allotmenteers were no more or less healthy than their neighbours, but for those over the age of sixty-two the ones with allotments scored better on every single measure of health and well-being. It may be that these benefits are simply because gardening helps people to relax; half an hour of gardening has been found to lead to a significant drop in cortisol levels (a commonly used measure of stress). It might also be due to the regular, gentle exercise associated with gardening, or to the health-giving properties of the food grown, or to something else less easily quantified. It has been argued that allotments help to build communities, getting people out of their houses where they often live in isolation and into a situation where they are hoeing and digging alongside like-minded people – potential friends.

This leads me to the one area in which allotment-food growing is vastly less efficient than conventional farming: it requires huge numbers of people. Mechanisation and large fields allow a conventional farm to operate with minimal labour; indeed, a modern arable farm can be run by just one person, who might hire in contractors to help out at the busiest times. As a result, less than 1 per cent of UK jobs are in farming, down from 22 per cent in 1840 (and compared to the global average of 40 per cent of all jobs being in farming). The industrialisation and mechanisation of agriculture has led to the collapse of rural communities, the closure of village shops, pubs and schools. Producing food the way I do in my garden requires quite a lot of work (though I do have a full-time job so it has to be squeezed into weekends and evenings). You cannot mechanise the growing and harvesting of lettuces grown between rows of potatoes, or the picking of mangetout peas rambling among broccoli – at least not until someone invents a very clever robot. But is it a bad thing if growing food requires lots of people? After all, one thing the world is not short of is people. Ninety thousand people want an allotment right now, without any encouragement or prompting. But what if we had another 'dig for victory' style campaign, supported by the government? In the Second World War 10 per cent of the food we ate was produced in allotments and gardens, from an area of land that is estimated to have been less than 1 per cent of that covered by conventional arable crops at the time. How about giving councils the power to compulsorily purchase farmland adjoining towns and cities? You might think this is an outrageous suggestion, yet construction of the new HS2 train line will require compulsory purchase of a much larger area of land, including hundreds of people's homes. Perhaps we could spend a small percentage of the £3 billion currently given out in farming subsidy each year to help support allotments and encourage people to grow their own fruit and veg in their gardens. It could pay for free training events, to encourage uptake of allotments and subsidise their cost, and perhaps it could be used to provide free vegetable seeds. If we did so, I suspect that we could get far more than another 90,000 people back onto the land. Every new allot-ment created on former farmland would increase food production, increase carbon capture into the soil, increase biodiversity, reduce pesticide use, and improve the health of ageing allotment owners (so reducing the burden on the National Health Service).

Of course, encouraging people onto allotments will not, by itself, solve all of the world's problems, but it is a step in the direction I believe we need to take, a step towards appreciating where food comes from, towards growing healthy, pesticide-free food for local consumption in ways that can also sustain a great diversity of life. This approach could be scaled up, taking advantage of the prop-erties that make allotments so productive. There are various mod-els, none of them given serious consideration by the mainstream. Agroforestry is one such, and permaculture is another, systems that have a lot in common with one another. Both incorporate the principles of growing multiple crops including perennials in close proximity, and on protecting and nurturing the soil, regarding it as the most basic and valuable resource we have. Agroforestry ba-sically means incorporating trees into farming. At its simplest, it might involve growing lines of productive fruit trees on pasture which is used for grazing animals or for free-range hens to roam. My orchard, where my chickens and turkeys peck about, is an agroforestry system of sorts. The trees provide multiple benefits, including an edible harvest such as apples, shade for livestock or for shade-loving crops, firewood or building materials, browse for the animals, mulch for other crops, improved drainage, reducing flooding and holding the soil together. Other tree species might be included because they fix nitrogen from the atmosphere, boosting soil fertility. In the tropics, coffee is commonly grown as a mono-culture, with the attendant problems of soil erosion and high pest pressure necessitating high levels of pesticide use. Coffee is nat-urally a shrub that thrives in shade, and it can be grown much more sustainably using taller rainforest trees to provide that shade. This approach vastly increases the numbers of species of wild birds, mammals and insects living in the plantations, reduces the pest pressure, suppresses weeds, and provides more reliable pollination for the crop. This 'shade-grown coffee' also sells at a premium because of the significant environmental benefits it provides. As a result, the area of shade-grown coffee is increasing – great news for wildlife. Unfortunately the growing global demand for cheap coffee is driving the expansion of monoculture coffee plantations at an even faster rate; it may not be sustainable in the long term, but it is quicker and easier just to plant lots of coffee bushes and not worry about growing trees to shade them.[57]

Permaculture is a little harder to explain, and is to my mind a little woollier; it seems to me that it is more of a philosophy than a science, focused on working with nature rather than against it – something I would of course wholeheartedly endorse. It was invented in the 1970s by Bill Mollison, a scientist at the University of Tasmania, along with his PhD student David Holmgren. Mollison was inspired by watching marsupials grazing in the lush temperate

---

[57] Similar principles apply to cacao, which is commonly grown as a monoculture in full sun but is a species that naturally grows in shade beneath rainforest trees in tropical South America. My colleague Mika Peck at Sussex University is leading a project to save the critically endangered brown-headed spider monkey, of which only about 250 individuals survive. While a core area of forest has been purchased in western Ecuador to protect the last significant fragment of rainforest in which the monkey thrives, Mika and his team have been working with local cacao growers to surround the forest with a protective ring of shade-grown cacao farms. In return for preserving the tree cover and preventing hunting of the monkeys, the growers are given a premium price for their beans.

Tasmanian rainforests, and his notion was to build systems in which humans could live as part of functionally complex and interconnected, sustainable, living systems. He advocated protracted and thoughtful observation of the interactions and functions of organisms in any particular area before attempting to 'consciously design landscapes which mimic the patterns and relationships found in nature, while yielding an abundance of food, fibre and energy for provision of local needs'. In practice, the schemes Mollison came up with involved growing multiple useful plants together, from trees and shrubs to herbs and fungi, along with encouraging both wild and domestic animals. I can't make up my mind if Mollison was a genius visionary or a mad hippy, or both, but clearly his heart was in the right place.

While I'm on the subject of eccentrics and alternative forms of agriculture, I guess I must mention biodynamic farming. This is a concept developed by Rudolf Steiner back in the 1920s, essentially a negative reaction to the very early days of chemical agriculture. Steiner was concerned at apparent deterioration in the health of crops and livestock that he attributed to the growing use of artificial fertilisers. Biodynamic farming has much in common with organic farming, prohibiting the use of pesticides and promoting many very sensible practices including crop rotations, setting aside 10 per cent of the farm for nature, and generally looking after the land and producing healthy food. This is all great stuff, but unfortunately biodynamic farming also includes an element of what seems to me to be witchcraft or magic. I've been lucky enough to be shown around a biodynamic farm and I was mightily impressed by the range of fantastic crops they were growing, but was somewhat taken aback when the farm manager explained how each year he stuffed a red deer's bladder with yarrow blossom, left it in the sun to fester for a while, then buried it over the winter before digging it up and using it as compost. As you know I'm as keen on compost as any man, but that seems like a pretty inefficient and bizarre way of making it. He was also keen on grinding up quartz rock and burying that in a cow's horn for six months before sprinkling it about, and his planting schemes were influenced by the phases of the moon and their conjunction with the zodiacal constellations. I do try to keep an open mind, and I'd be delighted if someone could show me some evidence that this actually works (I've looked, and there doesn't seem to be any), but to me as a scientist this all seems quite bonkers.

Sadly, the existence of some well-meaning but clearly flaky practices in 'alternative' farming make it all too easy for the vested interests in mainstream industrial farming to paint it all as the realm of dungaree-wearing tree-hugging nutcases.[58] It is easy to argue that this mumbo-jumbo nonsense can't possibly feed the world. Yet the central themes of these alternative ways of growing food are sound ones that are supported by science: look after the soil; grow a diversity of crops; encourage pollinators and natural enemies; minimise or eliminate pesticides and fertilisers; compost and recycle. All just common sense to a good gardener.

Imagine a very different world. A world in which most people have access to a garden or allotment, and grow their own food, so that our cities and towns are surrounded by a network of vibrant, productive, sociable growing places, where the chirping of sparrows and buzzing of bees mingle with the chatter of growers comparing

[58] Interestingly, some modern farming practices have no more credibility than sprinkling quartz powder from a cow's horn. The United States Environmental Protection Agency recently reported that neonicotinoid seed dressings on soya beans were entirely ineffective, yet 30 million hectares were being treated each year at a cost to farmers of $176 million. Farmers should beware of agrochemical sales reps selling snake oil.

the size of their courgettes, swapping their surpluses, and sharing seeds. Beyond that, imagine that instead of those vast green deserts of wheat or rye grass pasture, we had small, sustainable farms practising organic agroforestry schemes tailored to the local soil and climate, producing fruits, vegetables, chicken and eggs for local markets, grazing cattle beneath the orchard trees for milk and cheese. More, smaller farms would mean getting more people back onto the land, which could revitalise rural communities. Instead of giving huge subsidies to support industrial farming, this is where our money should go: making small-scale, sustainable agriculture viable. Whatever your view on Brexit, it frees us from the Common Agricultural Policy and provides a golden opportunity to turn farming on its head, to make the radical changes that are urgently needed before most of our wildlife and our soils have gone. We should have government-funded experimental farms doing research into how to optimise this type of agriculture. If a gardener or allotmenteer can get forty tonnes of food from a hectare of land without any training or research and development to back them up, imagine what might be possible if we took a scientific approach to properly evaluating the best practices. Researchers could investigate which combinations of crops grow best together, develop crop varieties best suited to this form of farming, test how to boost populations of useful insects such as earwigs, and work out how best to ensure that the organic matter content of soils slowly grows over time. With this approach to growing food we could have a truly sustainable farming system, in which wildlife thrives and people have access to plentiful, locally produced and nutritious food. If you really want to leave your grandchildren a healthy planet to live on, it's time to get out in the garden and dig.

My sixteen favourite garden plants for pollinators

Many flowers are attractive to pollinators, with different types of insect varying in their particular preferences. In general, herbs and cottage garden perennials are good, and annual bedding plants are best avoided (because they have been intensively bred and have often lost their rewards or become so misshapen that insects cannot get into them). This list includes my absolute favourites, all guaranteed to suck in insects from miles around and keep your garden buzzing. So far as possible it is based on scientific studies, or at the very least I have grown the plant myself and can verify that, in my garden, it is a magnet for pollinators. There are of course many other great plants for pollinators; exclusion from this list should most definitely not be taken as an indication that something isn't worth growing.

Bush vetch, *Vicia sepium*	A member of the pea family, this unobtrusive native climbing perennial carries small purple flowers through late spring and summer and is constantly alive with the hum of carder bees.

Catmint, *Nepeta racemosa* and related species	Natives of southern Europe and Asia, there are more than 250 species of *Nepeta*. *N. racemosa* is one of the best, a sprawling, robust perennial plant, with lilac flowers through late spring to late summer. *N. x faasenii* 'Six Hills Giant' is especially good for long-tongued bees. Lovely perennial, a cottage garden classic, every garden should have some.
Plume thistle, *Cirsium rivulare* '*Atropurpureum*'	A great plant for male bumblebees in high summer, this species is not spiny like its wild thistle relatives and is quite at home in a flower bed. However, it does spread vegetatively and can take over a bit. Propagate from seed or root cuttings. Flowers from July to September, up to 1m high.
Comfrey, *Symphytum officinale*, 'Bocking 14'	A very hardy perennial, great for the back of a herbaceous border or a forgotten corner where it will look after itself. Very long flowering period, from May to August, and one of the very best plants for bees. Visited by long- and short-tongued species, the latter often robbing from holes bitten in the tops of the flowers. Comfrey can also be chopped down regularly and used to make excellent compost. Can grow 1.5m tall or more, and will smother smaller plants nearby. Propagates best from root cuttings.

Dahlia 'Bishop of Llandaff'	*Dahlia* feature in few lists of recommended plants for pollinators, but open varieties such as this one can be fantastic magnets for bumblebees (avoid the 'cactus' or 'pompom' varieties). Brilliant red flowers and purplish foliage, growing up to 1m tall. Tubers are sensitive to frost, so best dug up and stored for the winter.
Field scabious, *Knautia arvensis*	Lovely native meadow perennial, one of my particular favourites. Our wild field scabious is found on chalk downland, but it seems to cope on a range of garden soils including my wet clay. There are many garden strains and species available, but I'd stick with the native one. I love the powder-puff blue of the flowers, and bees, butterflies and hoverflies seem pretty keen too. Flowers in July and August.
Meadow cranesbill, *Geranium pratense*	Most hardy *Geranium* species are good for bees, and there are dozens of easy-to-grow species to choose from, but if I had to pick one I would go for this beautiful native, which is at home in a flower bed or naturalised into grassland.
Giant hyssop, *Agastache foeniculum*, 'Blackadder', 'Blue Fortune' and 'Blue Boa'	A great perennial plant for bees, originally from North America. Needs a well-drained soil otherwise it tends to die over the winter. Grows to about 1m, with spikes of blue flowers in summer that bees adore.

Lavender, *Lavandula x intermedia*, 'Gros bleu'	No garden is complete without lavender, a stately mauve-flowered perennial on sale in every garden centre. However, get the right type; the more common English lavender (*L. angustifolia*) is less attractive to pollinators, and Spanish lavender is worse still.
Lungwort, *Pulmonaria*, 'Blue Ensign' or 'Trevi Fountain'	A great very early-spring nectar resource for hungry queen bumblebees and, if you are lucky, for the wonderful hairy-footed flower bee. An easy perennial to grow, happy in shade beneath trees or in full sun.
Marjoram, *Origanum vulgare*	A great all-rounder, easy to grow, attractive to heaps of different pollinators, and good for cooking too! A perennial native, growing to 0.8m tall, loves a sunny position. Avoid the golden and variegated garden varieties.
Pussy willow, *Salix caprea*	Native trees, growing to 10m or more. Sallows are dioecious, being either male or female. Both sexes produce catkins in early spring, and are very important sources of food for queen bumblebees and many early solitary mining bees. Since the male trees produce pollen and a little nectar and the females only produce nectar, it is best to grow a male if possible. Dwarf and weeping varieties can be bought for smaller gardens.

Sicilian honey garlic, *Allium siculum*	Many *Allium* are attractive to pollinators, but this one is the best in my opinion. Rather odd, pendant cream-and-magenta flowers that drip with nectar in early summer. The perennial bulbs can be bought online and, despite being from southern Europe, they seem to thrive in my garden.
Sneezewort, *Helenium*, 'Moerheim Beauty'	Heleniums have attractive daisy-like flowers on tall stems in warm, glowing oranges and reds which are very popular with bees of all sizes, but particularly with some of the smaller solitary bees. Seems prone to dying off in the winter in my soggy clay garden.
Thyme, *Thymus polytrichus* subsp. *Britannicus*	There are a number of wild and cultivated species, but this one is perhaps the best for pollinators. Thymes also attract hoverflies and honeybees in abundance. A lovely, low-growing, rambling perennial plant for a pot, the cracks in a patio, or the front of a border.
Viper's bugloss, *Echium vulgare*	A stunning biennial wild flower growing to about 1m, flowering in July and August and absolutely loved by bees of all types for its copious nectar. Likes a sunny, well-drained site, and given this will freely self-seed.

My top twelve berry plants for birds

Many garden plants are good food sources for birds, providing berries or seeds, which can be particularly valuable in the winter months when food is in short supply. This list is based only on my own observations, rather than scientific experimentation. Some of these plants are also attractive to pollinators when flowering, so provide a double whammy for garden wildlife. All but the firethorn and Oregon grape are natives to the UK, and hence support other creatures such as caterpillars, which eat the leaves.

In addition to the list below, most cultivated fruit trees and shrubs provide fruit that birds love to eat, but you may find yourself fighting them over it.

Blackberry, *Rubus fruticosus*	A common wild plant, also available in thornless cultivated varieties, the flowers are very attractive to insects, and birds love the early-autumn fruits (which also make a fabulous jam).
Blackthorn, *Prunus spinosa*	A great hedging plant, and the snow-white flowers are popular with solitary bees such as the orange-tailed mining bee in early spring. Purplish fruits last into the winter if you do not pick them for making sloe gin.

Crab apple, *Malus sylvestris*, 'John Downie'	Crab apples have beautiful blossom in spring and the small, sharp fruits hang attractively into winter when they are consumed by birds. The fruits also give zing to cider or apple wine, and are commonly used for jelly.
Dog rose, *Rosa canina*	The flowers are attractive to bees, while the red hips are popular with birds in winter.
Elder, *Sambucus nigra*	Frothy cream flower heads in summer which are strangely unattractive to insects, but make an unusual though sometimes insipid sparkling wine. The dark purple berries make a wonderful port-like wine, or you can leave them for the birds to gorge themselves on in late summer.
Hawthorn, *Crataegus monogyna*	Attractive blossom in May, often visited by hoverflies and some bees, followed by abundant red haws in autumn through winter.
Firethorn, *Pyracantha coccinea*	An abundance of small white blooms in summer that are highly attractive to pollinators, followed by clusters of attractive bright red berries in autumn, also makes a great hedge.
Honeysuckle, *Lonicera periclymenum*	A lovely climbing plant with exotic purple, yellow and cream flowers with a strong scent that attracts moths by night and long-tongued bees by day. The soft red berries are soon scoffed by birds.

Ivy, *Hedera helix*	A much maligned plant, often chopped back mercilessly and treated as a weed. The plain green flowers are hugely attractive to butterflies, bees, hoverflies and wasps in early autumn, providing food when almost all other flowers have finished for the year. The dark berries then feed birds through the winter.
Oregon grape, *Mahonia aquifolium*	Flowers in December and January, and favoured by winter-active buff-tailed bumblebees. The purple, tangy berries in spring are a tasty snack for us humans, or a welcome treat for blackbirds and thrushes.
Rowan, *Sorbus aucuparia*	An elegant small tree, with frothy white flowers and bunches of red berries in autumn.
Wayfaring tree, *Viburnum lantana*	Bees, butterflies and hoverflies visit the flowers, while blackbirds, fieldfares and waxwings (if you are very lucky) eat the berries. Dormice and wood mice are also said to enjoy the fruits.

Make your own wormery

A wormery is a great way to recycle kitchen scraps into highly fertile compost for your garden in just a few weeks. Note that it isn't suitable for dealing with large amounts of garden waste, so if you have a reasonable-sized garden you really ought to have a compost heap too. There are lots of commercial varieties of wormery available, or you can make your own. At its very simplest, all you need is a large plastic or wooden box or bin, ideally with a volume of at least sixty litres. Drill lots of 12mm holes in the bottom, and lots of 8mm holes in the sides. Put at least 5cm of old compost, or bought (peat-free) compost, or coir in the bottom. Add as many compost worms as you can lay your hands on – ideally a few hundred. The stripy red brandling worm (*Eisenia fetida*) and its slightly chubbier cousin the compost worm (*Eisenia veneta*) are the best bet, and both are likely to be common in your garden compost heap, or your neighbour's heap. Otherwise you can buy them online and get them delivered. Sprinkle on some kitchen scraps. Most food waste is fine, including raw and cooked vegetables, tea bags, coffee grounds, eggshells, and small amounts of cooked rice and pasta. You can also add small amounts of weeds or other garden waste, and shredded paper. Avoid fish, meat, bones, grease and fat, and lots of cooked food such as pasta and rice, as these will attract rats. Add a little at a time to start with. The wormery needs a lid, and is best situated on bricks to keep it off the ground and help drainage, and in a shady spot where the worms won't get too hot in summer.

Some of the fancier commercial designs allow the processed compost to fall from the bottom, ready for use, but with this home-made system you simply keep adding waste until the bin is full. Once it is filled you tip out the compost and start again, reusing the worms, which should be mostly in the top few centimetres.

If you really get in to your wormery, you might like to read George Pilkington's book *Composting with Worms*.

Further reading

Lymbery, P.J., *Dead Zone: Where the Wild Things Were*, Bloomsbury, 2017.

Lymbery, P.J., *Farmageddon: The True Cost of Cheap Meat*, Bloomsbury, 2014.

Pilkington, G., *Composting with Worms: Why Waste Your Waste?*, Eco-Logic Books, 2005.

Thompson, K., *The Book of Weeds*, Dorling Kindersley, 2009.

Thompson, K., *No Nettles Required: The Reassuring Truth about Wildlife Gardening*, Eden Project Books, 2007.

Thompson, K., *The Sceptical Gardener*, Icon Books, 2016.

Walker, J., *Digging Deep in the Garden: Book One*, Earth-friendly Books, 2015.

Walker, J., *Digging Deep in the Garden: Book Two*, Earth-friendly Books, 2016.

Walker, J., *How to Create an Ecogarden*, Aquamarine, 2011.

Organisations you might consider joining

Buzz Club A small charity that I helped to found, a membership-based club in which scientists and members of the public work together to find out what insects are living in our gardens, how their populations are changing, and what are the most effective measures we can take in our gardens to boost their numbers. https://www.thebuzzclub.uk/

Buglife Focuses on conserving the UK's invertebrates (insects, spiders, slugs, snails, etc.). It is actively involved in creating habitats for insects across the UK, and vocal campaigns against the worst pesticides. https://www.buglife.org.uk/

Butterfly Conservation The oldest charity focused on insects anywhere in the world, Butterfly Conservation does great work to look after both butterflies and moths. https://butterfly-conservation.org/

Bumblebee Conservation Trust A great little charity, involved in habitat creation for bumblebees and other pollinators. It also runs 'citizen science' schemes such as 'Beewalks' which is gathering valuable data on changing bumblebee populations. https://www.bumblebeeconservation.org/

The Earthworm Society of Great Britain A delightful organisation which promotes appreciation of earthworms, and runs a national recording scheme. It is keen to recruit more worm recorders since at present data is very sparse, with no records from some parts of the country. Why not give it a go? https://www.earthwormsoc.org.uk/

Royal Society for the Protection of Birds Although primarily focused on birds, the RSPB has extended its remit to encompass all wildlife. A big and powerful organisation, it currently manages more than one hundred nature reserves around the UK. https://www.rspb.org.uk/

Wildlife Trusts Every county or region has its own wildlife trust. Between them, they manage about 2,300 nature reserves, from remote woodlands to city nature parks. The wildlife trusts have an extensive volunteer network, and do much to help children engage with nature. Contact details for your local branch are readily obtained online.

Wildflower seed suppliers

Bee Happy Plants
https://www.beehappyplants.co.uk/
A great range of unusual and pesticide-free seeds.

Cotswold Seeds Ltd
Cotswold Business Village
London Road
Moreton-in-Marsh
Gloucestershire
GL56 0JQ
https://www.cotswoldseeds.com/

Emorsgate Seeds
Limes Farm
Tilney All Saints
King's Lynn
Norfolk
PE34 4RT
https://www.wildseed.co.uk/

Index

DG indicates Dave Goulson.

Index